"YO'D MEK A PARSON ~~SWEAR.~~

FOND MEMORIES OF OLD NOTTINGHAM

by

JOY JAMES

Joy James

xx

ACKNOWLEDGEMENTS

A huge thank you to the following people who helped me with this book;

COVER PHOTO: Pym Street looking down to St Ann's Well Road in the 70's. Midway down the photo on the right is my beloved Moffat Street.

G **Thornton** took the photograph and kindly allowed me to use it for the cover of my book. I was astonished when I saw it, for Pym Street IS the original "Effin' 'ill", the steepness of which mam moaned constantly about! This great photo can be seen at **www.picturethepast.org.uk** who also generously allowed me to use it.

This book is primarily intended for my three daughters; **Laura**, **Cindy** and **Zoë**; my grandchildren **Phoebe Pickering**, **Joseph McKie**, **Hattie Pickering**, **Sam Walker** and baby **Toby Walker**.

Kerry Moor – a good and much loved friend.

Jackie Simmons - who constantly encourages me and so kindly proof read this for me.

Alan Bailey – who nagged, chivvied, and constructively criticised my work, until he realised he was flogging a dead horse and gave up.

I am not a rich woman, except perhaps in friends……

ISBN 978-0-9563644-01

Prologue

Mam was a strong, harsh, loud voiced, no nonsense violent woman who took no prisoners. She was, she'd be the first to tell you, and in no uncertain terms, as tough as old boots, afraid of nothing and no-one. As you read this, you may think I have been hard on her but on the contrary, it's the exact opposite. I want this to be a testimony to two people who did the best they could with whatever means they had to keep us kids together. However, whilst what you are about to read *is* the truth, I have often wondered just what sort of young life she herself had that made *her* the way she was, for surely don't we teach as we've been taught, by example? Since parenting does not come with a tried and tested manual, she did it the only way she knew how, the way she herself must have been bought up, by the

" Don't do as ah do, do as ah say, else ah'll brain yer" rule. Why?

"Be'cos ah said so".

And guess what? *I did exactly the same.* I hit my kids. I am not proud of it, but strangely I am immensely happy with how they have all turned out, in spite of, or dare I hope, because of me.

In retrospect, considering the deprived times and but for mam's fiery temper, my parents didn't do too bad a job of rearing us in those appallingly bleak times. At least they managed to keep us six, later 7 kids together, somehow fashioning us into the people we ultimately became from the mean raw materials life had put at their disposal. Dad was a kind, placid gentle soul who never hit us so it was only mam's brutality I feared. She didn't just ill treat me; she did it to all of us to a greater or lesser degree, although thankfully, she did mellow as she got older. She undoubtedly loved babies passionately but was not so fond of children, especially lippy ones like me. I can never ever recall sitting on her knee, unless it was to 'earn' my fish and chip supper. Any time I went to give her a hug, or hold her hand, I was roughly shoved away and even the good night kiss I nightly gave her was always perfunctorily wiped away on the back of her hand.

My siblings too can also recall painful incidents concerning the harsh treatment she meted out. My step brother, younger than me by some 13 years, told me of a time when she threw a table fork at him in his early teens and it stuck in his head. He went into shock as blood poured down his face. She made no attempt to remove the fork or assist him but carried on with her tirade. I had my nose broken, both ears perforated, my wrist deliberately scalded with a poultice and, at aged 13, I was knocked unconscious. Many a time I was kept off school till the bruises healed. Even so, I personally would have sooner been beaten black and blue than be subject to one of her vicious verbal tirades. It was no accident that at a very early age, one by one we all escaped this spoken and actual physical violence by whatever means possible.

Mickey left school and went to work with our dad. He seemed to like his job and worked well at it, but mam took his entire wage packet and merely doled out a few pence back. This went on for about a year and then I too went to work. I began as a sewing machinist at a company called Jersey Kapwood, later Jersey Fabrics which made Marks and Spencer underwear for ladies. I very quickly became a fast and skilled worker and, once on piece rates, my earnings soared and I was soon earning more than dad. Like Mickey before me, I too had to give my mother an unopened wage packet and was given half a crown a week back (12p) and this had to cover clothing, shoes, bus fares to work and lunch money. After a couple of years of this, Mickey was the first to leave home at 17, signing on with the RAF. Our mam was furious. She would be one wage packet down of course and took him back to the recruitment centre the next day to "to bleedin' well un- bloody - sign him". But she'd met her match in the duty sergeant who refused her request and Mickey, to his relief, was in.

I was next and left home at about the same age after a particularly nasty plate throwing incident. The shards of crockery cut my face so badly it bled. Aunty Pats' words "One day you will land her such an unlucky blow," raced through my head and it suddenly dawned she might one day kill me. After a miserable, sleepless night, I left the next morning with all my worldly goods in a brown paper carrier bag. I caught the X99 bus from Nottingham to Birmingham and the only place of safety I could think of, Aunty Lizzie's house and there I remained for a year before striking out on my own.

So it was that one by one, we all left home and out of all of us, I was the only one to return aged 20 and walk down the aisle on my dad's arm. Sad to say mam's life was never a bed of roses, although that does not excuse her, as extreme hardship and grinding poverty were common to most folk back then. We were living through the war and post war years and life was an endless struggle against dirt, penury and hunger. Every crust we kids ate was a crust hard won by dad, our only bread winner.

I know almost nothing about 'dad's' family and only a little of mam's. I believe she was one of six or seven children born to my grandma Polly Anne Warner. She passed away long before I was even born. Two children died in infancy, one a girl named Joan whom I believe suffered from Downs Syndrome, and a boy Sidney. She must have grieved greatly for the boy baby as she later went on to have another son and named him Sydney. At one point the family lived within a mini skirt length of the Nottingham Castle in a run down backstreet named Jessamine Cottages, directly opposite the world famous 'Trip to Jerusalem' Inn.

My grandfather Joseph Warner was, judging by his photograph, a big brute of a man I would not have liked to meet in a crowded street in broad daylight, let alone a deserted dark alley at night! A self taught honky tonk pianist, he left his family and ran off with a woman named Rose along with her 3 year old child Rosie. Mam told me grandfather was not above coming back to Nottingham again from time to time and putting grandma in the family way before wending his way back down south to Rose yet again. But there is no way of knowing if this was so. It has to be said, mam and truth were not natural bed fellows.

Even so, grandma must have had a hard time of it, trying to raise her family alone. She was handicapped by one leg being considerably shorter than the other, causing her to limp badly and she wore a built up shoe to compensate. Grandfather's new common law partner was several years younger than he but had the necessary wherewithal to set them up in style in a sweetshop/tobacconist in Plymouth.

Grandma died quite young and when his partner Rose died some years later, he married the younger Rosie, who was by now, effectively, his step daughter. That seems to me to be an odd thing to do. Though of course, the shop must have lawfully passed to Rosie on her mother's death and I just wonder if that was the reason he married her.

Through a long standing feud between mam and her family, I only met two of her brothers, Sydney just the once and her youngest brother uncle Joe, whom I was to meet twice. Once when I was about 7 or so, and the second meeting was in my 50's and was the most unpleasant experience I can ever recall, but that is another story for another day. I also knew her only sister Aunty Lizzie who was the elder and that too is another story. Suffice to say the two women remained lifelong enemies and not without a good valid reason on my Aunt's part. Are you sensing there's a man in there somewhere? You betcha, Aunty Lizzie's husband!

My mother met and married one Cecil Lowther, her soldier husband - whom I have presumed to have been my biological father - after a whirlwind 6 weeks courtship. Their resultant marriage seemed to have lasted just about as long and sadly I was never ever to set eyes on him, he being long gone before I was even born.

(One of the jobs I had to do as a child, was to take the long walk into the city every Tuesday after school, go to the Guildhall and collect the 10/- a week (50pence) maintenance my father paid for me, quite a generous sum in those days. The value of that money was doubly, trebly instilled into me and by the time I reached home, my fingers would ache from holding it tightly and safely in my hand. If he missed a week and I had to come home empty handed...fortunately for me, he rarely missed.)

My Parents subsequent if somewhat highly unlikely union was to prove lifelong and they would go on to add four more children to the family. 'Dad' was a hard working, gentle soul with a quick racy wit and an all round love of life and his family. I loved him dearly, as did we all. They made an odd looking couple, he being as thin as mam was fat, as tall as she was tiny – she was well short of five foot, as tidy as she was slovenly, as placid as she was fiery, as prudent as she was spendthrift, as industrious as she was lazy, as quietly spoken as she was loud of voice with a soft and gentle manner as she was violent. He saved me from many a childhood beating.

Mam was never physically violent to dad as far as I can recall but her vitriolic onslaughts were just as cruel, if not even more painful. Her treatment of him made no difference to our dad and in my younger days when I mistakenly saw things as either black or white, I used to wonder why mam treated him so badly and, more puzzling, why he put up with it. Why? One never to be forgotten day, for the memory is seared into my very soul; I was to discover what was to me, a surprising answer.

I was married by this time and had two kids. Every Saturday morning I called in on my parents, as was my wont in those days. One day I found Dad sat alone in the kitchen idly watching mam through the window as she scrubbed at an old door mat laid over a table in the backyard. She was really giving it some welly. A few years previously she had lost all her teeth and would not wear her false ones unless she had guests or was going out and so they lived on the corner of the mantelpiece, alongside her cigarettes and lighter.

Deep in concentration, she attended to the task at hand and was absent mindedly chewing hard on her gums. I looked at dad, who in turn was studying her and he had a tender smile on his face as he watched her work.

"Just look at your mam," he said gently, quietly, "she looks like a cow chewing the cud."

He said it as sweetly and reverently as Cary Grant might have said of Carole Lombard:

'Look at her, isn't she the most beautiful woman in the whole world.'

Time stopped as I stared open mouthed at him. Tears welled up in my eyes and a huge lump formed in my throat, that to this day has never quite gone away, for in that moment, it was as if someone had switched the light on for me and in one of those life changing experiences that come like a bolt out of the blue, I suddenly understood. He loved her. There is a photo in the book of my mother when she was in her early 20's and I think you will agree with me, she was a looker. In her youth, she entered and won a beauty pageant in London, winning the top prize of £100, a small fortune then. But at this point in time, she was a much older looking woman of about forty five and was grossly overweight. I had never known her own a lipstick, scent, pretty clothes, even a deodorant, let alone use them. *She didn't need to do anything to please him. He loved her.* From that moment on, I envied my mum. I don't know if she realised it, but she was a very lucky woman and had the love I have since strived for all my life and never found.

In the mid sixties, Dad had to retire through ill health and because they were not married, his pension was pitifully inadequate. It was explained to him that if he were to get a divorce and marry mam, his pension would practically double to encompass her also. Dad told the official he would have wed mam donkeys years ago but he could not afford aa annulment. Legal aid was explained and arranged for him and he got divorced. It was a very proud man who secretly married mam a few months later.

Whatever mam did, I have long since forgiven her, I was probably an impossible kid, I am an impossible woman. She was my only mam and without the strength she instilled into me, perhaps I would have been a very different person to the one I am today. I am not sure if that's a good or a bad thing. But I am reasonably proud of what I have achieved in life. It was mam who, by example, default even, taught us all to be strong; to stand on our own feet and not rely on others; to come out fighting when the bell rang; to dodge and fend off what life threw at us and despite its unerring aim, I think I for one have managed to do just that.

It's been a bitter-sweet if somewhat painful experience walking the remembered streets of my childhood again and the more I write the more I recall of the old St Ann's Well Road; Moffat Street, the Bluebell Hill and Pierrepoint, Schools, the street aunts and uncles, the Cavendish and Empire cinema's, the times, places and people that made me who I am and coloured my life so richly and, at times so bizarrely.

In 1967 I made a pilgrimage back to 80 Moffatt Street. I took my then two young daughters Laura and Cindy to see where I had grown up. I had not been back for many years and got out of my car with an odd mixture of feelings. To my surprise, the street seemed much smaller than I remembered but affluence had steadily reached even this previously deprived area and cars of every age, shape, size, colour and repair were parked outside their owner's house, their wheels half on and half off the pavement. Our old house had hardly changed if at all. The front door was still painted black and maybe it was imagination that made me think I could detect at 'rat a tat tat' height, some tiny tin tack holes and hear the echo of my dad's triumphant laughter. But because they no longer had a slave to keep them white, those doorsteps had aged to a blackish grey. I could not see through the window, covered as they were by heavily bunched up net curtains, protecting the occupant's privacy. I said a silent, tearful farewell and within a few more years it was demolished. Only now does it occur to me to wonder why I did not knock on the door and ask, beg even, could I go in for one last time? I will always regret that I didn't. And yet, don't they say 'never look back?'

So, here it is, in black and white, my young life laid bare. If you lived in St Ann's in those days, if you can recognise one thing in this book, one half remembered mannerism, one risqué cuss word, one incident that makes you smile but you don't know why, one tiny memory that stirs nostalgia in you, then be aware a small, scruffy little girl was watching and listening and *you* are in this book. You helped me to write it. Thank you.

Eee, it's been a funny owd life....an' ya know what? *I ent done yet!*

GLOSSARY

Sad to say, I can't help but notice the *real* old Nottingham accent is slowly dying out. I suppose with a city such as ours with its many races and multiculturalism, it was bound to happen, but I mourn its passing nevertheless. It's a difficult dialect to mimic and of the many TV plays and films based in and around this city, neither actor nor actress has yet managed the pronunciation successfully, the nearest anyone seems to get to it is a sort of Yorkshire burr. Sue Pollard doesn't count....she was born here! And I, playing the barmaid in the BBC serial 'Reznick', set in Nottingham a few years ago, most certainly got it right! Though, even my accent was criticised in the local press by a certain Mr Billiald. Ah soon purrim right!

But there are still odd pockets of the lingo in daily use and only a short while ago I overheard something that could *only* have been said, heard and more importantly understood by someone born and bred in this my beloved city. I had gone into a café and the male customer in front of me asked for a

Bacon cob.

"Teetin or teetout duck?" the assistant asked.

"Oh teetin," replied the customer.

I howled with laughter. And another example I overheard in Clifton, Nottingham a mere few weeks ago;

"Ah went raund 'er 'ause t'tek catalogue but she weren't in."

She were not in?

So, come on now, have a go… let's get you talking and understanding 'Nottinghamese'!

Annall	Also.
Allus	Always
Annit	Hasn't it?
Atta	Have to.
Ayup	Traditional greeting
Ast	Ask.
Bat	Hit.
Batchy	Daft.
Boozer	Hostelry, pub.
Cadge	Borrow.
Cadger	Incessant borrower.
Chelp	Answer back in a cheeky way.
Cob	Bread roll.
Coggin	Apple core.
Corsey	Pavement.
Dicks	Head lice
Dinnit	Didn't it?
Dintah	Didn't I?
Duck	A term of affection used equally by both sexes to both sexes.
Essa	Ever so.
Eyya	Have you?
Eyyabindahn?	Have you been down *to the football match?*
Eyyagorrer?	Do you have?
Eyya gorrowt	Have you got anything?
Faunt	Found
Frock	Dress.

Gerr'off	Get off
Goyin' or gooin'	Going.
Guzzunder	Commode or under-bed pot.
Gorra	Got a.
Hoity-toity	To think oneself better than.
Innit	Isn't it?
Jitteh	An alleyway leading to the backs of terraces.
Ligger	Liar.
Lippy	Too quick to answer back, cheeky.
Mardy	Cowardly.
Mashin'	Brewing tea.
Messen	Myself.
Nowt	Nothing.
Owd	Old or hold.
Owt	Anything.
Oyya	Are you?
Oyya-beya-sen	Are you alone?
Pobs	Stale bread soaked in tea.
Pods	Baby's footwear, usually knitted.
Scrat	Anything meagre spread on bread.
Shintin	She isn't at home
Shunta	Shouldn't have
Snap	Lunch
Swing fo' ya	Someone is in serious trouble.

Tab	Ear
Tinna or tint	It is not.
Towd	Told.
Tuffees	Sweets, oddly coffee was pronounced correctly.
Twist	Spoons of tea twisted up in a scrap of newspaper.
Wannit	Wasn't it?
Wesh	Wash.
Wiggin'	Usually applied to kids listening into adult conversation.
Yerssen	Yourself.
Yev	You have.

If there are two words that define the Nottingham twang its 'Gerr'off'. To truly say it as it's colloquially said in these parts, you have to sound hyphenate the 'Gerr' from the 'off'. So say it thus; *Gerro' phf.* That's it!!

Yo've gorrit nah?

CHAPTER 1

NEW ARRIVALS

It was a pea souper of a night in the midst of the 2nd world war when we did our 'moonlight flit' and moved to 80 Moffat Street, in the St Ann's Well Road district of Nottingham. This secretive move was done, as its name implies, under cover of darkness. It was deemed necessary to escape the local gossip and owing a few pounds worth of debt also played its part. My parents were married but not to each other. In those days there was still a taboo attached to living 'over the brush' left over from a more prim and proper Victorian era and although the practice even then was quite common, it was frowned upon and not to be flaunted.

So to all extents and purposes, as far as our new neighbours were concerned, we were just a typical 1940's family with three kids. Dad had two, Mickey aged four and a half and Eileen, no more than a babe in arms and at some point, Mam, rather belatedly it appears, had taken me from my aunt's care where I had been almost from birth. For reasons unknown to me, although born in Ipswich, I had been cared for by my aunt Lizzie and spent most of the first three years of my life in Aston, Birmingham. This aunt later told me that mam, by now living with the man I grew to know and love as 'dad', forcibly took me from her and I was brought to Nottingham to begin life with my new family. I was never to see or hear from this aunt again until I was in my early teens and when we did finally meet up, I had no memory of her. Oddly I have no knowledge of what must surely have been a traumatic time for one so young, except perhaps a trip to London I took with mam though I can trace my feelings of isolation back to those early days. She had to produce me in the high court where her divorce was to be heard, divorce being a rare occurrence back then.

I vividly remember taking the train with her and it must have been very early in the morning as it was quite dark. The train was jam packed with soldiers going home on leave or back to the front. Some were lying on the floor sleeping, others slept curled up on the seats and there were quite a few of them who were injured and wearing bandages. I can even recall what I was wearing; a beige circular skirt with a matching bolero and a white lawn blouse with multi coloured embroidered dots all over it. When we reached London, I recall being desperately tired and asking mam to carry me. We were stood by a new brick wall and she slapped my legs and made me walk. Then there is a yawning gap until we went back to the station to return home and we were with several people all come to see us off. One of them gave me a shilling – a lot of money then and I dropped it and watched as it rolled off the edge onto the tracks. I dived to get it and someone pulled me back just as a train went thundering by. Another of the party gave me a brown paper bag with nougat bars in it and as I wanted to know if they were all the same inside, I bit into every bar and got another slap. When I recalled these events many years later, mam was astonished at how well I could remember it, for I was barely three years of age.

Our flit had been necessary because the gossiping neighbour-hood womenfolk hereabouts had known poor Albert King's wife had buggered off with another man and left him with two youngsters to bring up and they also knew mam had answered his advert for a live-in housekeeper.

Stood in small gossiping groups on the street corner, probably wearing their old man's flat cap on their heads and wrapped up against the cold in garish hand crocheted multi-coloured shawls of varying degrees of cleanliness, the local women discussed the flighty young piece that had moved in as poor Albert's housekeeper.

It wasn't long before those self same nosy neighbours noticed there seemed to be a lot more going on in that house than a spot of cleaning and polishing! Hence the moonlight flit. Dad piled all we owned onto a hand cart, plonked us kids on top and undercover of darkness and fog we set off for our new home, the big iron wheels clattering noisily on the cobble stones. These poor upright and unsuspecting folks in this run down, though not unpleasant terraced street were mainly sedate, older, goodly and Godly folk, some even retired. As soon as we moved, mam became Mrs King and I was immediately divested of my given surname Lowther and also 'adopted' my new dad's name. Now I too was a King. But there was nothing 'Kingly' about our family. By the morning light, our new neighbours were to find out we were poverty stricken, common as muck, loud and scruffy, indeed the very sort of people you do not want moving in next door to you. Every living thing in our new street, from the peace loving residents down to the pigeons on the roof were about to have a rude awakening, quickly finding out why our dad labelled his noisy family 'the brass band'. Soon we were to bring new life to that terrace, most of it rolled up in the bedding on the back of our hand cart!

Our new house was reached via a steep road mam called 'Effin' 'ill' but it was only when I started school and learned to read, I found out its actual name was Pym Street. On my first day at the Bluebell Hill Infants and junior school, I was asked by my teacher, a Miss Castle, where I lived. I replied parrot fashion as I had been taught by mam, both my address and the Co-op divi number; "80, Moffat Street Miss."
"Where is that?" she asked, meaning whereabouts in Nottingham? St Ann's? Sneinton? Carlton, Mapperley, the City? They all ran into each other, at most over a scant mile or two.
"Dahn effin' 'ill," I had innocently replied and tearfully wondered why I'd been so soundly slapped.

Mam was nothing if not an accomplished cusser and could have earned a degree in the art. She could most certainly out-swear any man I ever met. More, she would and could easily, split a perfectly normal, respectable word in half and tuck a profanity squarely in the middle, as if it had always belonged there! In her defence though, Pym Street was really steep and I think she cut her swearing teeth on it. Many's the time she spat out that and other choice utterances as my step brother and I helped push our pram, fully laden with shopping and baby Eileen, up this hill. We were on our way home, from the Home and Colonial grocery shop or Sneinton fruit and veg market, where mam had us pick up and secrete under the pram blankets, any odd discarded vegetables, cabbage leaves, potatoes or bruised fruit. Stopping midway to catch her breath, she'd heavily and somewhat precariously plonk her large bottom on a narrow terraced wall, carefully avoiding the sharp metal stumps where black ornamental iron railings had been removed 'to aid the war effort' in some mysterious way.

Thus settled, wheezing and puffing, she'd wipe the sweat from her face on her all enveloping wrap around floral pinny, scratch a match on the bricks and light up the hand rolled tab-end kept in readiness behind her tobacco stained ear. Thus settled she'd inhale deeply, the fire racing quickly along the loose packed hand rolled cigarette sending a curl of blue smoke rising from the glowing end. Her harsh scowling expression softened and a look of utter bliss would pass over her face. From beneath the potatoes, cabbages, onions and other miscellany of scavenging and shopping pinning Eileen down in the pram, there came a wail of discomfort. Mickey quickly silenced her by shoving her dummy in her mouth and now, in the ensuing silence, we waited patiently as mam smoked the tab down to a lip scorching fraction of an inch.

Mam, an entrenched smoker all her life, saved even the tiniest of tab ends in an old pipe-tobacco tin. This dubious and no doubt toxic mix was kept moist with a supplementary piece of cut potato. She added to this foul smelling tin daily, sometimes even picking up the odd long butt from the pavement. When she was out of fags and money and she was invariably out of fags and money, she'd clumsily roll her own with a small Ritzla cigarette making machine. Sat on the wall in a fug of nicotine bliss, she took a last short puff then looked hard at the stub in her orange stained fingers, studying the remains very carefully. Deciding there was nothing worth saving of the quarter inch butt, she ground the glowing end underfoot, carefully avoiding the inevitable hole in her shoe. Now she'd cough, spit, wipe her mouth on the palm of her hand, the palm of her hand on the back of her pinny, stretch and look up at the seemingly Everest of an 'effin' ill' yet to climb and her features settled back into their customary scowl. Sighing, she prepared herself for the final push for home. Teeth gritted and snorting the last of the blue grey smoke dragon like out of her nostrils, she'd say; "Come on you kids put yer backs into it then. Ohh, this effin 'ill is enough to mek a parson swear. It's un – bleddy – ending an' gets longer be the soddin' day, 'it'll be the death o' me one o' these day's, yo'll see! Come on then, gi' it some elbow grease, push the thing then, push......"

Just a couple of hundred yards short of the peak, the last street on the left was ours. Moffat Street was neatly cornered by a cobbler's on one side, a chip shop the other and, in the middle, a creepy air raid shelter leant towards the chip shop. Dad said this was lucky for us these were all on our doorstep as; 'yo' allus gunna need one or t'other on 'em.' This road was if anything, even steeper than Pym Street but the section we had to traverse, was a whole lot shorter, as mercifully it levelled out a mere hundred yards further on. As we climbed, we put our young backs into the push, taking as much strain as possible off mam. There must had been a time when this cobbled road was shiny and new, the houses marching briskly like rigid Roman soldiers in perfect union up the hill. Now, either side, the rows of grey, two and three storied terraced dwellings, their continuity broken by dark jitty's every dozen or so houses, leaned into each other precariously, looking for all the world like a drunken chain of dishevelled and arthritic old men shuffling up a mountain side. Just when we thought we could not push one more step, the road levelled out and number 80, the first on the left past the jitty, was ours.

This three storied house, the beginning of a row of six, was considered 'posh' locally because they were the only ones on the entire street with an enclosed front porch and also one of the few with electricity, gaslight still being more the norm in those days. Leading up to the black painted front door and enclosed within the porch, were three stone steps which mam painstakingly whitened with a pumice stone every week. Only don't try to find the steps or the house now, both are long gone, except here in my memory. My parents may well have left behind the local gossip by this move but as mam could not manage money to save her life and times were exceptionally hard, the 'by the skin of your teeth' escape would be a brief respite with the debt mounting very quickly again, as needs dictated, and they dictated often.

Any memory my brother Mickey and I had of our previous home is long gone. Mam said, as kids, we scathingly referred to it as the 'black house', though she didn't know why. Well, assuming 'black' to mean not good, if the one we had left behind was the black house, lord only knows why we moved to number 80, since it didn't even have a lavatory. Mind, even though the one we had left behind *had* a lavatory, it was not something to boast about as being what was known as a paddle lav. Mam recalled this involved a sort of wooden paddle that 'floated' a little way down the pan and the other end of it stuck out of the outside back wall. When solids hit the paddle it caused it to drop the faeces below, out of sight and then spring back into position. Tired of 'Rum –

stick – a bum', 'dobby' or 'statues', the local kids would quietly observe an unsuspecting neighbour entering the loo and with perfect timing, wait until a critical point in the defecation was reached and then jump down hard on the back end of the paddle. I am sure your imagination has furnished you as to the outcome of this action. Screamingly funny or agonisingly painful depending on which end of the paddle you were.

But not only was there no toilet, nor was there a bath, not even a galvanised one to hang on the back wall. There were six houses and five toilets. Six houses, five hanging baths. There was a hook where one had once hung and would one day hang again, but that was all. Mickey and me pondered long and hard as to why there was no lavatory. I mean, there was a space where one should have been, so did the builder forget? The empty space, some 8ft away from the house, was handy though in that it was a convenient spot for mam to keep our dustbin, a boon since they could stink foul and crawl with maggots in the hot summer months and everyone else had to have theirs right under their living room (kitchen) window.

In its absence, we had to share a toilet with our next door neighbours, an elderly couple who were extremely kind to us. It was quite a trek down the yard and was a simple brick box, built back to back with their next neighbours' toilet and had a shared, heavily leaking roof. Its crumbling walls were distempered with a whitewash which forever came off onto our clothes. We hadn't been there long when, kids being kids especially we kids, in the absence of a sheet or two of toilet paper – in our case a scrap of the Daily Mirror – the distemper took on a less than salubrious hue! The nice old couple next door gave up on it and left it to us, they in turn, sharing with their 'cleaner' neighbours.

Another good thing about this house was its proximity to the jitty which gave access to the back of the terrace. It was fortunate, meaning as it did, we never had to use our front door, and neither did anyone else, it being taboo to put even one foot on our mam's pristine white steps. Every Friday, 'top to bottom' cleaning morning, she'd get down on her knee's and scrub them, pumice stone on stone, worn smooth by countless generations of feet and scrubbing. As she did so, her fat bottom swung hypnotically in rhythm with the rolls of fat under her arms, the blackened soles of her feet showing through her ill fitting pom-pommed and ragged slippers. The steps took some time to do and her knuckles often bled as she caught them on the stone. Eventually she'd stand up, arms streaked with ribbons of dirt, place her hands on her lower back to ease the ache that followed, step back, admire her work, throw a warning look at nobody in particular and the road in general, sling the dirty water down the street drain and after taking one last look at a job well done, slip slop her way back down the jitty. I have stood and watched mam do this chore over and over, little knowing that by the age of six, Mickey and I would be doing this and a few other jobs besides to earn our weekly sixpence pocket money. It did us no harm and might just have done us a bit of good but I can still taste the childish resentment even now.

The daily newspaper played a very important role in our lives, and it had to be the Mirror mind, not the Sketch, mam considered that paper too down market even for us! The Mirror was an absolute must. It not only kept us abreast of what was happening in the war ridden world but also with what Jane, Garth and Belinda were doing in their colourful black and white cartoon life; they kept mam up to date on juicy murders and salacious stuff whilst the Nottingham Evening Post and News told her of the local jumble sales and whist drives. One of her favourite columns in this paper was headed Houses to Rent or Exchange. This she would scrutinise before selecting one that excited her.

"Oh listen Al, this sounds nice. Three bed-roomed mid terrace, parlour, sitting room, large kitchen, bathroom, Ohhhh a BATHROOM! Private backyard, with small garden, two an' a tanner a week. (12.5 pence) Refs required. Suit us would that. Just imagine, eyyin' us own bathroom eh? Do you know where Bunbury Street is dad?"

Since dad was a born and bred Meadows area man, if he didn't know, no-one did. Usually he'd lift his head from his racing paper, peer at her over his glasses and confidently say; 'Ah know that street ah do, that's in the Meadows thar'ris,' or St Ann's or Carlton, or any other surrounding district, dad seemed to know them well from a boyhood of living and later working in the city. On this occasion however, he jerked his head from his racing paper, drew in a sharp whistled breath and as though speaking of the most vile place in England, said;

"Yo' don't want ter be even *thinkin'* o' movin' there. It's a bad move is that. Yo've got the rotten stink o' Bitterlin's bone factory all soddin' day an' night, the bleddy tannery on Trent bridge, football fans screamin' an' yellin' every weekend, it bleddy well floods every winter an' yo' etta live upstairs wi' nowt but candle light, we better off stayin' 'ere woman." Whether or not it was true, only our dad knew but he breathed a silent sigh of relief when she seemed to accept what he said without question and, turning the page, moved onto the Hatched, Matched and Despatched column (Births, Marriages and Deaths!)

The 'contents of wills' was another particular favourite. This 'who left what and to whom' column fascinated mam. She often drooled over the seemingly huge fortunes left behind and said she wished someone would die and leave her a lot of money and then would immediately qualify it by saying they didn't actually need to die, just leave her their money. Other pages also provided them both with many an unfinished crossword, made colouring books for us kids, polished windows, furniture, lino and shoes; obligingly tore into neat little squares for the lavatory, made a crisply pleated fan for the fire grate in the summer months and blotter like, helped dry freshly mopped floors, lined all the cupboards and drawers, wrapped dad's daily work lunch of two perpetual cheese sandwiches - thus protecting them against the copious rust in his 'snap' tin, became a tablecloth and even, albeit briefly, packed several pages deep into our holed shoes, gave us scant protection against rain and snow. On the very bottom of the back page was a small 2"x 4" blank bit labelled STOP PRESS. This precious piece was torn out and used as stationary for notes to teachers and shopkeepers.

Indeed once, when mam had no fags, I saw her roll a cigarette out of that scrap of paper too, though the ensuing coughing fit made it an experiment not worth repeating. And one sheet could and would be used more than once. For e.g.; when taken from the table, it went on to polish shoes before being twisted into 'log' shapes and used to light the copper fire on washday. Not a bad pennies worth....except, we didn't *actually* pay for it! From the day we moved there, Mr Ball the local newsagent was told in no uncertain terms to keep off mam's front door steps. He plaintively questioned her as to how he was supposed to reach the letterbox without the use of them? Mam said that was his problem but if he didn't she would soon take her business elsewhere. He tried to get round this obstacle by using an old sheet of newspaper to stand on but mam complained that the print came off onto her white steps and so he spread a bit of brown paper kept in readiness in his newspaper sack. Thus the poor gullible man managed to deliver the tabloid according to her demands.

After a few weeks he was to wish he hadn't, for the day predictably came when he wanted paying but he was out of luck. In our house, the money ran out twice as fast as the week. He walked down the jitty and knocked on our backdoor, thereby joining a growing number of people to whom mam owed money. It always fell to us kids to do mam's whispered bidding, answer the door and tell him; 'Shintin'. (Dad said it sounded like a China man's name!) This chore was something we became very adept at. *(I loathed it so much; I grew up with a hatred of debt. To this day, other than the Derbyshire building society to whom I once owed my mortgage, I have never owed anyone anything!)*

As kids, we hated this job, it being an almost daily chore encompassing anyone who actually dared request money for their goods and services! Since everything in those days, i.e. rent, milk, insurance, club, coal, etc were all paid for, and the money collected by men at the back door, being repeatedly told, week after week that mam wasn't in, led to the men becoming verbally quite nasty to us, hence our hatred of the job. Mr Ball, after trying and failing many times to trap mam and collect his just dues, stopped delivering the papers but not his, if somewhat loud, demand for payment. Very early every Sunday he took to knocking long and loud on our front door. "Ya can't say yer norrin nah can ya?" he'd boom, his normal, patient, polite manner having been used up several weeks before.

"Where's me bleedin' money eh? yo've 'ed yer papers, nah pay up ya schemin', robbin' gets"

This not unreasonable, but each week successively louder, door thumping request for payment, went on for numerous Sundays and then the newsagent boldly started to stand on the steps without benefit of anything underfoot. The ensuing black marks, on the white surface were a red rag to our mam and she nagged dad constantly about it.

Now, Sunday in those days, was strictly observed as the Sabbath, a day of quiet rest and contemplation, so this ongoing early morning fracas woke our neighbours and embarrassed and riled our mild mannered dad. He opened the bedroom window and threatened to throw the piss pot all over him. But it was no great threat, as it was not yet quite light and dad could not see him anyway as he was hidden from view sheltered under the porch, defiantly standing on mam's forbidden steps. Dad slammed the window shut and tried to get back to sleep.

Weekly, Mr Ball stood his ground, loudly repeating his demands to be paid again and again.
"Yo'll not be gerrin' any Sunday rest until yo've paid me, ah'm warnin' yo," was his weekly parting shot as he gave up....for now! After several annoying weeks of this crack of dawn, neighbour waking, knuckle thumping theatre, dad had an idea, an idea which afforded him a devilish grin.

The following Saturday evening, still smirking fiendishly, dad took out his shoe repair kit from the bottom cupboard and opened a small box that held the tiny little nails with which he bi-weekly repaired our shoes. He tacked dozens of them - each being not much thicker than a dressmakers pin - into the door at just about 'rat a tat tat' height. Early the very next morning, the slumbering peace was shattered for the last time by one thump of the door followed by a yowl of pain, plus a string of un-Sunday like oaths. Dad smiled, turned over and went back to his sleep. Poor Mr Ball never came back again. But it was to be many a long day before we got our newspapers delivered once more.

Now, with only a small whistling and oft screeching valve radio to keep us abreast of the warring world, mam had to wait until dad got home from work bringing with him whatever papers his workmates had left behind - even the Sketch being grudgingly welcomed - or cadging, begging and borrowing off the neighbours, going so far as to even read the fish and chip wrappers! No matter their age or grease, they were precious and we had a use for them.

There was a time when another strange visitor bravely knocked on our front door. Mam angrily swung it open. I was stood warily behind her skirts and saw a tall gent dressed in a

long brown military style raincoat, wearing a trilby hat and
carrying a clipboard and pen. He politely doffed his hat to
mam from his great height.

"Good morning," he began, "would you be Mrs King?"
Mam glared down at his well polished shiny shoes plonked
squarely on her work.

"Never mind 'oo I am, gerr offa them bleddy steps, ah've
spent all bleedin' morning' cleanin' 'em," she loudly warned
him.

"I..I'm sorry."

The man apologised and hurriedly stepped backwards down
onto the pavement, leaving a distinct black mark on the step.
From this somewhat reduced and disadvantaged level, he
tried to reassert his status, looked up at her and asked in a
stern voice;

"I repeat. Are you Mrs King?"

"Who's astin'?" mam said through clenched teeth, scowling
at the dirty mark. He went on to explain who he was and
what he was doing there. Someone had made a complaint to
the NSPCC that we kids were being ill treated and he had
been sent to look into the allegations. With a sound like the
roar of a lion, she leapt off the top step. I recognised that

sound and, tiny as I was, knew he had about one sixth of a seconds warning or she would have him. But thankfully he moved with the required lightning speed and sped off. She chased after him down the street and round the corner past the chip shop. He lost his pen in his flight and as mam returned, she picked up the pen, victoriously holding it up as a trophy and breathlessly slip slopped her way back up the hill.

"It's an ill wind as does no bogger any good." mam said triumphantly, "we got us selves a nice new pen!"

He never came back. Mam then set her mind to the 'who did it' game and came up with the elderly, kindly Byewater couple who lived next door. What bought her to this conclusion was an incident that had taken place a few months previously. It was during my summertime convalescence after having my tonsils out at aged five. When I came out of hospital a few days later, I was surprised to find we had a new baby. My sister Sandra had been born during the brief time I was away. Now, mam clearly had no time for me or anything else except the new baby, a baby that screamed day and night and only stopped when mam picked her up and stuffed her huge tit in her mouth. I was horror stricken

44

watching her suck the nipple and seeing the greenish tinged
milk run down her chin. Yeuk. I had been told by mam that I
must go out in the street to play, as the hospital doctor had
said I needed as much fresh air as possible.

"And don't yo' be sittin' in all that muck on that corsey in yer
nice clean clo'se, an' stay off them front steps," she
admonished me. But all my street friends of course were in
school and I found it hot, sticky, boring and tiring to simply
stand alone doing nothing. So, my childish logic reasoned,
mam could not see me if I sat on the cool steps within the
shelter of next doors porch, out of sight of her. I had only
been sitting there some short time when the door opened and
Mrs Byewater threw a slop pail of dirty water all over me. All
hell broke loose. Mrs Byewater tried to explain she had no
idea I was there and how could mam think she would do
something so nasty to a little girl just out of hospital and it
really had been an awful accident. She simply did not see me
there. But mam did not believe her and never spoke to this
woman again. I was as sure then as I am now that it was an
accident. This sweet lady continued to pass on her left over
food items to us and could always be relied upon to find

sixpence when we pointedly reminded her that today was our
birthday.

Although generally speaking the 'don't stand on the steps' rule was rigorously enforced there were *some* exceptions to the rule. I do recall the Dr's Lynd and Nelson always used them, and there was one special man who was allowed, no encouraged, to use our front steps, even do a Fred Astaire in hob nailed pitch black miners boots up them if he so chose and that was the hero of the day, the man who emptied the meters. He was the most welcome of visitors and his whereabouts were keenly tracked from street to street as the cash strapped families waited on his ever nearer lucrative call.

This was one man to whom 'shintin' did not apply, he *GAVE* us money you see and what a ritual that was. The electric and gas meters were on the wall just inside our cellar door. Out would come his torch, which he expertly clenched in his teeth to light his way, needing as he did, two hands to remove the very heavy metal cash box. This he'd then slap onto the kitchen table with a noisy clatter. Now he'd open it, tip it out and more money than I had ever seen in my young life would race and spin out. He would tell us we could keep any coins that fell on the floor. Coiled like springs, we waited to pounce on any wayward pennies but he was so skilful and swift he never allowed a rolling coin to hit the floor, smacking them flat to the table with the palm of his hand. Winking at us kids but casting a questioning look at mam and "tutting" through disapproving pursed lips, he'd find and remove all the 'foreign objects' masquerading as coins of the realm. These consisted of bottle tops carefully hammered into the exact shape of a penny, foreign coins, bits of plastic and even buttons carefully filed to fit – needs must when the devil drives or the gas pops out!

There then came the ritual played out in every house he ever visited; of mothers scolding their kids for treating the meters as toys and shoving these foreign objects in the slot. Our mam and dad even tried to kid us that these meters were money boxes and pocket money pennies could be saved in them, but I think we were a bit too cute for that. Sighing, he'd push the foreigners to one side, but their escape into light was short lived, mam putting them back again the second he had gone. (It pleased her no end when these were finally inherited by the family who took over our house when we moved some years later!)

Now with unbelievable swiftness, he counted the coins 2 at a time and stacked them 12 deep into neat piles each equalling one shilling. As tidily regimented as the Terracotta Army and about the same colour, the rows grew and marched across the table. After calculating how much was owed to the company – minus of course the value of the 'foreign objects' - a few of these stacks were handed back as rebate. We would eat, mam would smoke tailor made cigarettes, the local shops tills were awash with pennies and our clock would tick again for a few affluent days.

Taking pride of place in the centre of the black shiny slate mantelpiece and worthy of note, was our old timepiece. Save for the tinny alarm clock at dad's side of the bed, this was our only means of tracking time and whether it ticked or not was a measure of our finances at any given point, for it literally ran on pennies! In retrospect, it was a large, Westminster chiming, highly polished, elegant, mahogany and brass, melodious sounding beauty I suppose, but it was without doubt a temperamental article that only dad could manage. Every Thursday night, pay day, he took out a large brass key from his waistcoat pocket, opened the domed glass door on the front, put the key into the hole, slowly and oh so carefully wound it before lodging one brass foot on a pile of two, three or four pennies. It was an exercise that took some time and skill to do as, according to their age, the coins varied in depth and had to be the exact right thickness, else the clock stayed silent. Trial and error finally won and the clock seemed to sigh and begin to tick again. He'd carefully put the key back, shoving it deep into his breast pocket, step back with evident satisfaction and give mam a stern warning look that advised her not to touch it again, but it was a look that was lost on her and we all knew it. Thus tilted, the clock would faithfully tick and sing its tuneful melody for eight long days and nights, well 2 or 3 anyway, for it was a foregone conclusion that once mam's purse was empty and she needed a penny for the gas or the electric meter, or even for a packet of five Park Drive cigarettes, she'd remove the coins and the clock would stop once more.

It drove dad crazy. Since we were still many years off either of them owning a simple wrist watch, mam bought down the brass twin belled one from their bedroom and used it whilst the Westminster chimer took a breather until next payday. Dad had to then remember to take the clock to bed with him and many was the time he would dog wearily climb those steep stairs to go to bed, automatically reach for the clock to wind and set it for the morning, only to find it was still downstairs on the kitchen shelf! I well remember one heated argument when dad asked her why she couldn't just get the time off the radio instead of nicking his bedside clock. Mam replied that was a good idea and she didn't know why she hadn't thought of it. In future, she vowed, when the leccy went out, she would use the pennies from under the clock so as she could get the leccy back on just to hear the time and sod the penny needed for the gas meter to cook his tea and he could have 'ifit' for tea! (If he could catch it, he could eat it!)

There was a 'knocker up' man named Billy, a local man who lit the street lights at twilight and who also put out the flame at dawn and for only one penny a week he would tap on your bedroom window to waken you but dad wouldn't or, most likely couldn't afford such luxury. Many a verbal scrap took place between my parents over the removal of the pennies from under the foot of that clock I can tell you.

Many years later, now married with a child, I was living in the now long defunct Durban Terrace, Hyson Green, in an old, horribly run down house that had been previously boarded up and condemned as unfit for many years. It made 80 Moffatt Street look like a mansion. When we took it on, the last half a dozen or so stairs were missing, as was the floorboards under the kitchen sink. We had to pay to get these repaired ourselves and also to have the gas and the electricity put in. The house had two rooms up, two down and an outdoor toilet. The sitting room was no more than 10ft square and in the cellar, there were four pit props holding the sagging floor up. There was just enough room for a chest of drawers and a small sofa. Over the course of a few hours, footsteps vibrating on the prop held floor caused the drawers to ease out little by little, until the whole chest ultimately toppled over unless caught in time. Life was really tough. I lived in constant fear that the floor would eventually give and we would all be plunged into the cellar below, along with the glowing coal fire! But when the house finally did give up the ghost, the floor held and the roof caved in!

I regularly popped in to see mam, who at this time was living on Bobbersmill Road, Hyson Green. One day she was sat talking to a local woman friend nick-named the Duchess on account of - relative to the area and the poverty of the times - her fortune though how much of a fortune, nobody ever knew for sure. As we chatted, mam was trying to get the clock to work by putting the usual pennies underneath its right foot but it had other idea's and refused to work. She lost her temper and swore she would get rid of it and get a new one by the end of the day.

"'appen it just wants a clean," offered the Duchess.

"Ah've gen it a good wesh many a time in the bleddy sink, burrit meks not the slightest bit o' difference."

Mam was not joking. I asked her if I could have the old clock as I didn't have one at all.

"Yes, yo' c'n ev the bleddy thing, eeyar…" and so saying, she threw in the corner where it smashed into smithereens. An ignoble, if somewhat erratic end to a mischievous timepiece.

CHAPTER 2

IT'S RAINING - GORRA BE WESHDAY!

Our jitty being the first on this side of the street not only gave access to the back of our house but to all the others left and right. It was a shelter from the rain for passers by, a place for us kids to play, a way of knowing dad was home by the echoing of his squeaky bike wheels and heavy booted footfall bouncing off the walls into our back kitchen, or, under the cover of darkness, made a nice courting spot. There were three steps up to our yard on the left and three down on the right. Either side, the yard was shared by all the other houses and it was possible to go down ours and travel almost the whole of the entire street - and it was quite a long one - without ever coming out onto the front. In our part of the yard, there were a couple of loose floor tiles close to the back doorstep which, on wet days, could squirt thick black mud up the back of your legs. This most unpleasant experience was to be avoided if at all possible! In the long communal back alley, paved with the same dark blue, criss-cross patterned, quarry tiles, washing festooned the yard, in varying shades of white or even cleanliness.

It was set in stone that every Monday was wash day, come rain, hail or flood, for no housewife worth her salt would let the weather interfere. Very early in the morning, dad would light the copper fire for mam before leaving for his work. By the time she got up, the water would be boiling and the first lot of washing would begin. She would ladle out some of the hot water into the dolly tub, sparingly sprinkle on Oxydol or Persil and begin by ponching the nappies and sheets through the resultant foam.

Since this action was taking place in every house in Nottingham, the smell of soap powder and bleach overrode the usual stale household smells and refreshingly scented the whole street. Almost every house seemed to have a baby and pretty soon nappies, the first of the whites and having been dunked in Reckitts Dolly Blue, ours *were* sparkling white, were propped up in the yard like so many flags of surrender – quite an apt description I guess. Lines of laundry, according to the weather, either blew in the yard, or hung limply from the overhead pulley and dripped like indoor rain, sizzling onto the hot hearth.

When mam and the street aunts put their sheets out, they were at the mercy of all who needed to access the back. Mostly folk cared enough to try not to touch them if at all possible and lifted them gingerly with two cleanish fingers but to us kids, the sheer joy of running a fevered brow through a cool, wet, soap and fresh air scented sheet, on a hot sticky day was absolute bliss and once, I memorably ran the whole length of Moffat Street there and back doing just that! As mam pegged ours out on the lines, she would glance at some of the other women's wash disdainfully and mumble under her breath that she would not bother to hang out such filthy garments and a little elbow grease would not come amiss.

I had learned at a very early age that where cleanliness was concerned, we were different to other people in some strange and to me, unfathomable way. For a start, our muck was quite unlike anyone else's, ours being superior in some aspect. Having been taken to the house of a casual friend of my

mother's one day, she later recounted to dad the place had
been filthy. As we partook of our simple evening meal, she
regaled him with somewhat exaggerated tales of dirty floors
and hearths, smeary windows, fluff and stuff under the table.
"..an yo' shoulda seen the state o' the cup she gen me to drink
me tea out on, it were bleddy disgustin'. Ah couldn't drink it
an' it were still on the shelf when ah left."
I glanced down and in my innocence said;
"But look 'ere mam, we got fluff and stuff under our table
annall."
She must have been in a good mood that day for she clouted
me on top of my head with the *flat* side of her knife and told
me;
"But that's our muck ya silly sod yo'. An' it's different when
its yer own muck and watch yer chelp, yer've got too much
lip yo' ev, an' yer gerrin' far too bleddy big fer yer boots."
My chelp? - My lip? - My boots? The subsequent stars I saw
from the knife blow did nothing to enlighten me!

This long continuous yard was bordered by a small, street
long brick wall some three foot high. Into the bricks was set a
high metal fence which was a safety barrier over a steep

sandstone cliff that dropped to a street some 50 to 60ft below us. It formed the dead end of a street running vertically under and away from us. Think of it as a cross, as Upper Beacon Street ran vertically uphill opposite our front door, so Lower Beacon Street, ran to the main St Ann's Well Road at the back and Moffat street sat on top of a cliff and ran horizontally between the two. Only the black, lead painted, pike staff shaped iron railing of the same ilk of those cut down on Pym Street, kept us kids safe from that enormous drop.

Family legend has it, some time previously, two officials came a-knocking on our door and told dad that, as there was a shortage of metal, the railings would have be cut down within a few days to 'aid the war effort'. With great dignity, dad pointed out the treacherous drop to the street below and informed the official just how many children lived along this terrace. He told them they would be condemning these kids to certain death and they would cut it down over his dead body. Our dad could talk a mean fight! But they took heed, left the railings intact and never came back.

I had painful personal experience of this railing. The stretch of bank below our houses had the only greenery around and it was fun to stand on the wall, hang onto the railings and look down at the flora and fauna that lived there. One warm sunny day I was watching a small mole or mouse scurrying along stopping at this plant or that flower. As I watched, I had one of the spikes in my mouth. Oh the horror of all that lead paint I can almost hear you thinking. The paint wasn't the problem, my foot slipped and you do not want to know the painful outcome. Though I can tell you that most of the hurt was from my other end after I ran screaming and bleeding to my mother in those days of 'pay as you go' illness's and accidents!

This lowly road below the bank was a feature in our lives that afforded us great entertainment. It was a small grossly over-crowded street of two storied houses, mostly occupied by newly arrived Jamaican and Irish families, the latter of whom for some reason took to scrapping every Friday, Saturday and Sunday nights. I suppose having a boozer seemingly on every corner in those days didn't help. As soon as the pubs turned out, the occupants would begin arguing and fighting and one by one, all the neighbours in our yard came out. They sat down in some considerable comfort on seats bought out from their own kitchens. With arms resting comfortably on the wall and noses pressed into the iron railings, we all looked down on and enjoyed a front row seat, much like the Romans did at the Coliseum. On looking up and seeing the line of figures watching the show, the protagonists often raised their fists in anger towards the onlookers and threatened them with violence. But the neighbours merely laughed and shouted down to them causing even more uproar. If the neighbours were worried they didn't show it, but later, in the darkness of their beds, it may well have been a very different story.... In those days there were few telephones and it could be a long night before the clanging of the police 'Black Maria' bell signalled the end of the night's floor show. But even the mopping up was worth the watch and only after the ambulances had left with the odd broken body and the police had calmed things down somewhat, was the show considered over for another night. The previous weekend's rowdy events then became the core of the next days 'post wash' gossip, as the women hung out their laundry and cackled over the weekend's proceedings through a mouthful of dolly pegs.

I remember vividly looking down on another, sadder spectacle through those self same railings; the funeral of two little girls –English and Jamaican - aged about six. They were friends and had gone to the park to play. They got caught in a storm and sheltered beneath a tree. It was struck by lightning and they were both killed instantly. Their funeral was a sombre but spectacular and terribly sad event.

A factory stood at the top of this street making highly flammable celluloid products. It was immediately under the rock and therefore under our house, and I was actually sat on the lavatory the day it exploded and caught fire! I don't think it was anything to do with the war. Pandemonium broke out as you can well imagine. I recall racing past the huge wall of flames and into our house screaming for my mam. I ran over glass and debris into every room, even braving the upstairs in my hunt for her. To my horror, I could find neither she nor the baby and my mind had them both blown to smithereens. Panic ran through me and I frantically scoured the street calling and looking for her. I eventually found her obliviously drinking tea and smoking in a neighbour's house. When I breathlessly and tearfully told her about the fire, it appears the two women had heard the explosion and thought it to be thunder. As I recollect, no-one was actually injured but the folks round about soon got wind that there was some insurance payout to be had. Every house claimed for satin eiderdowns, Egyptian cotton sheets, mattresses, feather pillows, counterpanes, carpets, easy chairs, bedside rugs, and curtains for every window in the house. The insurance assessor sarcastically said he was amazed at how modest these houses seemed from the outside when the insides held such riches. Within days of the delivery of the replacements, the items for sale in the miscellaneous column of the Evening Post doubled. We ate well around that 'clock ticking' time too!

Having dodged the aforementioned loose bricks in our backyard, the first room in our house was a miniscule scullery no bigger than 5 ft square. This was where our food was prepared and cooked; where mam did the weekly wash and where we all took our daily ablutions – or, as far as we kids were concerned, did or did not according to how cold the tap water was, or even if there was any tap water, as frozen pipes were normal in the winter. It was also where, on a devilishly dark night, the trip down the back alley to the lavatory was a no go and mam had a pee in the baby's potty and tipped it down the sink! It seems that we kids were not the only ones afraid of the bogeyman.

The brick walls of the scullery were lead painted a very dark green and it was sparsely furnished with a shallow, chipped, mustard coloured sink, with one cold, permanently dripping brass tap. There was a horrid spider ridden, soggy space beneath, which also housed our cane washing basket filled with dirty clothes and a galvanised ridged dolly tub and ponch. A ponch being an implement that was a sort of upside down, colander shaped and holed dish, made of copper and joined onto a stout broom type handle. It was used to remove dirt quite effectively by dunking it up and down onto soaking clothes, though it was hard, back breaking work. Next to the sink, a removable, slimy wood draining board covered a 'copper' in the corner, this being a deep basin shaped bowl which had to have a fire lit under it and was for the aforementioned family wash. It took its name from the metal it was made of. Outside the back door, was an old fashioned mangle with a huge iron wheel which afforded us kid's great fun as we turned it and watched as the water was squeezed out of the clothes by the huge wooden rollers. Mam eventually got a modern one with a fold down enamelled top which also doubled as an additional scullery work surface. Above the black iron, three burner gas cooker, was a shelf which housed a few chipped enamel saucepans, a couple of roasting tins and that was about all we had as a fitted kitchen in those days. Notwithstanding, mam was a good cook and turned out some delicious food in there; stew that had simmered gently sometimes for days and which stuck to your ribs, tripe and onions poached for hours in milk and, finances providing, with a few sausages dropped in as well, mouth wateringly light pastries, egg custards and delicious, oh so scrumptious and fondly remembered mince pies. I love mince pies but have yet to taste one half as good as those she made.

A towel hung behind the backdoor on a roller and was a dubious shade of multi coloured stripes on a white background with an exceedingly black centre which got blacker as the week progressed, it being changed only on wash day. On the wall to the right of the towel, hung an old and much steam damaged mirror into which dad squinted daily as he shaved. Since the kitchen was lit by no more than a 40 watt bulb, the only other light came from an 18" square window, too small to warrant curtains. It was difficult to see what you were doing and everyone moaned as to the uselessness of the mirror. I was considered vain for I spent a lot of time staring into it. To me, its damage portrayed a misty fairy tale castle set in a far off land, in which lived a beautiful princess with long flowing hair and diaphanous film star gown. Not at all like the image of the ugly little girl that sullenly stared back at me through its hazy imaging. Podgy faced, cow brown eyed and with the short mousey hair which mam cut into the 'pudding basin style' haircut of the day, in which I sat with a basin on top of the head and any hair that fell below it was unceremoniously chopped off with our blunt scissors. The 'styling', I hasten to add, having nothing to do with fashion and everything to do with our family's finances. Mickey had to have his hair cut by the barber and should have thought himself lucky but I was always made to accompany him with orders to tell the barber to take plenty off the top and sides. Oh how he hated the barber and would plead with me en route not to tell him what mam had said, but to let him keep some of his hair. I felt for him and really wanted to do as he asked, but I knew and so did he, that it was more than our very lives were worth not to follow orders. He used to come out looking like a shorn lamb, a *sorry* shorn lamb. I thought him lucky; at least his hairstyle was far too short to accommodate the head lice that I was so often plagued with.

The kitchen was one step up and was the warmest room in the entire house, come to think of it; it was the ONLY warm room in the house. Here was where we congregated and did most of what families did back then, played board games like Ludo or snakes and ladders or even enjoyed card games with our parents. Generally though, we kids entertained ourselves, drawing, colouring or painting on old newspapers whilst dad read his racing magazine, mam knitted, pegged the next hearth rug or sobbed her way through the latest episode of 'Little Orphan Annie' on radio Luxembourg, which we received via the crackling wheezing valve wireless our dad had built into an old box. Thus we lived through long bitter winter evenings as the icy wind howled down the chimney and sent sparks cascading into the hearth like wayward fireworks.

Sometimes though, if mam was of a mind, she would tell us stories of when she was young. They seemed far fetched to my, even then, vivid imagination. But I recall she told us she had been in service as a young girl. Unfortunately by the time she reached the working age of 14 in 1932, servitude in the big houses had long since gone, seen off by a combination of the war and the Wall Street crash! Another of her stories told of the time she ran off at 14 with a married Irishman and how her dad beat her swain up and fetched her back dragging her by her hair. Yet another told of how she worked for an abortionist doctor and assisted him as he did the deed whilst riding around London in the back of a taxi! Then there were stories of working in the sweet shop owned by granddads partner and how she stole vast amounts of money and hid it under the lino in the hopes of passing it on to her poor old mum (who died at 32!) She was proud of telling us she was a Yorkshire lass born and bred in Dinnington. I later found out from her sister she had actually been born in Pinxton in Notts! But in reply to our plea's of 'Tell us about the olden days eh our mam?' she narrated story after story and we lapped it up, unwilling to face the icy cold wet bed that awaited us. With the glowing coals constantly shifting in the grate and dad snoring softly in his chair, we lived through the winter evenings with the wind spitefully freezing our ankles and noisily bouncing a rousing tattoo up and down on the scullery doormat. And so, without even the knowledge of TV, video or electronic games we managed to amuse ourselves quite well.

But there were some games mam played that I didn't find amusing and which were enjoyed by my siblings rather more than me. One involved me standing in the corner of the room alongside the dresser and with my face to the wall. Mam had a large steel 2 handled pan that contained several balls. These ranged from ping pong to tennis to cricket and every size in between. I would think there were about a dozen of them. She would then throw them one by one at my back as my siblings laughed. When she had exhausted her supply, I had to crawl about the room, pick them all up, hand them back, return to my original position and the 'game' would begin again. None of my brothers and sisters ever had to stand in the corner, just me. Another of her sports was to play the 'what will I buy you if I win the pools' game. It always begin the same way: Mam would ask:

"What would you buy me kids, if you grow up to be very rich?"

"A fur coat mam", we would say almost in unison, "..a real fur coat." And then the hated game would begin;

"Mam tell me what you would buy me if you were rich?"

Mickey always went first. Mam's imagination would instantly click into play and she would paint a mental picture.

"I will buy you the biggest fort in the world," she'd tell my brother, extending her arms to indicate it would be half the width of our sitting room and near half the height,

"Inside will be a troop of soldiers dressed in blue uniforms, some on horse back and some holding rifles to guard it against the Indians. All around the stockade will be hundreds of Indians all trying to get in and being driven back by the soldiers."

Mickey's eyes would light up as he 'saw' the toy come to life.

"Ave the Injuns got head dresses on eh mam?"

"Oh yes, red blue and green feather head dresses, long and colourful right down their back and thick war paint on their faces ."

"My turn, my turn. What can I 'ave eh mam?"

Eileen, her eyes shining in anticipation, was next.

"You shall have a double jointed china doll with tiny white teeth. If you tip her forwards she will say 'mamma'. I'll knit it a beautiful pink coat and hat and she will have a lovely white satin dress and have tiny white leather shoes and pretty socks on her feet. And what'll you call her?"

"Daisy, An' a pram mam, can I 'ave a pram annall?"

Mam didn't consider it greedy to ask for the moon when she played these 'imagine if we were rich' games.

"Oh yes your Daisy will need a nice new pram."

"An' she'll want somewhere to live annall eh mam?"

"Yes, so I will have to get yer a big dolls house too."

"What will it look like eh our mam?"

Mam would describe the house so well, I could see it. There then came a painful silence as they waited for me to ask.

"Go on our Joy, go on and ask mam what she will buy you."

I would hesitate, not wanting to join in the 'fun', knowing only too well what the answer would be. They all waited expectantly and praying this time the answer would be different, I would finally and reluctantly ask:

"What will you buy me mam?"

"A packet of hair grips."

*They would all laugh and so would I. I cannot say in all
honesty these games actually caused me physical pain. Maybe
it's me, maybe I didn't have a sense of humour and maybe
even unto today I don't have the required sense of humour. I
thought I had. It seemed mam had special ways of hurting and
humiliating me and she aimed many cruel vocal jibes at me.
But the cruellest by far and the one that hurt the most even
unto today, was when she repeatedly told me I was not her
child, she had picked up the wrong baby in the hospital and
someone somewhere had the baby she loved and she was
stuck with me. That did leave its mark.*

In the dead centre of our living room was a large oak
polished top table which also doubled as an ironing board,
baby changing table, games table, pastry board and it came in
handy for actually eating off too. It was covered in - money
permitting - oilcloth, or snowy white linen (used only for high
days and holidays), but more often than not, the good old
pages of the Daily Mirror sufficed. There was the usual milk,
brown sauce and vinegar bottles permanently sat in the centre,
whilst overhead a brown spiral sticky insect paper, studded

with the black bodies of flies caught in agonising death throes, hung from the light cord and lazily twisted and turned in the rising heat of tobacco smoke and the fire. A huge Victorian fireplace dominated this room and was our family's only source of heat and hot water. Mam Friday polished this with black lead until it gleamed to a mirror shine throughout the summer but the fire was kept burning day and night in the coldest part of winter, so polishing it at that time of year was impossible.

To one side of the fire was a small oven in which bread and stews made of a tanners worth of scrag end and tuppence worth of pot herbs could be slowly cooked to utter rib sticking perfection. On the other, in the same sized space was a receptacle which we filled with water and which boiled in the heat, it then had to be carried with great care in a ladle to the sink in the scullery for our ablutions or washing. (*Once, eager to get back into mam's good books after some misdeed or other, Mickey and I decided to wash the kitchen floor whilst she had a nattering session round aunty Bet's. Mickey got the blue rimmed white enamelled bowl out and held it as I carefully poured the boiling water into it.*

We were just small kids and had no idea that heat travels quickly in metal and in an instant Mickey could no longer hold it and dropped it, straight onto his bare legs. Frantically trying to help my screaming brother, I rubbed his sore legs and the skin came off under my fingers.)

Either side of the grate were round fancy iron trivets which could be pushed in and out of the burning coals. A soot blackened kettle singing softly sat on one, whilst on the other, kept warm by the heat, sat a tea pot, its acrid stewed smell competing with mixed scents of cigarettes and polish, soot and smoke, damp, urine, sweat, bleach and stale cabbage. On ironing day, our two flat irons were also heated up on those trivets. Propped up in the corner of the hearth was a stout stick, 'punishment for the use of' and it was well used! On the opposite side, hung a long brass toasting fork which we kids fought for the right to use in order to get closer to the warmth of the fire and risk our legs being burnt to a resultant plaid. The floor was laid with alternating red and blue-black quarry tiles carried through from the kitchen, with only a hand pegged hearth rug giving any underfoot comfort.

To the left of the fireplace and opposite the window was the staircase and to the right, a large built in cupboard that held our families treasures. These consisted of; a Willow pattern tea set which I loathe even unto today and with good reason as you will soon learn, a dictionary with a broken spine and consequently the section E to F missing, a dog eared, well thumbed medical book showing all the likely symptoms of all the known diseases we were likely to encounter in our entire lives from dengue fever to fallen arches, and due to mam's misinterpretation, did!, a leather bound and battered old bible presented for good attendance to one "_____" and there was the rub. The name of the recipient had long since faded away and both mam and dad claimed heated ownership of it. There was an ancient square tin chocolate box that still held the deliciously haunting scent of long gone chocolates *I* had not been privy to I was sure. The picture on the front depicted a snowy street scene of the backs of a couple of children peering into a 'dressed for Christmas' Victorian toyshop window. The children's mother, an elegant lady in a long green crinoline dress - hands stuffed into a brown fur muff – is forever acknowledging a gentleman in a morning suit who is doffing his shiny top hat to her. This box contained all our penny insurance policies, ration books, doctor's cards, tally man cards, rent book, birth certificates and anything else considered sacred or valuable to a poverty stricken family that had less than the customary nothing. Beneath this, another smaller cupboard, musty, damp and overrun with spiders and silverfish, held the family shoes, one could almost say shoe!; twists of newspapers for the coming fires and there was also an old wooden, lid-less box containing dad's last and shoe repair equipment which he used to questionable effect on our footwear every other Sunday night. Everything in there came out covered in white damp spores and it was as well to shake the shoes before wearing them, the wriggle of an indignant silverfish between the toes being not at all pleasant!

Directly opposite this cupboard and alongside the scullery door, was another cupboard of similar ilk. On the first shelf was our everyday dishes and plates, tin cups and jam jar 'glasses', from which we drank the finest wines, champagnes and spirits....well, the occasional glass of lemonade but mostly Gods own wine from the dripping brass tap in the scullery or more often acrid stewed tea, coloured and sweetened with condensed milk or saccharin to mask its bitter taste. On the shelf above, was our larder which held our meagre weekly rations and limited other foodstuffs; ancient dusty boxes of Symington's table creams, a tin of Colman's mustard, Monk and Glass custard powder, penny Oxo cubes, a blue half lb bag of sugar and right on the very top shelf in the furthest corner, quite out of reach of prying fingers (or so thought my mother!) a large tin of fruit meted out to each house by the government via rationing every summer and spirited away onto that 'unreachable' top shelf until Christmas. The recess next to this cupboard was where I stood whilst mam played her ball 'game' and next along this wall was a truly beautiful piece of furniture, a dresser made from a golden coloured wood. It had a huge mirror which reflected the fireplace and was mam's absolute pride and joy. The day came when Sandra, aged about 2, stood on the table and entertained us all by dancing. She could see herself in the mirror from this vantage point and as she whirled this way and that, the small glue pot she was inexplicably holding in her hand, fell from her grasp and smashed the mirror to smithereens. Mam then took off the high back and now had a modern low sideboard that was very much in keeping with the trend of the day but it was a crying shame and I fancy it would be worth a lot of money today in its original state. Either side of the fire were two matching easy chairs for my parents and four hard back ones jutted out from under the table in the centre of the room. On the far wall opposite the scullery were three doors. One led to the front room, an adjacent one led to the cellar and the third to the staircase.

That front room was our mam's absolute pride and joy. The cellar was my own private torment, of terror and unspeakable horror. If the devil himself was ever sent to plague me, I found him down that cellar.
"Joy? JOYEEE? Get dahn the cellar an' gerrus a bucket o' coal up will ya duck?"
Now, just hold it right there dear reader. I don't want you running away with the ridiculous idea that I had been given a choice here. This was not an invitation, no matter its sweet guise, this was an order from the very top. It was a job usually done by Mickey but in his absence, it fell to me. If it was daytime, I could bravely, happily even, make the trip without benefit of light as the odd thing was, once you got down the terrifyingly dark narrow steep steps and turned the corner

where the stairs further narrowed to almost nothing, daylight entered this basement via an ornamental iron grate through which the coal was delivered. If it was sunny, totally unafraid, I would happily dawdle as I watched the way the iridescent coal dust swirled and danced quite beautifully in the suns rays. But, in the twilight or complete dark, my heart began to thump and my hands to sweat as I reached for the empty galvanised bucket kept at the side of the fireplace alongside the punishment stick.

Gingerly I'd open the door to the yawning black hole and stand in utter terror. There was an overhead light which sometimes, provided it was not needed elsewhere in the house, even had a 40 watt bulb to light the way, for the stairs were treacherously steep. So what on earth was it that troubled me so? The terrifying bogeymen that mam used to scare me half to death with in order to ensure my good behaviour at all times? Partly, rats and mice running over my feet? Yes, that too, darkness? Oh absolutely. But that's all too simple. The biggest fear of all was, of all things, the light switch. It was brass, more, it was faulty and could and often did, give out a nasty shock. Cowardly I would stand staring at my yellow metal torment, trying to pluck up enough courage to touch it. I would give it a personality and politely beg it please not to hurt me, not today. Whilst I hesitated and silently pleaded, my hands got wetter and wetter.

"Ayo you got that bleddy coal up yet? Yo'll 'ev this fire out in a minute…where ya gone forrit, bleddy Newcastle, ya' dozy mare? Ah'll wring yer neck in a minute."

I didn't doubt it, not for a minute and fear rose in my throat and threatened to choke me, but then, so did mam! And, once the coal had been collected and hauled up the steps, there then came a repeat as the switch now needed to be turned off and the same danger of electric shock faced me.

So the torment went on, day after day, month after month. Then once, whilst in this state of mortal fear and terror after a particularly bad shock the previous day, I had what I thought was an absolute brain wave. I would turn the light switch on with the coal bucket handle. How simple was that? I could not understand why I had not thought of it before. No worries. I would use the handle, the *galvanised metal coal bucket handle!* Innocently I lifted it up and confidently hooked the handle over the brass switch. As metal touched metal, there was a deafening bang, the bucket shot out of my hands and fell down the stairs sparking and crackling all the way and our house blacked out totally! Ironically I did not get a shock. The switch however was burned out and had to be replaced by the landlord with a brown bakelite one, a *safe* brown bakelite one. To this day my mother never knew I was to blame for this. Maybe blame is not the right word to use here. The danger of a shock was now gone for the cellar users, but low down on the other side of the same wall in the kitchen, was another brass switch. This one also gave out shocks, only they were twice as painful and powerful. As mam mopped the kitchen floor, even splashing the faulty plug was enough to knock her to the other side of the room.

As you have learned by now, our family really was living on the proverbial breadline. It must have been a nightmare to our dad trying to keep his growing family healthy and fed during those years. Our good neighbours on both sides passed their leftovers on to us and we kids gratefully wolfed them down. In retrospect, I just wonder what on earth we put in our dustbin, since we ate everything given us. The heavy clump of dad's steel tipped boots echoing down the jitty heralded his return from work and was the signal for us to run out and grab his left over cheese sandwiches from his saddle bag. Curled and dried to a crisp from being in the hot heavy atmosphere of a lace making factory for eight hours plus and often with the clear black oily imprint of his fingers on them, they were nevertheless nectar to us.

Very often the only food we had in the entire house was several days old stale bread. We kids managed to eat copious amounts of it by spreading it with whatever was available in the cupboard. Bread and lard sprinkled with salt was delicious, as was bread and brown sauce, bread with treacle, spread with condensed milk or tinned thick tomato juice, even, when mam wasn't looking, bread and sugar sneaked from our meagre rations. But sometimes, the bread was so rock hard, it was too hard to eat and mam dunked it in warm saccharin sweetened and water thinned, condensed or sterilised milky tea for us. Dad labelled it 'tea pobs', though the funny label did nothing to improve the look or taste of the mushy meal. But when we were hungry, and we were *always* hungry, such food was manna from heaven. Bread with vast amounts of cabbage and mash was our staple diet.

Of a Saturday we had a fried breakfast of a tiny 2 inch square of fatty bacon, 2 half slices of crisply fried bread and tinned tomatoes or puree. Sunday, proper tablecloth day when mam could be bothered, we had a roast dinner and again a 2 inch square of invariably fatty meat with lashings of mashed spuds, a large Yorkshire pudding and a huge heap of cabbage. Sometimes, as an extra special treat, mam would make us a rice pudding or an egg custard and we'd fight for the right to scrape clean the empty dish. Sunday tea we had bread and plum jam. When the jar was finished, trust me there would be not a smear left of the rich red contents. Mam would occasionally open a precious tin of fruit and serve it with evaporated milk, referring to it as 'cream', but again, this was never ever eaten without a slice of bread spread with the yellow axle grease that passed for war time margarine, the taste of which lived up to it's implied name, Nor could we even eat something as simple as an apple without benefit of a slice of dry bread. I can honestly say as a child there was never a day I left my parents table unable to eat another mouthful and absolutely nothing was ever wasted. Got a bit of mould on the bread? Pick it off and eat the rest. Brussel sprouts smothered in blackfly? Cover them with gravy the kids will never spot them. And we didn't dare say we didn't like something. Only rich kids had likes and dislikes and there weren't too many of them in our neck of the woods.

To this day the only food I dislike is sardines.

And if there was little or no food in the house, there was precious little warmth. Once we left the comfort of our kitchen fire, the cold of the rest of the house seeped through to our very bones. The upper storeys were reached via a staircase off the kitchen. The narrow jute carpeted steps - a mirror image of the steep cellar stairs - led the way to two bedrooms on the first floor and another uncarpeted flight revealed an attic right at the top.

The bedroom over the kitchen was the warmest and was toddler Eileen's room. It overlooked the back yard, was bleak, austere, whitewashed and held her cot and nothing else. The uncurtained window had a broken and therefore unused roller 'blackout' blind and the bare wooden floor was devoid of any comforting mats. Eileen slept blissfully in this back bedroom, little knowing she would one day be usurped from her bed into the freezing cold attic sandwiched between Mickey and me.

The attic was reached via a second uncarpeted narrow dark staircase. If the rest of the house was cold, this was absolutely freezing; sub zero in the winter and stiflingly, unbearably hot in the summer. Both conditions had to be tolerated as there was never a fire lit in this fireplace because of our safety, or more likely cost and the sash cord of the window was broken and being extremely heavy, the window could only be opened by a strong pair of hands and so remained shut during the most suffocating of summers.

Once or twice a year, mam, unable or unwilling to pay a window cleaner, would climb the attic stairs with a bucket of soapy water and a few pages of newspaper. Opening the window, she would prop it ajar with the stout stick kept in the corner of the room, ease herself through the gap and sitting with her back to the street her large bottom hanging over the sill, remove the prop and lower the window onto her legs. Now with her legs securely trapped, she would clean the panes. *She was three storeys high!* But mam saw it as another sixpence or so saved.

It seemed that everything in our house had at the very least a dual purpose use and that included the window prop. It pains me to say, that this stout stick had another use and my backside had personal and intimate knowledge of it quite a few times! But in the starkness of that room, at certain times of the year, there was heart wrenching beauty too. In the harsh winter the frost did magical things to the windows and we woke daily to find the glass panes had been mysteriously dressed overnight in a lacy ice curtain of incredible artistry. Exquisitely beautiful flowers and leaves crept into every corner of the glass and left behind a tracery of such majesty it quite took my breath away.

Although as I have said previously there was a street light immediately below our attic window, its mean light did not reach high enough to offer us any comfort. The un-curtained window hadn't had the obligatory black out blind during the war, it hadn't needed one, being pitifully dark save for what I perceived to be, the terrifying glow of moonlight. There was a dangerously bare, light cable hanging from the ceiling but it could never light our way because the fitting was missing. The uncovered live wires offered no danger to us kids though, since it needed a ladder to reach and mend. This room held nothing but the double bed, its flock mattress and flock pillows welded into blackish grey wedges shaped by years of undisturbed use. Comfortable they were not. The bare wooden floor had a bucket for toilet use and several large tins and enamel bowls that were placed one inside the other in one corner of the room and were bought out and placed just so to catch the copious drips of rain that found their way into the room by way of the holed roof. When it did rain, the resultant 'ting ting ting' of the drops dripping into those containers was almost a lullaby compared to the devilish noises that came rushing down the chimney on a windy night. Because we were on top of a hill and right at the top of the house, the fireplace was no more than a yawning black hole down which the wind would yowl, screech and scream rattling the window and door and sending me scurrying under the bed clothes into the urine scented, steam-bath atmosphere and relative safety of Mickey's back.

On the other hand, at least the yowling drowned out the scratching and skittering of the mice. One night, the noise from the mice went on and on and I was so afraid, I screamed for dad to come upstairs and begged him to catch them. But he laughed his head off.

"There's bogger all for 'em t'eat even if they gorrin the bleddy kitchen neh' mind in the attic. Nah get to sleep ya daft sod. Yo're a proper little worrier yo' are, allus whittling abaht summat and nowt."

Although I dare not contradict him, I knew him to be wrong. Yes there *was* something to eat in the attic, us! We had bed bugs that ate off us didn't we? All four legs of our bedstead stood in empty tomato puree tins filled with paraffin but our bugs were smarter than the average. They just walked up the walls and dropped on us as we slept, leaving behind red marks that we scratched and made worse. I was sure the mice would find a similar way to attack us.

Our bed was always sopping wet. One of us had a weak bladder and it wasn't until I slept alone for the first time at aged 11, to my surprise, I realised it was me. Since mam didn't know which of us had done the deed, when she remembered she'd clout us both, thus ensuring she got the guilty party. I apologise here and now unreservedly for all the beatings poor Mickey had to endure for my weak bladder. It was warmly wet when we got out of it in the morning and I swear it had a rainbow arcing over it. And it was just as wet, only horribly, freezingly so, when we got back into it at night.

The act of actually getting into bed in the winter took real courage. The wet mattress struck cold on our young undressed skin, our 'pyjama's' being vest and knickers and the second we were in it, we didn't dare move. To do so was to have to touch an un-warmed spot and it sank its ice cold teeth into us like daggers. In the suffocating summer heat, it would have been almost a pleasure to get into a cold wet bed, but in the airless room, it had spitefully dried by the time we got into it. As you can imagine the stench was pretty bad and permeated the whole house

I was a fearful child; afraid of, and in this order, my mother, the dark, the moon, the horrors of the cellar; Maureen and Carol who bullied me so cruelly at school, dogs, my teachers, the scampering attic mice and bugs, the dark airless bomb proof shelter at the bottom of our road, the picture of Christ covered in blood hanging on the cross just inside the door of the Salvation Army, thunder and lightning, the air raid siren, the baleful sound of the night trains hooting from the nearby Union street station and the bogeymen that mam constantly warned and worried us about. If I ran fast, I could dodge mam sometimes but there was no escaping the nightly horrors and torments of the attic.

On a still darker than dark night I would almost choke with dread when the call of nature was actually strong enough to wake me and I had to use the bucket stood in the far corner by the window, Mam insisted, as it was too big to go under the bed, it had to stay close to the wall, lest we got out of bed in the night and accidentally kicked it over. In the dead of night, it seemed to be a million miles away. I'd try to hang on to my sleep and wriggle away the need to go but I would eventually have to wake Mickey up with a firm nudge in the ribs.

"Mickey….Mickey…"

"Gnnughh"

"**Mickey**…"

"Whaaat?"

"Will yer sing fo' me, I gorra use the bucket."

"Lah dah de dee…" followed by a yawning silence save for the splashing of urine in the bucket.

"MICKEY…. I ent done yet…yo' gotta keep singin'…"

"Oh 'urry up then" he snapped irritably, "….lah dah dee dah…"

I'd hurriedly drip my way back to the bed as he quickly descended into sleep again. This middle of the night 'safety' ritual was used by both of us I might add. Our bedding owed nothing to the comfort of either feathers or down and everything to the left overs of the First World War. There were neither pillow cases on pillows, nor sheets on the mattress. Our bed covers consisted of an old khaki greatcoat, a small single blanket of indeterminate hue that might once have been prettily coloured around the time of the Crimean war, and a grey Air Force overcoat that dad would fetch off our bed every winter morning and wear for his long cycle ride to work.

Dad's workday routine was always the same. I must have been a very light sleeper for I invariably heard the alarm go off – it would 'ting' just the once and he would instantly stop it dead in its noisy tracks; I heard him make his way up the creaking attic stairs, pad across the floorboards to our bed and oh so gently lift his coat off us as we slept. Then, just as softly, he'd creep back down both flights of stairs, carefully avoiding the really creaky ones lest he wake his beloved family and only when he had reached the kitchen and closed the stair door firmly behind him would he give vent to the permanent racking chesty cough that plagued him all his life. He thought it most unfair that mam, who smoked like a trooper, never ailed a day, whilst he, who just had the odd one now and again, suffered so badly with his chest. Having breakfasted on a cup of tea and a slice of bread and scrat, he'd quietly leave the house and cycle the eight miles to his workplace in Beeston. He got paid every Thursday and handed his entire pay packet over to mam more often than not unopened, saying he didn't need money. She gave him a few shillings back and he was a contented man and mam a contented woman!

Each Friday mam was up early doing a lightning fast, top to bottom house clean before heading to town with her bulging purse. There were times though when waiting for him to come home from work and lay his weekly treasure in her lap was too a long a wait and in the school holidays, we would often walk halfway to Beeston and wait for him to join us as we happily paddled in the University park pool. At lunch time, he would happily cycle the couple of miles or so, hand over his money and we would share a meagre picnic with him before he returned to work and we took the long walk into the city where mam spent his hard earned wages.

In later years, mam took to going out at night to a local whist drive and she would leave us kids with dad. He would kindly let us stay up a little longer than usual and we loved this time for it held a very special treat for us. Almost as soon as mam had gone, he'd push his glasses onto the top of his head, casually get up, stretch and agonisingly slowly it seemed to us, take the few steps to his work jacket hanging on the inside of the cellar door. Mickey and I would stiffen with expectancy as we heard the sound of the latch. He would turn his back on us so we could not see what he was doing but there came another much loved familiar sound, a crackly noise that pleased us no end and widened our grins. We'd exchange delighted conspiratorial looks. Dad would come back to his chair and we'd search in vain for the booty, but his hands would be empty, 'it' being well secreted in one of his many overall pockets. After a few hour long seconds, he'd smile mischievously at us, put his glasses back on, pick up his racing book and continue where he had left off for what seemed to us to be an interminable age, and then some. Now, mere seconds later, he'd reach into his pocket and matching us with the grin, set down on the table his only treat for a whole week's hard graft, his beloved Mars bar.

As we watched goggle eyed and salivating with excitement, slowly and ceremoniously he'd unwrap it exposing the rich milky brown, undulating ridges of delicious creamy chocolate. With a practiced eye, he'd mark it with a sharp knife in the family tradition of 'one cuts - the other chooses.' This action instantly freed the delicious scent of the chocolate and it would dart straight into our nostrils. He would cut it into perfectly equal sections, giving each of us a piece. He could have waited until we were in our bed and had the whole treat to himself but I am sure he would not have enjoyed it nearly as much. Our dad may not have fought in the war, may not have won a medal but he was a hero to us just the same and oh I still miss him......

I have a lovely memory of him; he is standing hand on hip, endlessly stirring the pot of tea he has just made. He is gazing down onto a vista of a thousand St Ann's roof tops and chimney pots. Even as a very young child I would wonder what he was thinking and I would know it would be to make things better for us. He must have wanted warm satin edged blankets for our beds, new shoes for our feet, food aplenty for our table, warmth for our bodies. Oh and he would have loved a set of teeth! He had false teeth most of his life but the ones he had were many years old and had worn right through on his top set. Naturally they didn't adhere too well and when he nodded off in his chair after dinner, they slowly dropped down giving him a comical skeletal look. But teeth were right at the bottom of the 'desperately needed' list. He worked every hour he could at his respected trade of twisthand, making a world famous exquisite Nottingham lace that he could never have afforded to buy in his entire life.

He always did his very best and somehow, even as small children, my siblings and I knew it and it was more than good enough for us. So our dad need never have had cause to regret our poverty stricken state, it was not of his making. And even though he was not my biological father, I can honestly say he never treated me any differently to his own blood children, yet I always felt alone and isolated from the family in a way I cannot explain. But in common with the rest of the 'King' children, I loved him dearly.

There were so many things he could not buy us, but bless him, if he couldn't afford to buy us new shoes, he could at least keep the sad sorry buggers we had in good repair. To this end, every couple of weeks or so on a Sunday night, out would come the last, leather and tacks and leaving it as late as he possibly could, for he truly hated the job, he'd set to soling and heeling our footwear. Someone had once given him a huge sheet of really thick orange coloured leather. I don't know where it came from but I am sure it was never meant to be used for human's feet, let alone kids. Maybe a better use would have been for the heavy belts that ran some of the huge factories industrial machinery or for horse's saddles or even cart wheels maybe. We only had the one pair of shoes a year and as our feet grew, they went from being a size or two too big to a size or two too small and the backs began to split. Ripping his fingers to bits doing it, he'd sew the back seam up with steel-strong thread. Now he'd cut out and shape a new piece of leather which he would then tack onto holed soles already several layers deep. We grew tall fast in our house. Satisfied, he'd polish them until they gleamed, line them all up on the bottom stair and thankfully put away the paraphernalia until the next time. If dad hated cobbling them, and he did, we hated *wearing* the sods after he had cobbled them. The next morning, resplendent in our once weekly clean but ragged clothes and newly cobbled shoes, we headed to school hobbling up the hill, having very quickly found a rogue nail. By the time we got to the school gates a few hundred yards away, our feet were torn and bloodied and the backs were busted again. As soon as the nicer warmer weather came, mam had us in ugly black lace up plimsolls and I don't know who was the more relieved, us or dad!

CHAPTER 3

MEET OUR NEIGHBOUR; AUNTY BET'S!

We may well have been at the very bottom of the poverty ladder but mam would have us polite and well mannered at all times and to this end, we were required to call all adults of our day to day acquaintance, aunt and uncle. So we had a very smart and glamorous looking Aunty Ethel and her Garth like figure of a husband Uncle Walt who lived further up the street; we also had Aunts Marge and Pat, Flo, Joan and Uncles Wilf, Ted and Tom the milkman. But of all the several street aunts and uncles at that time, aunty Bet's was without doubt mam's favourite and a daily, if not sometimes hourly visitor. She lived further up the terrace with a family of five daughters and one son, ranging from six years through to teenage. The youngest was Patty. Aunt Bet's was painfully thin, tubercular thin and her favourite chair in our house was Sandra's baby high chair into which she slipped with consummate ease. There she would loftily sit, legs dangling comfortably for hours as our life went on around her.

The end result of a permanent fag kept dangling from the corner of her mouth was a semi circular nicotine stain. It spread and faded outwards and upwards, finally reaching her natural fair hair and turning it orange. I don't recall the two women had that such in common, she being as thin as mam was fat. Though they both smoked heavily, that's hardly something to build a long friendship on and that's just what their relationship turned out to be. Mind, I do recall they both enjoyed a risqué joke and they laughed a lot together, though sometimes, the joke was very much on Aunt Bet's.

I have to fast forward a few years now to a time round about 1950. There had always been door to door hawkers and salesmen earning their living knocking on doors and selling all manner of goods out of the backs of cars or even suitcases, with the debt being repaid weekly or in our case, weakly, to a man who came knocking for a payment hence the expression 'buying on the knock'! Mam was a sucker for them and 'bought' all sorts of things. The doorstep sellers became an everyday intrusion, selling a variety of goods: cook books, tea sets, clothing, encyclopaedias, a circular neon light that was going to save so much money, the salesman told mam, she would be rich by the years end, and memorably a washing machine!

This bore no relation to the famous Rolls washing machine, for this was manual rather than electric. It was a simple white enamelled metal box with a close fitting hinged cover which had a large fixed butterfly shaped paddle in the lid. Mam had to have one. It arrived and would not fit into the kitchen and so had to stand in the backyard. Dad bought a tarpaulin to cover and protect it. When closed, the paddle was agitated by hand, being pushed by a knob along a groove in the lid and then back down again. It was enormous fun when it first arrived and all the street aunts came to view it with their kids fighting for the right to have a go. But as they tired of it, it became merely another chore for Mickey and me. The idea palled after the newness wore off and mam discovered it was doing exactly the same thing as she herself had done for years with the ponch! Eventually rust began to creep up the sides and to me and Mickey it was a relief when it rotted its way into our family history.

One never to be forgotten day, for he was one of the few who did and lived to tell the tale, there came a salesman who knocked on our front door. Oh that peddler was good. As mam angrily threw wide the door ready to roust whomsoever for daring to stand on her steps, he threw a cupful of flour past her where it spread all over the lino on the front room floor. Before she could recover, talking non stop and before her very eyes, he edged past her and plugged this long red cylinder shaped machine into the power socket from where it sprang loudly to life. The noise was astonishing and I ran for cover behind mam's skirts. To mam's surprise, he slowly edged an attached black pipe towards the mess and sucked up every fraction of the flour off the floor. Its evident efficacy as witnessed by mam that day made it the easiest sale that man ever made. The age of the vacuum cleaner had arrived. I clearly remember it costing an impossible £9. Mam invited him through to the back kitchen, made him a nice cup of tea and they sat down to a smoke, a natter and another hire purchase signing ceremony.

In those days and for many years afterwards, women were not permitted to take out hire purchase agreements irrespective of their financial situation but it did not unduly affect mam, she expertly forged dad's signature on the bottom line!   Somewhere around here, a glimmer of an idea must have taken shape in mam's head, for she straight facedly told him,

"Ah tell ya what lad, ah know o' somebody else who'd want ter buy one o' these."

"Oh ay!" the salesman ears pricked up at the thought of two sales in one afternoon.

"Who'd that be then?"

"My mate Bet's, she lives just up the street. Finish yer tea an' ah'll tek yer to meet 'er."

He slurped his remaining tea noisily, stood up, picked up the vacuum cleaner and followed mam down the yard to aunty Bet's. Without knocking, as was her wont, mam went in.

"Hey Bet's," she called, "It's only me an' ah've bought somebody to see ya."

Bet's greeted mam, threw an "ow do" to the man and watched perplexed as he lost no time in showing off his product. He threw the sales recipe of a handful of flour all over her hearth rug.

"What the bleedin' 'ell do ya think ya doin'? Ah've on'y just done cleanin' that bleddy thing," she snapped at him, the cigarette in her mouth wobbling dangerously.

"Don't yo' be frettin' Bet's, yo' just wait an' see worr'e does next, yo'll be a–bleddy-mazed" mam said.

What he did next was take the brush from the fireside companion set, sweep all the coal dust and cigarette ash off the tiled hearth and onto the rug. Mam was by now struggling to keep her composure. Thinking there to be still more drama to be wrung from the situation, with the palm of his hand he swept the crumbs and table debris onto the rug too. Bet's face had a look of total bewilderment and mam's shoulders began to twitch. Now she saw the machine he was carrying for the first time as he dragged it across the room to first one wall and then another, hunting for the plug. He even went so far as to lift her curtains and move a small chest. Defeated, he asked;

"Where's your plug?"

"What plug?" aunt Bet's asked, puzzled.

"Your electricity plug."

Mam could hold it in no longer and howled with laughter.

"There aint no 'lectricity in this 'ouse mate, yo've bin 'ad!" Bet's said and then she too began to laugh.

So I retrospectively and respectfully conclude their friendship was undoubtedly built on need, respect and also, more than a little humour went a long way in those dark, humourless days.

Mam was the queen bee of the street women and they all came to her with their problems. The main one seemed to be how to get rid of an unwanted pregnancy. The fact that mam went on to have a relatively big family and clearly could not stop producing kids herself did not occur to the poor hapless women, such was their desperation. The street 'aunts' earned their title through their friendship with mam, but, if for any reason that friendship was broken, the ill fated 'aunt' would quickly revert to Mrs or 'tharr owd cah'. But that never happened with aunt Bet's. Although she had this large family, of her husband there was no sign. She told mam he was fighting in the war but dad said he had heard he worked at the local newspaper and lived in Bulwell with another woman. I never did learn the truth of this. Aunt Bet's youngest, Patty, sat side by side with me in school and we played at each others houses constantly. Mam loved Aunty Bet's company and could stand any amount of it except on washday. Bet's hated domesticity of any sort especially washing and did it only as a last resort and then not very well. When her teenaged girls needed a clean dress for a special dance or other social occasion, Bet's, a seamstress with albeit limited ability, would sooner make them a new dress than wash a dirty one and frequently did. And though she made them in many differing materials, the style, a 1920's shift with box pleats, was ever the same. Her sewing skills were well known though and folks came from far and wide to take advantage of them. She would mend a tear, turn a sheet, replace a zip or take up a hem for no more than a copper or two.

Aunty Bet's was a seasoned borrower and this frequent continuous habit annoyed the backside off our dad.
'Ayyup Feera," she'd say - seemingly unable to pronounce mam's given name of Vera - as she bustled her way into our kitchen, 'Ayya ya gorra twist ah c'n borrey?' or,
'C'n ya borrey me a shake of ya figginer bottle fo' me chips?'
Off she would go with whatever and often dad would reach for the vinegar bottle at the start of his evening meal only to find it missing. He would ask after it, knowing only too well where it was. Mickey would be sent off to Bet's and come

back with....an empty bottle! And once, memorably:

'Can I borrey your teapot? Our Florrie's comin' n yo' know worra fussy cah she is.'

Roughly translated, her posh sister was coming to tea! If we could be considered posh for living in a house with a porch, Bet's sister could be seen so for having a paid up rent book and a whole baby fox wrapped around her neck, its brush trailing permanently down her left shoulder. It was horrible. She wore it continuously regardless of season. It had all four legs, head and razor sharp teeth. Its glowing orange centred black beady eyes seemed to look right through you as though it was ready to pounce. And oh Lord, how it stank. No amount of Evening in Paris diminished the awful odour, though she drenched herself in it. She maintained that it was a Christmas gift given her by her late husband and was worth a fortune.

Dad was not at all enamoured of this woman and called her Sally Slick-Slack behind her back. He said the fox had been found on the Well's road, after having been flattened by a trolley bus. Her hubby had picked it up and Sally Slick-

Slack had worn it ever since! Today she was due to come for tea and aunty Bet's had been up since the crack of dawn to make her house fit for this minor royalty. So now permit me pause awhile here and tell you about the 'borreyin' of the legendary tea pot!

Most families then had those round dimpled metal teapots that could be safely put on a trivet and buried in the hot coals to keep warm. I'm not sure if you could have done that with a pot or china one.

"Mine 'asn't poured nowt burra trickle fo' months nah. The spauts all blocked up an' the tea tastes essa funneh. The on'y decent cuppa tea I gets is when I comes 'ere…put t' kettle on fer yer aunty Bet's eh our Mickey?"

Mickey, who worshipped at the very feet of her and would do anything to attend to her needs, hastened into the kitchen to do her bidding.

"So? Unblock it then." Mam said matter of factly, reaching the end of the row of the suspiciously small garment she was knitting. She lifted the empty knitting pin up and pushed it down her back to an itchy spot and worked it up and down with a look of sheer bliss on her face and then tucked the needle into her hair, laid the work in her lap and lit a nub end. "Ow?" Bet's asked.

Mam explained, being nothing if not practical.

"Well, worr 'appens is, over time, the strainer holes get smaller wi' the heat of the fire an' the 'ot water. Ya need to gerra small screwdriver, twist it in the 'oles an' mek 'em bigger."

Her words came out smoke shaped.

"I aint gorra small screwdriver, anywayup, I'm not like yo', ah can't do nowt like that. She'll be 'ere afore I've done pissin' abaht. I'll lend yourn for an 'our or two."

"Oh alright then. I expect it's the last I shall see o' me bleedin' screwdriver if ya' borreys it anyway. Tek me pot but send yourn down an' I'll do it fo' ya."

She left with a twist of tea, our still hot teapot and Mickey in tow to bring hers, which was almost identical, back to mam. She put down her knitting and turned her attention to the pot. Pushing the fine screwdriver into the spout hole from the inside, she twisted it. Then she moved onto the next hole and so on until all the holes were bigger and wider. Now she filled it with water and confidently tested it. But to her surprise, the water trickled out just as slowly as before.

Mam peered quizzically into the spout.

"There's gorra be summat stuck in 'ere," she said, puzzled. She poked pushed and prodded with the screwdriver for some considerable time, but could not remove the perceived blockage. Not to be outdone, she reached into her knitting bag and pulled out a very fine steel crochet hook. This she poked and prodded into the spout. After a little twisting, she hooked onto something solid but soft and carefully withdrew a very small, very wet, dead mouse.

The day was coming though when aunty Bet's borreyin' was to lose its charm. One evening she came in and asked mam for a couple of slices of bread for son Danny's work snap the next day.

"…an' scrat a bit o' marge or jam on 'em will ya?"

Dad looked up from his racing paper, peered over the top of his glasses and said, a touch sarcastically,

"Bet's, shall we dip 'em in our gravy fo' ya annall?"

She giggled.

"Stop larkin' about Al, yo' don't ev bleddy gravy till Sunday, an' I want it fo' 'is snap termorrer."

Though he tried to resist, his lips turned up at the corner.

"….no, I tell you what Bet's, ah've gorra better idea, we'll swap 'ouses wi' yer eh? Yo' come 'ere an' we'll go to yourn an' then yo'll 'ave everythin' yo' need."

Quick as a flash she quipped;

"Oh worra good idea Al, shall I order the 'oss and cart fer Wednesday?"

Despite himself he had to laugh out loud. But the time was ripe for the laughter to finish...at least for a while.

Tuesday was family allowance day – the street aunts called it 'cock rent day' - and the families leaned heavily for a day or two on its few shillings support. Thursday was dad's payday and Bet's was always at our house when he came home. She would borrow half a crown off him and pay it back faithfully the following Wednesday when she got her army pension (or as dad would have it, maintenance). One Thursday, she had been at our house for most of the day as usual but dad was inexplicably late and she had to return home to get her kids tea ready. She must have been watching for him coming home though, because almost as soon as he got through the door, she bustled in, threw herself into the high chair and said;

"Come on our Al, yo' late wi' me money ternight".

To everyone's shock, our normally mild mannered dad exploded;

"Well bogger me. If yo' ent got the cheek o' bleddy the devil yo' 'ev Bet's, even she," he threw his arm wide to indicate our mam, nearly knocking her head off in the process.

"...even she 'as the bleddy decency ter wait until ah've got me bleedin' coat off afore she rifles through me pissin' pockets looking fo' me 'ard earned wages. Yo' cheeky get yo', for yer nowt else. Eeyar...,"

He rifled through his pay packet and slammed a half crown down so hard on the table, it made the milk and sauce bottles jump and chink,

"'Ere ya are, ...tek it an' yo' know what Bets?, ya c'n keep it. Its more yourn than it's mine anyway. It's yourn six days a week an' its mine one day a week. Yo' keep it Bet's an' don't yo' be comin' 'ere borrowing nowt na more. Nah be off wi' ya."

Bet's face flamed with a mixture of shock and humiliation. She jumped up so fast; she overturned the baby chair in her haste and sped out of the door leaving the money on the table. That bought the three way friendship to a temporary end.

Mam was really angry at dad and begged him to apologise but he would not. Right was on his side he said, but I am sure over the next few months he wished he had kept quiet. It wasn't in his nature to hurt people in any way and I never ever heard him utter a bad word about anyone. But it was to be a while before the friendship resumed again and when it did, it was under tragic circumstances.

I got out of class one day to find Aunty Bet's standing waiting with the other mum's outside the school gates. I had never seen her there before, not ever and I looked around half expecting to see mam but she was alone. I had once asked mam why she never came to school to meet us, she had said 'ah got more ter do wi' me time than stand gossiping outside the school gates wi' them 'alf baked women.' I greeted aunt Bet's and told her Patty was on her way out and would have continued walking home but she grabbed me, held onto my hand and asked where Mickey was. I patiently waited with her and shortly both Patty and Mickey joined us.

"Yer've gorra come 'ome wi' me ternight, till yer dad gets back. Your mam's in 'ospital an' your dad's gone wi' 'er."

"Why? What's up wi' 'er? She worr alright this morning'

when ah took 'er a cuppa tea up." Mickey said perplexed. "She's lost the baby and she's 'ad to go into the 'ospital," aunt Bet's explained, "but don't you worry, she's ok, just upset that's all."

Mickey and I had had a vague idea that we six might soon be seven although mam had not said so in as many words. She had been knitting like crazy for several months now. Weekly she had bought cheap skeins of wool off Central market in beautiful shades of lemon, white, green and blue and we had stood patiently with our arms held wide holding the wool as she wound, wary of dropping it. She now had a drawer full of small beautiful lacy garments, tiny new vests and flannelette nighties as well as new soft snowy white nappies. Her tummy was fat at the best of times, so there was no way we could have known but this steadily growing pile of garments should have given us a clue.

We had tea at aunty Bet's that night and she allowed us to go into her front room and play noisy games until dad came to take us home about 7 o'clock. He and aunt Bet's discussed mam and the lost baby over a cup of tea and a sandwich she had made him. It was as if the row had never been and they talked easily, like the old friends they were and aunt Bet's was a tower of strength to both my parents at this awful time. Mam was delighted the two protagonists' friendship had resumed as though nothing had happened and dad himself began the payday loaning again.

A few days later, mam came home. She was sad and very quiet. We found ourselves tip toeing around her and trying to help as much as tiny kids like us could. I would sooner have her yell and scream than have her like this, I told Mickey. But, fate has an odd and at times, spiteful way of turning things around. Very soon afterwards, something much worse happened. Patty missed school. When I reached our shared desk one Monday morning, her seat was empty. I was just as surprised as the teacher, for I had spent a lot of the weekend playing at her house and apart from a bit of a cough, she'd been fine then. When I got home and told mam of Patty's absence, she told me Patty was poorly and the doctor had been. She had a cough and a cold but would soon be well again and as soon as I had done my chores, I could go and play with her. I hurriedly emptied the chamber pots, straightened mam's bedclothes and cleared the table before rushing off to see her. She was wrapped up in a blanket, lying listlessly on the couch in front of the fire, her face though unusually pasty had two artificially high spots of colour. I sat next to her, taught her what she had missed in school and brushed her long fine curly fair hair the way she liked me to.

But mam was wrong, Patty didn't get well, she got worse. I was allowed, no *encouraged* to spend as much time with her as I wanted and even, on occasion, to sleep over with her, though her fevered sweating and night long constant coughing kept me awake. After a few weeks, they took her into hospital. The aunts stood on the street or in our kitchen and gossiped in subdued tones, the words 'galloping tuberculosis' being fearfully bandied about. When she came out a few weeks later, she looked awful. Her eyes were sunken, she was painfully thin, drawn and tired looking. Her bed was brought down into the front room and she now rarely, if ever, left it. Doctors and nurses came several times daily and on the bedside table were numerous medicine and pill bottles and a small white enamel bowl containing blood stained cotton wool that had been used to wipe her mouth after a particularly bad coughing fit. I would pick off the bloodied bits and turn it into pretty dolly's and make them dance on her bed to entertain her.

As I came home from school, down Upper Beacon Street one day, I noticed the curtains pulled in aunt Bet's front room and when I got indoors, mam sobbingly told me Patty had died and gone to Jesus in heaven. She wasn't quite six. The first people at Bet's side at this awful time were my parents. They babied and even coddled her, to help her through this difficult time. I must have heard mam say a million times; 'I thought my own loss was bad enough but I cannot even begin to imagine what you are going through,' as the two women broke down over and over again. Then, a few weeks later I too began to cough up blood...

On account of my association with Patty, the doctors took no chances and I was immediately whisked away to the Children's hospital. It turned out I too had the disease. It was a nasty time for me as, along with all the other patients, I was not permitted any contact at all with visitors. I was several months in the sanatorium and spent most of the time sleeping and crying. Daily I was subjected to endless time out on the balcony in the open air. When winter came on, the staff did, what to me seemed so odd. Notwithstanding the elements, they still wheeled my bed out onto a veranda and there I lay in the bitter cold with snow lying thick on the ground and falling softly on my bed. I had to eat some weird things too. I remember being spoon fed raw liver and it was not nearly as bad as you might think. In time I was moved up to the first floor at the front of the building and recall one day looking out of the window and seeing mam, aunty Bet's, Mickey and Eileen walking down the drive below, coming to see me!

I watched them approach with mounting excitement, waving all the time as they made their way down the snow packed path before disappearing into the hospital building beneath my window. I was ecstatic and raced out of bed to the door. I tugged on it but in my weakened state, it was far too heavy for me to open and I was unceremoniously bundled back into bed by one of the nurses. I fixed my eyes on the door, waiting with bated breath. But several minutes later, it opened and a nurse came in with a bag of books, some flowers, a doll and sweeties etc and told me my visitors would not be allowed to come in and see me as I was too poorly. I ran to the window and watched them as they walked away and I screamed and sobbed long after they were out of sight.

But, unlike poor Patty, I was lucky and lived to tell the tale. When I eventually left the hospital some months later, all the lovely books and that beautiful doll had to be left behind as it was thought that they may well have harboured germs having been in the T.B ward. They were like treasure to me as they were the only toys I owned....except for the beads. Defining the quilting on our mattress, were small pom-pom like tufts and secreted beneath one of them, under my pillow, were four tiny glass bugle beads - two red, two white. When you own nothing else, you would be surprised at how a bit of ingenuity can turn such tiny things into a world of play. Often sent to bed supperless and far too early for bad behaviour, mummy, daddy, the twins and I had some amazing times and adventures on that blackish grey mattress. So the loss of those wonderful and oft remembered possessions I had to leave behind was great.

I went home to convalesce and spent a few days in mam's bed until even that was driving me potty and I longed to go out and join my school friends in their street games. It was agony watching them through mam's bedroom window as they tobogganed down the icy stretches of Upper Beacon Street, slamming into the wall out of sight, under the window. Eventually mam gave up trying to keep me tucked up in a her warm bed and made me a make-shift one on the front room sofa in front of a live fire and I was able to watch the kids and talk to them through the glass in comfort. At night though, I was still carried up to our cold wet bed in the attic. Gradually over a period of several months, I did get well and was eventually told I could return to school but I was way, way behind the others in my studies and took a long time to catch up.

A new girl, Brenda, was sat next to me in what had once been Patty's chair and we too became good friends. She lived with her mother, father and two younger brothers in Turner Street. She was now the eldest she told me, because her brother had been killed in the war. I spent as much time with her as I had done with Patty. If I thought I was hard done by with the amount of chores I had to do, Bren was worse off than me as she was forever doing housework or running errands. Her mam, an incredibly industrious woman, always seemed to have a sweeping brush welded to her hands and I never saw her without her turban which was tied so tightly to her head it was impossible to even see the colour of her hair, or even if she *had* any hair. Her dad, a tall thin man in navy blue overalls, was just a ghostly face behind the net curtained window whenever I knocked on their door and called for Brenda.

"Go away, she's not coming out." He would shout through the glass, or:

"Yo'll etta wait, our Brenda's busy just now."

And I would wait, patiently and sometimes for hours. Brenda became a regular visitor to our house but I never once set foot in hers.

One day I'd waited longer than usual for her to come out to play and my backside became numb from sitting on her front doorstep. At first the activities of the neighbour across the street held my interest. She was washing her windows and at the same time having a conversation between her and a disembodied child's voice from indoors, regarding something that was lost. The woman told her where IT was and the child looked.   First in the top left hand sideboard drawer, "Its not there our mam," came the child's voice. Next she was exhorted to look in the table drawer.   This action drew the same response. Now the next place to search was behind the clock and finally the top cupboard alongside the fire-grate. It surprised me that she never lost her temper with the child, but carried on slopping water onto the windows as the child searched. But even that interlude palled and I lost interest.

I took out a piece of chalk from my pocket. In class that day, 'Miss' had lost her temper with one of the boys on the back row and had thrown her chalk at him. It had broken into several pieces which I'd gathered up and given back to her. But there was one tiny piece I had missed and on the way out of class I'd picked it up and secreted it in my pocket. Now I began to draw on the pavement. Carol had shown me a new pattern that was racing round the school and I tried to draw it. It was a simple series of bars, some going this way and some that. But try as I might, I could not get the hang of it.

I moved a little further and found a fresh patch of pavement to practice on. And suddenly, I saw where I was going wrong. I was putting some bars the wrong way round. Once I realised my mistake and righted it, it was easy peasy. I drew it again and again, any smooth clear surface I saw, I copied this pattern onto and was just doing it on Brenda's doorstep when the door opened and her dad stood there.

"WHAT THE HELL ARE YOU DOING?" He thundered at me. Fear gripped me and I froze to the spot. He grabbed hold of my shoulder tearing my dress in the process and hit me hard across the back of my head. I saw stars and began to scream. Again and again he hit me and I kept yelling 'Ah'm sorry mester.' The woman over the road stopped her window washing and began running towards him, screaming loudly at him to let me go. She slapped him again and again with the dirty wet rag she had in her hand. Doors began to open and folk rushed into the street. After what seemed to be a lifetime of blows, some men yelling abuse at him, pulled him from me and bundled him back into his house. Brenda, her mam and other neighbours gathered round me as I sobbed and shook with shock.

"That's Mrs Kings' gel off Moffat Street" someone said in the melee. She put her arms around me and with a couple more folk led me away still shaking and sobbing. I was more afraid of mam seeing my torn dress and tried to pull free but the kindly neighbours would have none of it.

"Don't tek me 'ome," I sobbed, "mam'll kill me, look me frocks all ripped an' ah drew on that man's step with the chalk I nicked from school."

"No she won't duckie, no she won't."

And on this lone occasion she didn't.

Brenda and her family moved away very quickly and I never saw them again. It took a long while for me to realise the sin had not been in making a mess with the chalk, it had been in him losing his temper as he struggled to come to terms with the loss of his elder son in the war. The pattern I was drawing, I later – much later - discovered from dad was the once innocent sign for the rising sun, the Swastika.

CHAPTER 4

I GET A NEW COAT!

Our mam's front room was, not to put too fine a point on it, posh. Not quite as posh as the old folks either side of us or certainly not as posh as the Boultby sisters further down the street but posher than all the other street 'aunts' and that's what mattered most to mam! Even poverty was relative. In the back, mam had tobacco yellowed net curtains bunched tightly up at the kitchen window pane lest anyone see, even in a poor and lowly district such as this, just how much poorer than the observer we really were. But in the front room we had green sateen curtains gracefully draped back to allow anyone passing a glimpse of the room's finery. Not that many folk were tall enough to see in mind.

In pride of place was a green Rexine three piece suite, Rexine being a sort of leatherette fabric that owed absolutely nothing to leather. This was graced with handsome hand embroidered cream linen cushions covers embroidered not by mam I hasten to add, depicting crinoline dressed ladies, wearing frilly poked bonnets and gathering baskets of flowers from an equally stitched garden of every colour and hue known to man. Someone had been very busy with the needle for there were matching antimacassars and arm covers. The sofa was dead centre to the room and two matching chairs sat at right angles either side of the cream tiled fireplace. In this grate, there stood the most impressive, mirrored, brass framed fire screen. Hand painted with a spray of cream and pink coloured roses, it was lovingly polished till it gleamed beautifully where the sun hit it and if I half closed my eyes, the bevelled glass edges threw off all the colours of the rainbow. One day mam took it upon her self to try to remove the roses and she scratched at them for some considerable time with an old razor blade. The paint was hard to remove and the razor too blunt and she just succeeded in doing irreparable damage rendering this once fine looking fire screen absolutely worthless. On the mantelpiece sat a matching pair of dogs playing cricket, made out of some sort of hard, dull glazed cream pottery. They were really bookends, but since we didn't have any books worth displaying – err, since we didn't have any books, they made a nice pair of ornaments.

If I could have one or two things from my childhood home, it would be the fire screen and the bookends oh, and maybe the cut glass scent bottle from my mother's dressing table. (Maths was never my strong point!) There was a low built-in cupboard either side of the grate and on top of these were a matching pair of statues sat on the obligatory hand crocheted frilly doily's; a little girl shyly pulling out the hem of her green dress and a little boy whistling, with a fishing rod slung carelessly over his shoulder. Under the window, a polished topped table hid a Singer treadle sewing machine which only dad could use to good effect and on this sat an Alsatian dog climbing three steps. It had lost the tip of its tail and mam had coloured the white chalk in with brown crayon in an attempt to hide the damage. On the back wall close to the front door, was a china cabinet which mam kept securely locked, filled as it was, with all sorts of imagined treasures; the remains of the Willow Pattern tea service was now belatedly displayed here – minus one cup!, the bride and groom decoration off a wedding cake, a couple of sets of cheap drinking glasses won off the Goose fair bingo stall, a pearlised orange coloured glass bowl ditto, a couple of sepia dog eared photo's belatedly framed and other odds and sods carefully arranged in proud display on yet more cotton doily's. Mam cleaned and polished this room religiously and I could never understand why. After all we only used it to access the letter box in order to fetch the mail or the daily newspapers before they had stopped coming. Therefore the room never actually got dirty so I saw even less reason to spend so much time cleaning it. For most of the years we lived there, this room was rarely used.

Whilst I loved her as a person, I was not exactly enamoured of Aunty Bet's sewing skills. Oh I *had* been but she was later to go on and make me something that pains me to think of even unto today! I can distinctly recall the first time she had put her sewing skills to good use on my behalf and that had coincided with V.E day. A few days earlier, mam was folding up her laundry when Aunty Bet's came bustling in. She helped mam fold her one and only pair of sheets and mam sighed at the threadbare state of them. They had already been torn down the middle and had been given a few more months wear by Aunty Bet's re-sewing them with the outer edges now forming a centre seam. Mam said they were 'uncomfortable to sleep on' and were again showing centre wear.

"It's no good Bet's, I shall 'ave to get some new sheets wi' me next club cheques," mam said wearily. "But the bleddy kids all need new cloe's an' shoes and Al's just gorra 'ave some new shoes this time. He keeps sayin' he don't wan' 'em, but 'e can't keep cycling to work in them hob nailed army boots an' that's a fact. They are that bleedin 'eavy, 'e has all on to change direction in 'em."

Most folk at that time used to buy into a useful system whereby they took out six monthly or yearly cheques from the Co-op. These were a sort of money order with which you freely shopped anywhere within the store. This was then repaid on a weekly basis and as one debt finished, you were free to take more cheques and could then go shopping again. There was somehow a little bit less shame in this debt, the Co-op having a bit more kudos than the regular 'flog at the door' tally man, though he too was a regular visitor to our house. It was more respectable and usual to take the Co-op cheques out in time for Christmas and provided mam kept up our repayments and we didn't have to shout the China man's name 'Shintin' out too often, took them again in the summer. Ours had to cover so much of course that new sheets weren't exactly top of the desperately needed list.

"Tell ya what mate, I could mek 'er a new frock outta this owd sheet, then you wunt etta buy 'er one an' ya could afford to buy some new sheets."

Mam opened the sheet back out and examined it carefully.

"What wi' this bit of owd rag? Yer kiddin' me right? Ah c'n see me bleddy 'and through it."

"It won't look like a bit of owd rag be the time ah've done wi' it yo'll see."

The two women mechanically refolded it.

"Go on then, tek it, ah know you're a whiz wi' a needle but I think yo've met your match wi' this bit o' owd rag. If yo can mek owt outta this, ya can plait rain woman!"

Mam had shoved the sheet into her hands and Bet's had taken her 'borreying' for the day and gone home. A couple of days later, she had presented me with a dream of a dress. It was sleeveless, full skirted had two big patch pockets and a huge sash that tied into a dramatic bow at the back. It was the most beautiful dress I had ever seen let alone owned and it quite took my breath away. On the front round the edge of the square neckline, matching rows of tiny red and blue satin ribbons ran like tram lines and were repeated on the hemline and the tops of the patch pockets. This was so apt since red white and blue signalled the coming of the V E day celebrations.

On route to St Catherine's church for a thanksgiving service, our school paraded along St Ann's Well road waving our little union jacks in Victory. Although every single child wore something or other in the three colours of our flag, to show their pride and patriotism, I considered no one was better dressed than I that day. The street aunts somehow managed to scramble a few bits and bobs of rations together and do a party for the whole street. There were, by now, more than one of the local lasses courting a G.I Joe and they came through for us with food items and a few bottles of the good stuff for the adults from their NAFFI. The party was a warmer edition of bonfire night without the fireworks and the dancing in the streets went on till the early hours and we were allowed to stay up much longer than usual. I loved that dress and wore it and wore it until it was once more threadbare and it was a sad day for me when it eventually found its way into the rag bag to begin its final career as a floor cloth.

My next experience of aunt Bet's sewing skills was yet to come, in what turned out to be one of the worst winters. Just when we needed it most, there came a time when there was a shortage of and at times, no coal to be had and it had turned bitterly cold, a cold made worse by the aforementioned universal poor diet and lack of warm clothing. Icicles which began as a drip from a broken roof guttering slid and fell slowly, almost gracefully to the pavement, growing almost to the thickness of a man's waist, where it splayed out to envelop the pavement, block the street drains and as it crept down the hill, proved lethal underfoot. Our wet clothes hung desultorily from the pulley and took days on end to dry, adding still further to the dampness. Even the school boilers ran minimally so we were all bunched together in one class. We communally shivered a lot. Day after day there was no let up in the unremitting bad weather. Now, even our one and only hitherto dependable fire in the kitchen range gave out scant warmth. The home delivered coal previously rationed anyway, now all but dried up. Dad tried shovelling up the copious amount of slack there was down the cellar, added water to it and tried to burn that but it more often than not put the fire out. He tried logs, but they were too green and spit dangerously. He even brought home the oil soaked waste cotton he used to clean his works machinery. It burned brightly and warmly before dying out far too quickly. And even though it was waste cotton, he would have been sacked had he been caught taking it.

Then the coal storage depot at the bottom of Robin Hood Street started to have coal bricks delivered. These were made of the aforementioned coal dust but something was added to it to make it stick together. It was then shaped brick like and sold as fuel and burned very well. Mick and I were required to go and fetch them in our pram every week. It was an extremely unpleasant journey and we had to hold the pram back on the steep icy hill going down to the yard and now, fully laden with a cwt or so of coal bricks, push it hard uphill on the way back. The queues outside the coal yard were intolerable. Sometimes we'd be there for hours in the bone searing cold, stamping our poorly shod feet and trying to blow warm breath into our hands through the old socks we were wearing as mittens. We waited impatiently for them to be delivered and then for our turn. And we had to watch the men very carefully as they filled our pram, for mam believed they were apt to give short measure and there was all hell to pay if, when mam counted them on our return, she found there to be any missing. It was bad enough in any weather for any person but especially so for children as small as us. I was still frail having after my illness and although Mickey was that bit older than me, he was a small thin child too. With the thick ice underfoot, it was nigh on an impossible task for us. Many a time, the pram toppled over and we had to scrabble in the snow and ice to rescue the bricks.

Now, having just about caught up with my schooling after being in hospital so long the previous year, I could not now go to school as I had no coat. Mam had made several visits to Pownall's rag shop and the Sneinton market trying to find one but to no avail. This particular day, Aunty Bet's had sat with us whilst mam had braved the biting cold weather as she went to search the two rag markets yet again. She'd come back empty handed, bustled through the door, ousted me from her chair and pulled it further in to the fire.

"Gizza look at that fire, I'm bloody frozzen to death."

"Get yer mam a drink Joy, there's a good gel….got nowt then?"

"Nah, waste o' time an' bleddy bus fare."

Feeling guilty in some curious way, I rushed into the kitchen to make them a nice hot cup of tea. When I returned with the two steaming cups, the women smoked in companionable silence for a while as mam thawed out and her teeth ceased to chatter.

"Ah'll mek 'er one," aunty Bet's announced, "Eya gorra nowd blanket?"

"Yes, bleddy lots on 'em, all full of 'oles an' all on me beds, but none to spare." Mam replied.

"Do you think Jackie's ull ev any?"

"At this time o' year? Gi o'er, any decent coats he's 'ad are all on folks beds at night now aren't thi? Ah think ah got more chance o' C&A gi'ing 'er a brand new 'un fer nowt."

"Mmmm," Bet's mumbled through her smoke as she threw her miniscule nub end on the fire.

"Ah think ah know where there is one goin' spare. Leave it wi' me pal," she said. She turned to me and added,

132

"Ah shall mek yo' a nice new coat, one wi' big patch pockets like I done on that frock ah made yer."

Lulled into a false sense of security, I remembered how much I had loved the ribbon trimmed pockets on that beautiful dress she had made and had instantly got a picture in mind of the finished coat. It would be sky blue and made of a blanket like those on mam's bed, wonderfully soft and fleecy, so soft they felt like fur on the skin.

"Can I ev a blue un'?"

"You'll ave what she can gi' you," mam aimed a clout at me, but I expertly flinched away before it could land. Aunty Bet's gave me a conspiratorial wink, a wink that told me it *was* going to be the exact imagined shade of sky blue.

My sometime school friend Carol had a new winter coat. It was from Debenham's, an impossibly expensive shop to us, but then, when everything you owned was either from Pownalls or the rag market…. I had been in this shop many times with my mother and always felt uncomfortable, as though the staff were watching our every move. But we did not go in to buy; the only time we did go in was when mam needed a set of buttons for a new garment she had knitted. Oh, she didn't go in to *buy* them, under the guise of checking the sizes, one by one; she twisted the chosen buttons off the hanging garments until she had the requisite number plus a spare! As dad was laughingly fond of saying;

'It costs some folk only pennies ter live, burrit costs yer mam nowt!'

But Carol was taken to Debenham's at least once a month and got whatever she wanted. Their family home on Pym Street was directly opposite our road and was one of half a dozen built on top of a wood yard, the saw mill of which usually screeched all day long except for bank holidays. And yet, the house still managed to be a conventional one in every sense of the word. It had a front entrance via a sloping walkway, which brought you gently back down onto the street. But again, the normal entrance was round the back and straight into the scullery off the backyard, each house having a sectioned off private yard with its own waist high gate. It was paved with dark blue coloured, un-patterned, quarry tiles and had a shed as well as the lavatory. This three storey house was much larger than ours, indeed even the rooms were bigger and they needed to be for the house seemed always to be filled with adults.

Carol was the youngest by several years of a large family, the others all being grown and out working. It was overly flamboyant in its wealth and boasted high quality polished furniture and a dark blue velvet couch and matching chairs. Carols mam was incredibly thin and never seemed to sit down. She had once invited me to tea and on the appointed day, I sat at the dining table to a meal fit for, if you'll excuse the pun, a King. Bread sliced as thinly as you can imagine, was spread with real soft butter and home made jam; tea was served in cups with matching saucers and there was a large plate of delicious cake and biscuits to which I was free to help myself, but even out of eye and earshot of mam, I remembered my manners and refused a much wanted second slice of cake. It had been a lovely meal and when I came home and told mam of the delicious goodies and fine time I had had, she reciprocated by inviting Carol to come to tea at our house.

When we bustled in that chosen night after school, the table was strewn with the aunt's dirty cups, their saucers overflowing with fag ash and nubs from their gossiping sessions and mam hurriedly cleared it and wiped its cover clean with a damp nappy. Now she took the loaf and tucking it firmly under her armpit, spread the surface evenly with margarine and jam, then hacked off a huge chunk of bread plonking it down on the oil cloth directly in front of the intended recipient. She repeated this action, one per child, and then poured tin mugs of sterilised milky tea for each of us, before bidding us to tuck in. I was invited again to Carols many times, but she never came back to ours!

Carol's new winter coat was a warm, rusty ginger colour that perfectly matched her red hair. It had a cream and ginger fur collar, with a half belt at the back. She also had new winter boots of fine shiny brown leather with a fur trim round the ankles. But that was a dream too far. My new blue coat would be very fashionable just like Carols I decided. I wasn't too sure about it having a collar let alone a real fur one, but hey, I was getting a new coat and me and my parish oven sized gob lost no time in telling Carol at the first opportunity. When she pressed me, I described it as blue with big patch pockets. True to her word aunty Bet's started work. Within a few days she came hurrying through the door clutching a large brown paper carrier bag to her thin chest, leaving an odd, not entirely tobacco scent trail behind her as she came lightly into our kitchen and threw herself into the baby chair. "Mek me a cuppa and you shall 'ave what's in this bag," she had grinned, holding aloft a brown carrier bag. With trembling hands I hurriedly did her bidding and waited patiently as she took her first sips of the boiling hot liquid, scratched her match and lit up. With a twinkle in her eye, she handed me the bag. Eagerly I opened it. My first impression was grey! My second was that odd mysterious smell.

"Go on then," mam urged, "let's ayya look. Try it on."

I pulled it fully from the bag and it slipped from my hands onto my foot nearly fracturing my ankle. I hastily snatched it up and struggled into it. It was almost floor length, had a huge six inch hem and was made of an itchy, thick, heavy, grey, matted blanket. The promised patch pockets hung below my knee's, its huge saucer sized buttons were lost in even bigger buttonholes, it had a massive Peter Pan collar and it suspiciously looked and strongly *smelled* of aunty Bet's cat Whisky. As my eye noticed more and more grey cat hairs, it slowly dawned on me it *was* their cat's blanket. I wouldn't have been a bit surprised if it came complete with a whole family of fleas and it was so rough it was like wearing sand paper.

"It feel's just a bit too big aunty Bet's." I said weakly.

"Ah, it is a bit but ah'm better at mekkin' frocks than coats,"

"Yo'll grow into it." Mam said brightly. I thought mam was
right and probably by the time I was 27 it *would* fit me and
maybe by that time it might smell less awful too.

"Say thank you to aunty Bet's then!" mam demanded.

"Thank you aunty Bet's." I said, my voice sounding odd as I
tried not to breath in the pungent fumes too deeply.

"Now you can go to school tomorrow and get outta my 'air,"
said mam, lighting up another cigarette from the glowing end
of the finished one before stubbing it out in her saucer.

"Where'd ya get the owd blanket from eh Bet's?"

"It was our cats. But needs must….it stinks a bit an it could
do wi' a wash if truth be known Feera, But ah left it cos it'll
never dry in this weather, it wants a right windy day."

"Don't yo' worry midduck, ah'll do it the minute it picks up.
What's your Whisky sleeping on now then eh?"

"Daily Mirror an' its easier to keep clean."

She laughed a shrill laugh that turned into a coughing fit.

Mam bid me turn round so they could admire the back. They
both concurred I looked lovely and warm in it. It was thus

settled. I had my new coat and meanwhile, all I had to do was wear it and soon! Not to put too fine a point on it, I loathed and despised that coat from the very first glance. Aunt Bet's left to go home and I was just about to thankfully shrug it off when Mickey came in from school and saw it. Now I got an insight into what life with this hideous garment was likely to be at school. He roared with laughter and had a whale of a time teasing me.

"Oh our mam, it doan half stink." he had chortled.

"Ah know it does," even mam was grinning, "but it were very kind of her to mek it and she will 'ave to wear it for a bit at least so as not to upset yer aunt Bet's. She is so kind."

Mam must have seen the abject misery in my face for her voice softened a little and she winked and promised me

"Ah'll wesh it the minute it gets a bit warmer an' it'll probably shrink a bit too. And I shall still keep a look out at Jackie's to see if he's got one for you. You might not have to wear it for long anyway. But for now, needs must and it will just 'ave to do you for a bit."

"But mam, it really does stink…an' it's dead itchy."

She took it, held it to her nose and sniffed and pulled her head back sharply as if she'd been stung, her mouth turning down

at the stench. I honed in on her wrinkled nose reaction,
"See mam, can't you wash it now and put it on the fire guard
to dry? It'll be dry for school in the morning. Or I can stop
off school and 'elp you an' it will be dry the day after."
"Yo've lost too much time in school as it is, yo' not stoppin'
off one more day. There is no way that coat will dry in a
month of soddin' Sundays. Just wait till the weather picks up
an' I 'ave promised yer fust chance ah get, I'll do it fo' ya."
"Ah don't mind if it's a bit wet to put on termorrer."
I offered, pleaded. Mam scowled at me and sternly tugged at
the clothes pulley which dropped down to her shoulder level
with a clatter and she spread the coat over the bars and
hoisted it noisily back up again, securing it on a hook.
"There, you can't smell it now can you? That'll sweeten it up
no end come morning, an' ah don't want ter 'ear another
word!"
She gave me a look that signified the end of the conversation.
Mickey gave me one that implied it was just the beginning of
his! As we settled into bed that night, he began to chuckle.
"What?"
I was wary of my brother's laughter and didn't want to ask.
"Ah'm just thinkin', yo're dead lucky yo' are. Betcha there's

nobody at school termorrer who's got what yo' got."

He had this way of teasing and tormenting me.

'Putting ya on a horse and not letting ya ride it,' mam said.

All I had to do was ignore him and maybe he would go to sleep. But not tonight, I waited for the signs that would have told me he had nodded off, gentle snoring, an absolute stillness, but he kept wriggling to remind me he hadn't and just as I myself was dozing off, he poked me in the chest. The silence was broken by his repeated giggling. Still I waited until my patience even got on my own nerves. Suspiciously I asked;

"Huh? Ok smart arse, so what ave I got that then that they aint gorr eh?"

"Why, Yo' gorra real fur coat,"

"What yo' goin' on abaht, a real fur coat?"

"A CAT fur coat".

He laughed out loud and I kicked him hard in the shin but he still continued to chuckle maliciously as my face flamed in the dark. I turned over and shoved my freezing backside into him.

"It coulda bin a 'ole lot worse…" he began again.

If he was waiting for me to answer, he would wait a bleddy

long time, I decided. The silence lengthened. I was not playing his game and pretended to snore. He could sod off.

"**…what?**" I finally snapped.

"She coulda made it outta the cat!"

He laughed lustily and I got great satisfaction hearing my well aimed heel kick connect with his ankle and heard his voice change from glee to pain! I went to sleep grinning.

And so it proved to be at school the next day. Mam had been right and airing it out on the pulley had made a difference to how it smelled. As well as the cat stink it also had not so subtle undertones of tobacco and soot! Mickey 'cat' called me all the way up the hill, dodging every which way as I tried to thump him and when I got into the schoolyard, where Mickey left off, Carol took over and gave me hell.

"Ah thought yo' was gerrin a new coat an' it was goin' to be sky blue?"

"It is a sort of blue…" I said weakly.

She pointed to the sky.

"That's blue prat, that…" she pointed at my coat, "that's grey twit an' its NOT new.."

Then she caught a whiff of it and I was sunk.

"Ugh! It smells as if yo've pissed on it."

She pinched her nose, ran away and her friends followed all holding their noses and laughing. The only person who would come near me was Winnie and she had no sense of smell and was every bit as ragged as me. Mind, her ragged state was mostly self inflicted.

Long before it became known we all needed fibre in our diets, Winnie chewed all manner of things and so ate huge amounts of it. Books new at the start of term, were daily reduced to an ever deceasing circle as she nibbled mouse like at them. Absent mindedly she bit off chunks of her jumper and cardigan cuffs, having to bite higher and higher as the sleeves got shorter and shorter. She had no preference as to material, gnawing wool, wood and cotton alike. Everything she owned got the same treatment, belts, buttons, leather satchel straps, dolls fingers and toes, coat sleeves, and gym slip hems, indeed anything in fact she could get her strong teeth into. Oddly, she didn't bite her nails, whereas mine were chewed down to my elbow!

The two of us sat miserably together in a corner whilst Carol and her friends stomped round the playground making fun of me and faking cat noises. I was never so pleased to hear the bell signalling the start of another school day. Now Miss, standing down wind of me, got a whiff and made it worse by making a face and pulling back as I got near to her. She made me hang that blasted coat in the farthest corner of the cloakroom away from the other kid's coats. Henceforth my new nick-name was now 'missy pissy coat'. I wouldn't have minded so much (oh yes I would!) if the damn coat had been cosy, but it wasn't even the slightest bit warm. The material was too thick and stiff to hug my body, the sleeves too wide and the buttons would not stay in their holes. I did my best to persuade mam to wash it but my pleadings fell on deaf ears and had the opposite effect actually as she became equally determined I would wear it as it was and she never did give it the dolly tubbing it so desperately needed. So my hated coat became a fixture. As in all things in life I have found that for me, if they can get worse, they usually do. As a friend of mine is fond of saying;

'If it wasn't for your bad luck Joy, you'd have no luck at all.'

Never was a truer word uttered. If I thought myself unlucky, that blasted coat was about to cause me yet more angst.

The main St Ann's Well Road was a busy bustling thoroughfare of lots of businesses and retail outlets of every conceivable size, type, style and content. There were two cinema's - the Empress and the Cavendish, furniture, babywear and ladies dress shops, ironmongers, shoe shops, food stores, cobblers, pawnbrokers, tobacconists/newsagents and sweets, second hand shops, a bakery, dairy, a good few pubs and beer offs, post offices and, at a time when no-one had anything worth stealing and folk were able to boast they never had to lock their doors, there were even several banks! You name it; it was to be found thriving there. I used this road quite a lot as I ran errands for mam and our neighbours and the aunts and almost anything they wanted could be had along this thoroughfare. On the opposite side of this main road a smart tree lined avenue ran off to the left and was charmingly named Robin Hood Chase. This wide, gently sloping and spacious promenade of elegantly styled three storey houses would not have looked amiss in a smart Parisian boulevard. Although it was just a stones throw as the crow flies from my own humble toilet-less home, it was a very different world of grandeur and only rich folk like doctors and business people could afford to live there and it was in one of these lovely houses that mam got a part time job as a cleaning lady to a doctor and his family. The pay helped of course but so did the bounteous and delicious left over food that found its way to our table and store cupboard. Mam used to come home and tell us about the luxury these people lived in and how their only daughter, a little older than me, had dozens of exquisite china dolls, books and teddy bears lined up on shelves in her room. One day, mam promised, she would take me with her to play with this little girl. I would be not much more than seven or eight and the thought of those dolls had me pleading daily to be taken to see them. No amount of back handed dodged or received clouts stopped me and that day eventually came some weeks later. As I excitedly made the trip happily trotting alongside mam, my face beamed at the thought of being the one chosen to go with her.

As we neared the house – about half a dozen or so in on the right hand side - mam indicated with a nod of her head that this one here was where she worked. I eagerly turned to go up the path and was angrily pulled back as mam explained we could not use the front door but had to walk the long way round the back.

"Why we got to go raund the back eh mam?" I asked.

"Cos ah'm not good enough to goo in the front door ah'm just the skivvy an' ah gorra go to the back door, that's why."

We walked down the passageway (too posh to be called a jitty!) between the houses and turned right along the narrow path that separated all the houses from their long beautifully tended lawns and vegetable gardens. At the back door, mam walked straight in without knocking and I followed. We were in an amazing kitchen. It was almost bigger than our whole ground floor. In the centre was a really big scrubbed top work table and on every wall pale green painted cupboards and shelves held all manner of food stuffs. I was astonished to see several bags of sugar, named canisters of flour, rice and dried egg, innumerable packets of unopened tea and dozens of tins of all manner of foods stacked on the shelves. A shop could not have been better stocked. There was a huge range and a fire burned brightly in the grate which fuelled a large oven attended to by an immensely fat woman who I realised must be the cook. Whatever she was cooking reminded me that in my excitement, I had not eaten. Without stopping, mam brightly bid the cook 'good morning Dot' and got a glower in return. Young as I was, I instantly knew this woman did not like my mother. Mam seemed not to notice and went through the kitchen door into the hall and from the cupboard under the stairs took out a basket of cleaning materials and a carpet sweeper.

"Nah ah've gorra lot ter do," she wagged her warning finger at me, "so ah'll just tek yer up to meet Mary and then ya c'n play wi' 'er while I get on, and be'ave yerrsen an' if ya do, she might let ya play wi' 'er dolls 'ouse an' some o' 'er dolls."

As she spoke she was already trudging upstairs with me trailing behind her and she bustled into a room at the front of the house. I gasped. It was Mary's bedroom but it was oh so grand. Carpeted, wallpapered, and furnished with the comfiest bed I had ever seen in my young life and with a fire burning brightly in the grate. Either side of the grate, were recesses', in one stood a huge dolls house at play height, with a dolls pram big enough to hold a real baby occupying the other recess. Above, shelves lined the walls and had all manner of lovely dolls and books by the hundred or so it seemed to me.

Sat on the hearth rug was a young girl of about my age with long shiny brown plaited hair tied with two dark green satin ribbons.

"'Ere you are Mary ah bought mah little gel to play wi' ya." Mam turned to me.

"An' yo' better play nicely mind."

And she was gone.

"Hello" Mary said, "What's your name?"

"Joy," I'd replied shyly, "…can I evva a look at your dolls 'ouse?"

"Yes".

I walked over that soft carpet to the house and peered in through the tiny windows. It was wonderful and had everything that a big posh house might have, right down to cups, saucers, knives and forks, curtains and rugs, taps and even light fittings that actually worked. This house had the whole kit and expensive caboodle but in exquisite miniature.

"Can ya gerrinside?" I asked.

"Yes, I will show you".

Mary got off the floor and came and stood beside me.

"Oh! Pooh, you smell," she said, screwing her nose up. My face flamed and I stuttered,

"Aww n..no ah don't." but I knew I did. I smelled of pee.

"Oh please don't touch it; your hands are so dirty."

I belatedly tried to hide them behind my back. Knowing I was coming here, I had washed really carefully that morning, brushed my hair till it gleamed and had passed mam's cursory inspection. But I could not get my hands clean no matter how hard I had scrubbed. They were grimed with ingrained school ink and dirt lodged firmly under what was left of my bitten to the quick nails. I hurriedly moved away and stood in misery with my back to her looking out of the window onto the Chase below. I was aware she was scrutinising me and tried to speak to her but the words would not come out. There was an embarrassing silence that seemed to go on forever. After a while, she left the room, I followed immediately and went looking for mam. Mam had that job for a scant few weeks and then left under something of a cloud. Seems there were various foodstuffs and a canteen of cutlery missing from the kitchen and mam was questioned at some length by the doctor. She told him where he could stick the bleddy job and walked out. I have often wondered what happened to all those lovely dolls, books and the dolls house that I hankered after. This started me off on my dream of owning old dolls and a dolls house. I managed to collect quite a few original Victorian dolls and finally in my fifties, I got a large dolls house.

So as I dawdled along going about my errands, I well knew what Robin Hood Chase was like and often stopped to admire it through the ornamental railings that separated it from the very real world of St Ann's Well road. And yet, oddly, right on the corner of its elegant columned entrance was a rather dubious public toilet. It had an appalling bad name for some reason and we kids had it drilled into us by mam we were not to go into it for any reason. And I didn't, not ever....until that one, horrible, never to be forgotten day. I was coming back from an extra long errand and desperately needed a toilet and I do mean desperately. I neared it with trepidation and with mam's warning words ringing in my ear. Nevertheless, needs must and as I pushed open the door of the forbidden lavatory and went in, the stench was almost overwhelming. Only now did I understand how and where it had got its deservedly bad name. To my horror, the toilet bowl was overflowing, the floor sodden with urine and covered with piles of faeces, huge amounts of it. The stink was horrendous and I tried to get out a little too quickly, slipped and fell. I was covered in this filth. I came out in floods of tears and made my way to the first house along the road and begged its startled owner to help me. She had a kind sweet face and in an instant my ever ready imagination had me assuming this kind 'lady of the house' would take pity on me, come to my rescue, divest me of my filthy garments, wash me in sweet scented soap, wrap me up in a nice warm snowy white towel, sit me before a roaring coal fire with a drink of hot milk and give me a plateful of sweet biscuits to nibble on whilst she expertly cleaned and pressed my coat for me.

Oh boy was I ever wrong. Mam used to say my gob would get me hung one day, but I think my imagination would have given it a run for its money. She led me down the passage, through the kitchen into her spotlessly clean scullery, gave me a bowl with hot water and green washing soap and left me to it. Even though I was gagging at the appalling stench, I had no choice but to do it myself. I worked hard and somehow managed to remove some but by no means all of the filth. Then I had to clean myself up, for it was on my legs, bottom, hands and feet. Only one bright thought kept me going as I frantically scrubbed at the coat; now I was sure to get it washed, wasn't I? Only trouble was, I daren't tell mam where I had been, what had happened, what I had done and she never even noticed.

Gradually over a good deal of time, the smell on the coat lessened though every chance I got, I rubbed it with any nice sweet smelling thing I could find and wet washed it out sight of mam almost daily. It took a long time for that smell to fade and a good few years for me to grow into that coat, let alone out of it. I had my next 'new' second hand coat when I was 14. It was mustard coloured mohair, reasonably fashionable and smelled divinely of scent. Dad gave me the 10/- (50p) the price the young lady wanted for it. I wore it endlessly and loved it.

CHAPTER 5

WE GET A LODGER.

In the spring, first Mickey, then Eileen quickly followed by Sandra had gone down with the chicken pox and had had the pleasure of mam's bedroom for a few precious sick days. Though my brother was now up and about, he was still off school. I thought him to be skiving and was sure he was well enough to return but mam said Dr Lynd had told her all his spots had to be completely gone before he could go back to his lessons. I was on my way home from school and was dragging my hated coat on the floor behind me, trying to wear it out – having failed at trying to lose it. It was a cold day but I would sooner have frozen to death than wear this monstrosity. Mickey must have been eagerly watching for my return through our front room window, for he came running up the street to meet me in a state of some urgency. His face was still covered in hundreds of spots, liberally and comically dotted with the pinkish white 'cure all' Calamine Lotion.

"What ya doin' draggin' ya lovely fur coat in the muck? Yo'll cop it if our mam see's ya? Where yo' bleddy been till nah anyway?"

I ignored him. I was still angry with him for what he had said about me last night at tea. Each evening when I got in from school I had several jobs to do; peel the potatoes clear the table, make the beds, wash up and clean the scullery after dinner, but by far the most hated of my daily jobs was emptying the household piss pots. It was a standing joke in the family and they teased me rotten. That was bad enough but I had sufficient imagination to know what the kids at school would do and say if they saw me, so the later I did it, the less chance there was of being seen, since hopefully, they would be at their tea. It meant a long trek down the yard carrying first one then the other receptacle. Ours was a big metal bucket which, though heavy, was easy to manage but my parents had a much daintier pretty china one with an elegant handle. But dainty also meant small, so it was always over-flowing and would slop over the sides as I carried it down the steep stairs, through the kitchen into the scullery and out into the yard. When I got home after school, if mam was busy nattering at aunt Bet's house –and a lot of the time

she was - I would tip it down the grate under our scullery
window, but there was no chance of that today as the dreaded
chicken pox was racing rampant through the streets and mam
could not leave the kids, not even for a fag and a gossip. I
was not as lucky as my siblings and stayed extremely and
annoyingly well. Almost hourly I searched my body for the
tell tale spots mam said I was sure to get and which I saw as
my passage to 'mam's room' bliss. But not a one did I get. I
was, said Dr. Lynd, 'probably a carrier', mam said, as she
recounted his words to dad over tea last night Mickey had
quickly jumped in and said;

"Oh yeah, we know she's a carrier alright, ..a piss pot
carrier..." Mam had tutted at his use of the swear word, but
they'd all chortled anyway and I'd kicked his shins under
cover of the table. Now here he was dancing backwards in
front of me, his face flushed, almost sparking with excitement
and boy was he milking it. I somehow resisted the almost
irresistible urge to trip him up with my hated 'fur coat'.

"Where'd you think I've been, to London to see the queen,
day trip ter Skegness? I've been coming home spotty," I
retorted, "..an' stop swearin' else I'll tell our mam on you."

"Yo' do then, goo on, I dare ya. Then I'll tell mam about ya draggin' that lovely gorgeous fur coat in all this street muck, an' ah'll tell 'er who nicked that penny from under the clock annall!"

A chill ran through me, he *had* seen me steal the penny and had been holding it over me for months now. But for once, I knew I had the upper hand over him.

"Yeah smart arse, an' I ent forgot who put that hole in the fruit tin in the top cupboard and drank the all the juice….."

His face flared and I could see the fear in his eyes. Point to me I think!

"Yo' bin at 'ome all day then eh? Eyya done the beds emptied the pots an' cleared the table fo' me eh?" I continued.

"No ah ent. What time ev I 'ed? she's ed me runnin' errands all day an' cleanin' up fo' 'er annall an'mekkin' loads a cups a tea fo' 'er and aunh Bet's. Anyway, them's your jobs not mine.

That was true. We did each have our own jobs to do and he had, if anything, more than me. When dad was at work, he had to keep the fire going and bank it up, clean the lavvy, he also had to clear the table and clean the kitchen every morning so it was nice and tidy for mam to get up to, make her a morning cuppa before he left for school each day and keeping the backyard clean was also his responsibility.

"What do you want me for anyway?" I angrily demanded of him.

"Ah know summat yo' don't know our Joy. Wait'll ah tell you, just wait'll ah tell ya, you'll never, never, never guess, not in ten million trillion years …. Goo on evva guess."

"I know, we got shit wi' sugar on instead o' tea pobs fo' tea!" I practically spat the words at him.

"No, it's much better than that. Goo on, try again mardy arse." He loved playing this guessing game and any news was always a long time in the coming.

"I give up…"

Here we go again with the silence. One of these days, I would win. He tapped his foot and tutted with impatience.

"Awww, goo on then spoilsport, ayya another guess…."

But it seemed, I was not going to win another point today. Grudgingly I asked;

"Well go on then pain, I can see yo're just dying to tell me." He took a deep breath and held in the delicious secret just one more second before blurting it out.

"We gorra lodger." He announced dramatically.

I stopped dead in my tracks.

"WHAT?"

My incredulous voice thundered in the empty street.

"We 'ave, we gorra lodger," he repeated. "It's tharr owd man as our dad allus talks abaht, the one he wo'ks wi', the one 'e made them cod liver oil an' sugar sandwiches for."

I had heard dad mention old Ben many times at the dinner table. He was a work colleague and dad and the other men sometimes played tricks on him. He had us in stitches at mealtimes with his stories of what had happened to Ben that day. There was the time when the old man had gone for his usual after lunch, hour long ablutions. Leaving his workmates to do the work, he took a long leisurely time happy and contented on the lavvy reading the paper. One day, dad concocted a long hook and very gently slid it under the loo door and managed to hook the old man's pants out. That left him running bare arsed round the factory all afternoon searching for his pants. He was also a cadger. At lunch he would go round to every workmate begging food off them. One day dad took him the parcel of bread and cod liver oil sandwiches sprinkled with a few grains of our precious sugar ration. Ben believed dad when he said it was treacle and

159

wolfed it down with the inevitable consequences a few hours later. Our dad was alternately fond of, sorry for and angry at him all at the same time, his anger stemming from Ben's unbelievable meanness when it came to putting his hand in his pocket for anything, whilst dad knew him to be quite wealthy. He had neither family nor home of his own to spend his money on, so, dad reasoned, he must have it salted away somewhere. And every few months it seemed, he moved on living just about anywhere he could.

"You're fibbin' again." I found my voice and glared at him.

"No ah'm not, 'is names Ben, 'e's that mate of our dads, an' 'e's an owd man, about an 'undred, an 'e's gorran earring in his tab!" I was supposed to be the one in this family with the vivid imagination but this was a bit too much even for me.

"Yo' flippin' liar yo' our Mickey, for ya nowt else."

"See, that's all yo' know smarty pants. It's the dead Gods honest truth, cross my 'eart and 'ope ter die, if I dare to tell a lie"

He made the sign of the cross on his chest and spit on the corsey in the time honoured childlike way of proving truth. In a split second I had mentally gone through the entire house looking for anywhere we could put this lodger and came up with….nowhere! I was still not convinced, so I asked;

"Well where's 'e goin' ter sleep then ligger?"

Mick tutted, rolled his eyes and raised his voice.

"*I am not lying*, e's in our front room. Mam's gorrim a bed from Jackie's in there an' everythin' an' yo' got another piss pot to empty." He laughed out loud at his own joke.

"Ohhh, now I know yo're liggin'", I shouted, "our Mam wun't let nobody in that room, neh mind put a bed in there an' 'ave somebody sleep in it, you bleddy rotten liar you!"

"*Joy!*"

He sounded genuinely shocked at the cardinal sin and so he should, for I had used the one word mam could not abide. If we swore, that was worth a crack on the head with whatever she had to or in her hand. But if we used the word 'rotten', that was a full session with the punishment stick.

Inexplicably that word was absolutely taboo in our house.

"Our mam'll kill yo' stone dead fer usin' that word."

"Oh go on then snitch, tell 'er an' ah bet mam's just dyin' ter know who banged a 'ole in that peaches tin."

"Alright smart arse, ah won't tell on yo' if yo' won't tell on me. But yo' come in an' 'ave a look at Ben then an' we'll soon see who's liggin'."

He turned, ran down Upper Beacon street, barely turning his head to look for non existent traffic, before crossing the road at the bottom and throwing himself into our entry. I tore after him, wanting to bash him but I was struggling to put that damned coat back on before mam saw me. But he was way ahead and in my hurry to get him, I forgot the golden rule and hit the loose bricks. Mud squelched up my legs and all over my shoes and socks. I Looked down at the thick black stain splattered even on my coat hem and silently vowed I'd kill him. Stopping in the scullery, I wiped the filth off with our dishcloth, or maybe it was the floor cloth, they were both about the same dubious colour and off the same God only knows what or whose undergarment. I walked into the kitchen…and there I confronted what turned out to be nothing but the absolute truth.

Sat in dad's chair was the oldest, baldest, thinnest, boniest man I had ever seen. I was immediately drawn to what dangled and danced from his right ear, which was, as Mickey had so rightly reported, a fancy gold dangly earring with two large red stones, genuine and valuable rubies I was later to learn. His lipless mouth was set in a grim line, jaws clenched onto a short, time blackened clay pipe. Both arms and the backs of his hands were threaded with prominent blue veins running across and down his bony arthritic fingers. From his rheumy eyes and nose, a silvery snail trail raced down his paper thin skin which clung tightly to his clearly defined and oddly shaped skull. Dressed in the most threadbare of old clothes, he had on black trousers that came up under his armpits held in place by braces plus a wide, thick ancient leather belt, a black waistcoat shined with grease, a striped collarless shirt under which was a dirty yellowed, rubber buttoned wool vest and slung over the back of the chair was his coat. It was an old fashioned black frock coat complete with tails and had what had once been a vivid red satin lining, but was now stained a blackish brown with sweat and dirt. He was so different looking he was just plain scary.

"This is our Joy," said mam, "…this is yer Uncle Ben, say 'ello then…cat got your tongue as well as your coat?"

I was so shocked and speechless; I missed the jibe and stood rooted to the ground. Mickey had been, if anything, quite modest with the truth. I looked across at him stood behind mam's chair. He mouthed the words 'towd ya' and was watching my reaction, a smirk on his face.

"'ello," I faltered.

"'ello an' where ya' bin?"

His voice did not match his feeble frame and was surprisingly strong and deep.

"School."

"School? Waste o' bleddy time, I never went to no school an' I can't read nor write, never needed it an' its done me no 'arm not knowin'. On'y need to know 'ow to add me wages up an' I can do that well enough, eh Vera?" he cackled. "What's seven times eight eh? Come on come on…you're supposed to be the clever school gel."

His pale blue watery eyes burned into me.

"1x8 is 8, 2x8 are 16, 3x8…" I replied parrot fashion, the way I had been taught. He cut me off mid stream.

"7 x 8 is 56….see? I'm an owd man and ah'm quicker'n you. Waste a bleddy workin' time is school."

"Aw come on Ben, that's not fair. She's dead good at English. She can spell owt. Somebody asked 'er to spell 'necessary' the other day and she gorrit dead right".

Mam defended me.

"Oh right, if ever I want to spell necessary I'll know where to come then won't I?" he cackled like an old hen.

I was not sure I was going to like this old man and mam's next actions and words did nothing to change my mind. She reached across and took his coat off the back of the chair.

"Ben," she said, "I see there's a few rips in yer coat. Time yo' 'ed a new 'un."

"There's nowt wrong wi' that coat tharra few stitches wun't put right." he said defensively.

"Ah suppose that means yo' want me to mend it fo' ya?"

"A? oh arr, thank ya Vera, Albert said ya' would. That's a good coat is that. It's a coat to wear to the theatre or the opera really. See, look at the back, its got tails, that's what them long pointy things is called tails."

"Hmmm, I can see it is. Go to the theatre or opera often then do ya?" mam had a sarcastic edge to her voice but at this early juncture, it was lost on him. He'd learn. He went on unabashed.

"I gorrit at Jackie Pownall's rag shop an' all it cost was tuppence an' when I looked in the pockets I found a tanner." He giggled loudly and slapped his thigh, "Eee, ah ed ter laugh, ah've ed it 2 years already."

"Don't you get the tails caught in the bike wheels Ben?" she asked. He wiped the tears from his face on a dirty piece of

165

rag that sufficed as a handkerchief.

"No, ah used to, fetched me off it a time or two to begin wi',
but ah ties 'em up in the front nah."

Mam busied herself examining the many tears in the coat and
Ben said

"An' I've got some socks as needs darnin' annall."

I saw and recognised the warning look on mam's face but Ben
was new to the house and had much to learn.

"I'll get round to 'em soon enough Ben."

Her offer to repair his clothes did not go down well with
me. The elastic in both legs and both pairs of my navy
knickers had broken and I had asked mam many times if she
would mend them but she hadn't and I spent all day trying to
hitch them up, but as fast as I did, they fell down to my knee's
again. Now here comes this old man and in no time she is
sewing for him. Mam asked me to pass her sewing box out of
the cupboard at the side of the fire. As I passed, I got my first
whiff of him. It was not a nice scent but one I was to grow
used to over the coming months.

"Gerrin the front room an' mek Uncle Ben 'is bed up will
ya?"   Not an invitation I wanted to accept but then, as I'm

sure you've learned by now, it was not an invitation. I obediently went into the front room, closed the door behind me and stood stock still in shock.

This once beautiful room was now a mish-mash of Ben's and mam's stuff all jumbled together. It was not a good marriage. The sofa, two chairs and sewing machine had gone, having been taken upstairs into the back bedroom for the time being, I found out later. Everything else was shoved any which way to make room for the single bed mam had got from Pownall's second hand shop for half a crown (2s-6d). Though far from new, it was the cleanest bed in the house, though its straw filled mattress' level of comfort left much to be desired. Shoved under the window in place of the sewing machine were two stout cane chests, one on top of the other and on top of them was a large brown leather suitcase. One of the chests was a really big one, similar to the one that held all our school gym equipment, the other an identical, smaller one. With the suitcase they reached halfway up the window, making the room much darker and though the chests could be seen from outside, they did a good job providing Ben with some extra privacy. I really wanted to take a peek in those cane chests but they were secured with huge thick leather straps and I needed time and a chair to stand on to reach them. There was a small chair at the side of the bed which mam had put there for Ben to use as a bedside table. I sized it up as to whether it would reach the top chest, decided it would and made a mental note to look see as soon as possible. Piled on top of the mattress was a heap of second hand bedding and I busied myself making the bed. There were two grey army blankets felted to almost floorboard rigidity, a faded floral quilt, two flock pillows and an odd assortment of patched linen sheets and pillow slips. I busied myself making the bed and on shaking out the bedclothes, released a hundred years or more of concentrated mothball scent. As I went to the far side of the bed to tuck in the blankets, I noticed the plain white piss pot sat on the cream tiled hearth. It was an object I was to become very familiar with over the coming months and emptying it was not at all nice as he didn't just pee in it.

Ben moved in that very night and within a few days, fitted in as though he had always been there. Mam's once posh front room, previously deliciously fragranced with lavender polish, now took on Ben's peculiar scent mixed with mothballs and within a short time, mam refused to go in Ben's room, as it was now referred to, as she said the smell made her feel sick. I was then given the extra job of daily making his bed as well as emptying his pot. I found that if I worked very fast, I could succeed in holding my breath for the whole thirty seconds it took to make his bed and another 30 seconds to take out, race down the yard and empty his pot. This subsequent shortage of oxygen saw me stagger drunkenly from the lavatory after dumping it. Mam made him give me a penny every week for doing this most hated of tasks but every week it was a struggle to get it out of him. Now after being given the job of making his bed too, I had to nag him for the two pence mam said he had to pay me. He did eventually give it, but would do so grudgingly and often only at mam's insistence. On the brighter side, I would one day learn the wonderful secrets of those cane chests.

As Ben settled in with us, it got to a point where I could not imagine our lives without him. Apart from cleaning up after him, which was now my job, mam cooked for and continued to care for him, washing, mending and ironing his old clothes. Occasionally she would think some item of his apparel was totally beyond help and throw it out but he either fished it back out of the dustbin or replaced it with pretty much the same garment in the same dishevelled state sourced from Jackie Pownalls rag shop. But even she drew the line at his socks which she described as stiff as a board and 'more holey than righteous.'

She showed him the many holes and said he must have to THREAD his feet into them and insisted he get new ones. There then followed a scene that I will never forget. He begged and pleaded that she mend his socks. She steadfastly refused. He had to get some new ones. He got shirty with her and told her it was her *duty* as his landlady and his other landladies had done it without question. She told him it was no wonder he had to move on every few weeks if he treated his landladies like that. He told her that our dad had said it would be a pleasure for mam to mend his clothes. She laughed out loud and said she DID mend his clothes and believe her, it was no bleddy pleasure but she would still continue to mend them for him, she just drew the line at his socks.

On and on they went. She told him she didn't mend Albert's socks when they got that bad 'neh' mind' his. He fair *wept* with temper as she refused again and again. Finally he offered to pay her a penny a sock. She said she would never get rich that way and still refused.

"Ah tell yer what Ben," mam said, finally exasperated beyond more words, "...mend 'em yer-bleddy-self."

She took a bobbin of black cotton, stuck a needle into it and threw them into his lap, he snatched them up, grabbed his socks and stormed out. The next morning mam found one of his socks with all the holes roughly stitched up and she was unable to even get her hand in never mind he his foot.

Week in and week out the battle of the socks continued. He faithfully put them out to be washed and now, she just as faithfully threw them back on the bed for his return. One day, she had just about had enough and she tossed them in the dustbin. A little while later however, she envisaged him groping about in the bin and rescuing them, so she retrieved them and burned the lot. There followed one unholy row. He slammed into his room and, though he was nothing if not a gannet, ending his every meal by clearing each single morsel or mouthful left on anyone and everyone's plate, even going so far as to spit wet his forefinger and pick up each and every single crumb of bread from the Mirror tablecloth, he did not come out of his room for his dinner that night, such was his distress at the thought of having to spend his money. The next night he tersely asked her how much a pair of socks cost. Mam told him they were 1s/11p (8 pence approx) a pair, but she thought he would need two pairs. He whistled, swore under his breath and again slammed into his room making the very windows rattle. Mam smiled scenting victory. A few minutes later, he put a 2/- piece down on the table and immediately asked for the penny change.

"Eh, Ben, yo'll need at least two pairs. Ah'm not goin' all that way inter town for one. What ya gonna do when thi' need weshin' again? Yo need half a dozen pairs really but at the very least yo' need at least two, one on and one in the wash."
He glared at mam, turned on his heel and returned to his room, once more slamming the door so hard it rattled the windows.

"YO'LL EV THAT DOOR OFF'EN ITS 'INGES."
She angrily shouted after him. A few minutes later, he came out and slapped another two shilling piece on the table.

"Can yer gimme me tuppence change now?" he asked.

"Ben, ah ent got a halfpenny to me name just now. Ah shall ave to gi' it yer termorer." Mam answered stony faced.

"Yo'll not forget will yer?" he sounded alarmed.

"No Ben, ah shall not forget."

Her lips twitched at the corners. Those two pennies were to worry him no end. Several times that night he said words to the effect that she did remember she owed him tuppence didn't she? Several times she patiently affirmed she did.

The next night as he entered the kitchen after work, mam presented him with two pairs of thick warm grey socks. He looked at them every which way without comment and then asked for his change. Mam said he owed her another tuppence. He had a fit. Mam managed to get a word in and pointed out that it was a twopenny bus fare into town and a twopenny bus fare back. He told her she should have walked that's what her legs were for and demanded she give him back his money. She told him she had not gone into town for anything for herself or us, she had gone specifically for him and he should pay the bus fare or go himself and he could whistle for the tuppence change and he again slammed into his room. This money owed went on and on for some considerable time until he eventually gave in and told her she could keep it! Mam tried to keep the glee out of her face and voice as she thanked him. He never asked her to shop for him again!

I suppose he had been with us about 3 or 4 months when he had his first – for the want of a better description – funny fit. We were all sat at the table as usual having our evening meal when Ben started mumbling to himself. Then, as though in a trance, he got up, moved into the small space at the bottom of the stairs behind mam's chair and began to box an imaginary opponent, all the while giving a running commentary on who hit whom and where. He was reliving, we later found out, the legendry bare fisted Bendigo fight, which he assured us, he had personally witnessed as a young boy. His scrawny arms punched the air in an uppercut, or thumped out to the wall missing by a fraction as he cuffed the imagined challengers chin. Surprisingly nimble footed for one so aged, he dodged deftly this way and that, his heavy steel tipped boots sparking on the quarry tiled floor.

"An' e' 'it 'im wi' a right an' then a left hook ter the chin, an 'e dodged this way an' that, all the time 'e's lookin' for an openin' and the 'uge crowd is urgin' 'im on an' go-win' WILD…"

On and on went the fight and the commentary. Then, as abruptly as he had started, he finished and not at all sheepishly resumed his place at the table and finished his meal. He was breathing heavily, with sweat streaming down his red shiny face, his heart visibly pounding through his vest. We were absolutely astounded and looked at him and each other open mouthed. Mam had put her finger to her lips to warn us not to say anything or to laugh. But it was very difficult. He calmly finished his meal as though nothing had happened and dad later told mam he often did this at work. The next time it occurred, mam sent me and Mickey to fetch the aunt's Pat and Bet's and they too witnessed this wondrous sight and again, as quickly as he had started, he stopped and finished his tea seemingly oblivious to a kitchen of curious onlookers.

Ben was to share our home and influence our young lives for well over a year and now that he was adding modestly to the family income via board and lodging, mam started to spend a little time and effort on herself. She became aware of her body weight and went on a diet. To this end, she purchased Energen rolls, a lighter than light crispy bread alternative which she relished filled with wedges of best butter and thick chunks of fresh cheddar cheese. She ate copious amounts of cabbage which she loved at the start of her new food regime and hated with a passion a few days later. She gave up dieting and began instead to perk up her appearance.

I well recall the day she went to Madam Maisons to get her hair done and came back with her baby fine crowning glory shining like glass and plastered to her head in tiny waves. To keep this style crisp and get the most out of it, she bought some steel jawed monster hair clips that creased it into waves. Then she discovered the Twink home perm and aunty Bet's came and did mam's hair at our kitchen table and turned it into a halo of mousey brown frizz. Another change Ben's financial contribution made to our household that winter was mam could now afford to take her washing to the public wash house.

This was something else. Each woman rented out what was called a 'stall' in the laundry side of the beautiful Victorian building, the other side housing a couple of swimming pools with public bath cubicles occupying the other end. The stall had as much hot water as each housewife wanted, a glass rubbing board, a ponch, a boiler for the whites, a mangle and just a few steps away, a bank of hot dryers could be dragged out of the wall and the wet washing hung over its heated rods. It was then pushed back into the wall and the clothes were bone dry in no time at all. It made mincemeat of home washing. Now every Monday, we would go down to the washhouse straight from school, wait for mam to finish and then we would help push the pram back up Bluebell hill. Poor mam's knuckles would more often than not be bleeding from hard use of the scrubbing board.

Our parents could also afford to go out together and started going to the St Catherine's Whist Drive on a Saturday night, whilst Uncle Ben babysat us. Eileen and Sandra were put to bed before they left and we were supposed to go to bed at 7.30 but as long as we were quiet he would happily allow us to stay up until 9, sometimes even later if he dozed off in the heat of the fire. Indeed there were a couple of times when we had to race to get to bed as we heard our parents returning footsteps coming down the jitty.

Ben could be surprisingly good company, telling us some outrageous stories of his sea-faring days. He showed us on a map, all the countries he had been to, painting vivid pictures of far off lands. It was through these tales I think that Mickey was inspired to one day join the air force and travel. And it was from Uncle Ben I learned about the Nottingham boxing hero Bendigo, his hatred of his parents and also the meaning of the word 'atheism'. I had not been able thus far to see the secrets of the cane chests and to be honest, I had lost interest in them, barely glancing at them over this period of time. But all that was about to change.

CHAPTER 6

WE JOIN THE SALVATION ARMY

Routine was the order of the 1940's St Ann's. Almost every day was a 'something' day; Monday was washday, Tuesday family allowance day, Wednesday ironing day, Thursday dad's pay day and Friday house cleaning day. Very early on Friday mornings, spurred on by dad's pay packet burning a hole in her purse, mam got up and cleaned the house from top to bottom before setting off to enjoy the rest of the day in town. Saturday was threp'ney rush (kids cinema) day and Sunday; don't play/laugh/dirty your Sunday best clothes (what Sunday best clothes?) make a sound/'get out from under me bleddy feet an' get ter Sunday school' day!

My brother and I were by now reluctant Sally Army churchgoers and we had no one to blame but each other, something we did with monotonous regularity. A few weeks previously we had been sat on the pavement with some of our street friends. It was a warm day in early September and we were idly picking at the melted tar that was bubbling in the gutter. We'd discovered it made a passably good chewing gum if you chewed it and spat out the dirt several times and Winnie was trying it out. Carol pursed her lips disapprovingly at Winnie and began telling us about the Sunday school seaside trip they had just been on and how we ought to go to the Sally Army and go with them to reap some of its benefits. "We get to go to the seaside or 'ave a day in the country in the summer and we have a Christmas party annall. Santa comes and giz us a present and we get to play games and have cakes and trifle and stuff. It's dead good. You two should come." Win tried to blow a black bubble but the 'gum' wasn't that good and the black residue stuck. She began to pick the bits off of her lips and teeth.

"Yeah an' when we went to Skeggy last month......" Chas interrupted,

"I'm telling 'em not yo'." Carol gave him a push and went on with her narration.

"We went on a chara to Skeggy an' when we gorron it, they gen us a bag wi' an apple, orange, cake, chocolate biscuit an' a bag o' crisps."

Chas saw his chance and interrupted her again,

"An' a bottle o' pop, yer forgot the bottle o' pop…an they bought us an ice cream cornet when we got there annall."

"Shurruuup, ah towd yer, ah'm telling her."

Carol threw her leg out and cracked his ankle. He glowered darkly at her, pulled his sock down and rubbed at the reddening mark.

"….and then, on the way back we all sang Ten Green Bottles….it were dead good," he defiantly continued.

She gave him another thump on his shoulder and he punched her back.

"Pack it in you two; anyway, what's it like at this Sally Army place then?" asked Mickey suspiciously.

I was not like my brother, I jumped in with both feet but he had a suspicious bent and was a bit more cautious. Chas jumped up, gave Carol an almighty whack on the head and tore off homewards. Ladylike she patted her red hair back into place and continued, bravely ignoring the stars that swam in her vision.

"Its dead good, us mam's giz us a penny for the collection box an' a penny for the bus fare. We purra button in the box an' walk there an' back an' get some gob stoppers wi' the money."

"Yeah, but what do you *do* when you get to the Sally Army?"
Mickey asked, his head warily cocked to one side.

"We do all sorts o' stuff, like sing songs, bang tambourines,
paint pictures, they read stories to us, we say some prayers an'
then we come 'ome."

"Hey our Mickey it sounds dead good to me." I said.

"Look, all you have to do is go for a few months an' you get
to go to the Christmas party, then, if you don't like it, do what
we do an' pack it in an' then start goin' again in time for the
seaside trip." Carol explained. Mickey and me looked at each
other for a split second and tore down the entry.

Mam was nearing the end of her weekly ironing session and
the kitchen was stiflingly hot. Piles of finished laundry lay
neatly stacked on the edge of the kitchen table or over the
fireside chair and some gently aired on the overhead pulley.
The flat irons were heating up on the trivets by the live fire
and as we dashed in she exchanged the cooled one for a newly
heated one. Protecting her hand from the hot iron with a thick
cloth, she turned it upside down and spat on it, the spit sizzled
furiously before dying and leaving a yellow tobacco stain
behind. Now she rubbed its hot surface into a bar of green

washing soap and pushed it onto a wet dishcloth to clean it before beginning to iron the last of the whites. She checked the cleanliness of the iron's surface again and now her thick meaty arms slammed it down crushing the creased sheets into smooth submission. She pressed down hard ignoring the cloud of steam that surged into her face. Surprisingly she had a tuneful sweet singing voice and was singing along to a radio programme of Reginald Dixon at the organ.

Little pal if daddy goes away,
Promise you'll be good from day to day.
Do as mummy says and you'll never sin,
be the man your daddy might have been.
Daddy didn't have an easy start,
so it is the wish that's in my heart.
I want you to be little pal,
what I couldn't be little pal,
I want you to laugh, to sing and to play,
To be good to mummy while daddies away.
I'll pray every night little pal,
that you'll turn out right little pal.

If some day you should be

on a new daddies knee,

don't forget about me little pal.

We feigned patience as we waited until her song came to a tear jerking end that coincided with the finishing of the sheet. She laid it neatly on top of the pile, pushed a sweat drenched wisp of hair back with the flat of her hand, picked up the other sheet from the clothes basket and with the aid of her teeth, expertly folded it. She paused and only now seemed to notice us.

"Now what do the pair on ya want? T'int teatime yet an' ah don't know what we evvin, ah got no moneh ter buy owt. Ah couldn't afford a fly a pair o' garters."

"Mam, can we go Sunday school wi' the other kids?"

"When?"

"Next Sunday."

"Well ya can't go on Monday nah can you?"

I sighed silently. When we had finished a meal we were required to politely ask;

'Please may I leave the table?'

The answer was always;

"Well, ya can't take it wi' ya when ya go, can ya?"

No matter how many times, mam said it, we still had to repeat it and she still laughed. Mickey as usual left me to do the talking. He was no good at persuading her but, come to think of it, I wasn't much better. She wiped her steamy face on her pinny and the action made the wayward wisp of hair fall down again. She ignored it.

"Where is it?"

"The Salvation Army bottom o' Bath Street."

"What do ya wanna to go there for?"

"They said we can learn all about Jesus an' God an' angels an' stuff an' they gi' ya things."

"What sort of 'things'?"

"They told us we gerra birthday card on us birthday, they said we can go on day trips to different places like an' they said there's a party at Christmas with Santa an' food an' everything."

"Who's these 'they'?"

"Carol an' Chas an' Stan an' Jimmy Green an' Winnie, thi' all go, lots of the kids go, all the kids off the street go."

"Hmm".

'Hmm' was good. No, hmm, was more than good, it was

positively encouraging. If she had said no, no meant NO, just that and was not negotiable. But 'Hmm' meant 'maybe,' 'perhaps' even. Luckily for us she hadn't ended the negotiations by saying she'd 'think about it', thinking about it was not good either, by the time we had got to the top of the entry she would have forgotten all about it and it was not good to remind her.

Once, in the worst time of the food shortages, the government had suggested we eat rice instead of the now 'hard to get' potatoes. Mam had boiled it as per the government instructions and served it with the usual cabbage and gravy for our evening meal. It was awful and, hungry as we undoubtedly were, none of us wanted to eat what was on our plates let alone ask for seconds. But it was unthinkable to simply throw it out. Mam put it in the cupboard at the side of the fire and told us all to remind her that we still had to eat it. My brother promptly forgot all about it but I dutifully reminded her as she had asked. Over the next few days I bought it to her attention at the onset of every meal. Finally she lost her temper, took it out and threw it all over me as the family looked on and laughed. No, reminding her did not work. Bravely I took my begging one step further.

"Aw mam, please, we the only ones who don't go" I pleaded. "It will gi' us summat ter do on Sundays. It's boring 'ere wi' nowt ter do on a Sunday."

"Oh if all yo' want is summat to do, ah c'n allus find yer summat ter do an' that's a fact."

A tickle of sweat made its way down her neck, meandered onto her chest and into her ample cleavage. Irritated, she scratched it away. Then, just when I was convinced the argument was lost, she relented.

"Awww, I suppose so. But – let – me – tell - you," her eyes bored into us and she defined each word clearly and distinctly, wagging a warning forefinger at us that sent chills up and down our spines. "… I know you two boggers well enough, yo'll be wanting to go just long enough to get an invite to that bleddy party an' then yo'll want to stop gooin'. Yo' never stick at nowt, neither on ya. I ent forgot all that money I spent on them dancing lessons fo' yo," she reminded me for the umpteenth time.

Periodically she would bring up this thing about the dancing lessons she had paid good money for me to have. And that was the odd thing. I had no knowledge of it. You'd think something as good and as important as dancing lessons to a child obsessed with the stage might have left a tiny, weeny memory behind.

"Well, yo' either go or yo' don't," she went on, the tobacco stained finger still waggling in our faces, "yo' mek your minds up 'ere an' now an' yo'll bleddy well stick to it. Nah then, what's it ter be, go or stay?"

"We'll go, oh thank you our mam, oh thank you, we'll go," we both spoke in delighted unison.

"Ok then, ya can go. *But I am warning you.....*"

She raised her finger again but we never heard the last of her words, we were already half way down the entry, racing each other in order to be the first to share our easy earned victory with the street kids. The apparent effortlessness with which this weekly treat had been bestowed on us, should have been warning enough...

The next Sunday afternoon, suitably attired in fresh clean clothes, we excitedly got ready for our first visit. Mam gave us a penny each for the bus fare – half pence there and halfpence back - and a halfpenny each for the collection box.

"I shall want to see your bus tickets when ya get 'ome mind an' I shall ask the vicar how much ya purrin the collection box. Woe betide ya if ya spend it on owt else. I used to go to Sunday school messen when ah was a kid an' I know all the bleddy dodges, so don't think you can pull the wool over my eyes!"

Just her glance towards the punishment cane in the hearth was enough. Despite the 'mardy mardy mustard, can't eat your custard' cat calls of the other kids, we hurriedly and happily took the bus like proverbial lambs to slaughter. Having paid our half pence fare, we conscientiously saved the tickets, for we knew only too well mam meant the threats she had made.

Our Mickey said mam had got eyes in the back of her head. I believed that. There were many times when I had done something wrong and I was not sure whether mam had found out or not. Whilst ever I kept the thought of such a misdeed out of my mind, all was well, but the very split second I thought of it, so would she and she would rain thunder down on me. Eyes in the back of her head? She read our minds most like. But after what Mickey had said, the next time I had stood on her chair behind her and brushed her hair real slow, the way she liked it, I had looked for these extra eyes, but I had found nothing. But it was uncanny how she really did seem to know every move the pair of us made.

We got off the bus and were miles too early and waited impatiently for our dawdling friends to join us at the bottom of Bath Street. After what seemed like an age, they finally hoved into view coming down the hill, their jaws bulging with the colour changing gob stoppers they had bought with their purloined pennies. Finally reunited, we all trooped in together. Just inside the door there hung a really large coloured picture of Christ on the cross. It was terrifying. From the crown of thorns on his forehead, to the nails in his hands and soles of his feet, there was blood everywhere. This picture went straight onto my list of things to fear. For me, that horrific picture was not a good start and with sinking hearts, it took no time at all for both of us to decide we didn't like Sunday school one iota.

We spent the most part of the day on our knees, chanting prayers we'd never heard before, banged tambourines and sang songs we knew neither the words nor the tune to, sat with other kids we didn't know, read and were told stories containing a lot of 'thee's and thou's' we didn't understand or like and were greatly relieved when we were finally told we could go home by people we didn't know and didn't ever want to see again. When we got outside, Mickey and I just looked at each other, each wordlessly attaching blame to the other and made the return bus journey home in utter miserable silence. We were back just in time to help mam get the tea ready and she was keen to know what we had done. We tried to hide our disappointment and make it sound a lot of fun. She asked us for the bus tickets and we gave them to her. She scarcely glanced at them before throwing them in the fire. We had each been given a small brightly coloured scripture card from which we had to learn the words off by heart for the next weeks visit. Mine read:

"My spirit hath rejoiced in God my saviour and my soul doth sanctify the Lord."

I showed it to mam and she read it, then absent mindedly folded it to a point and used it as a toothpick to dislodge the meat stuck in her teeth, then that too went in the fire.

As much as we hated going, mam loved us gone and made much of the fact that she got an afternoon of rest and peace from us 'little sods'. And she did get her rest as nine times out of ten, she and dad would be in bed when we got back! We soon longed for the boredom of the previous Sundays and spent the rest of the week dreading going again. But at least we got some small pleasure from the thought of the coming Christmas party, though it was a fair way off yet.

One Saturday night, mam and dad had gone out to their usual whist drive and we were being baby sat by Uncle Ben. I was struggling with my Sally Army homework and I had to know the Ten Commandments off by heart for Sunday school class the next day. I was reading them parrot fashion from a pamphlet they had given me.

"Thou shalt not commit adultery. What's 'adultery' Uncle Ben?" He was filling his pipe, pushing the tobacco deep into the bowl with his long, claw like nails and didn't look up as he answered.

"It's about being an adult, what you becomes when…yer've all growed up."

"That can't be right. It sez 'shalt not'. I can't 'elp growin' up.

Does that mean I can't ever be an adult then?"

He lit the pipe and puffed short little puffs of grey smoke until it began to glow.

"Whaarr oyya readin' there anyway?"

"Sunday school stuff, about the 10 commandments. I have got to learn them for tomorrow. 'Honour thy father an' thy mother'." I chanted.

"You what," he roared, showering me with yellow spit, "honour 'em? If I 'ad my mam an' dad's coffins 'ere right now, I'd kick 'em into that bleddy fire. The lousy soddin' rotten bastards. Love 'em? I 'ated 'em," he shouted.

His astonishing outburst was so swift and loud that I flinched. I looked across at Mickey. His face too was shocked, his skin ashen. We were HORRIFIED.

"Oh Uncle Ben, 'ow could you? God can 'ere ya an' 'e'll punish ya." I said.

"God? GOD? What bleddy God? There's no god. What rubbish they teach you at them bleddy schools."

"Oh Uncle Ben, Ahhhh," his reply took my breath away. He placed his pipe in his saucer, stood up, bent down to my level and sprayed me with spit again as he said;

"I'll prove it to ya."

He raised himself to full height, placed his hands on his hips and glared in the general direction of the perceived heaven, the ceiling.

"God, GOD, can yo' 'ear me eh God? Come on then, show us yer power an' strike me down dead this very minute, go on then, do it, goo on, ah dare ya, goo on, ah'm waitin'…

"Glaring defiantly at some distant something, he went on "No you can't can you, you bogger, cos yo' just not there, are yer ya?"

Terrified, Mickey and me looked fearfully up expecting thunder and lightning, or a bevy of avenging angels at the very least to come crashing through the yellowed ceiling and smite him dead. We just about jumped out of our skins as the tension was broken by the burning coals shifting in the grate.

"See? Nowt, I towd ya so, din't ah? Din't ah tell ya?"

Heavily Uncle Ben slumped back into Dad's seat and began puff puffing at his now dead pipe and was soon snoring gently. I don't know what his parents must have done to him but this incident made me even more afraid of the dark attic than usual and I dived under the covers and prayed for him that night.

Another night he said he had something to show us and told us to wait whilst he sorted it out. He went into the front room and after a while, we heard the creak of the cane chest opening, followed by the rustle of tissue paper. He came back into the room with an armful of something covered in white paper. Placing the items on the table, he pulled his chair conspiratorially closer and very carefully began to unwrap the first of the parcels. It was a smoker's pipe. Mickey and I gasped. It was exquisitely hand carved out of a gold coloured wood,, in the shape of a lions head. The grains of the wood emphasised its long shaggy mane. It was utterly fantastic. The eyes were made of amber glass and when he lit it, as he now did, they glowed malevolently. Oh how we ached to touch it but he would not permit it. After a little while, gently and carefully he knocked out the glowing tobacco, wiped the still warm bowl out with his fingers and reverently wrapped it back up again. Next he took out a much smaller one. This was of a young Negroid woman's head with shiny black beaded eyes. She had a laughing face with the whitest of teeth, a curly head of carved black hair around which was a red and white spotted bandana. Her cheeks were tinted rosy red, as was her lips and her ears had tiny, real gold earrings.

She was utterly enchanting. Finally, with hands that visibly shook with expectation, he got out what he said was the most valuable. I was disappointed, it being a surprisingly ordinary pure white pipe with a miniscule bowl. Admittedly the very long slender stem was carved with hundreds of animals, odd buildings, people and flowers and it had never ever been used, but it was not a patch on the drama of the other two. He told us that the large cane trunk was full of other pipes too that he had collected from all over the world and as he took them back into his room, he promised he would show us more the next time. I couldn't wait to tell the kids at school. Only trouble was, Carol didn't believe me. I had even dragged Mickey over to her and got him to tell her the truth but she still wouldn't have it.

"Show us then…" said my old adversary, "I dare you, go on, show us!"

"I can't they're in a chest in his room an' I can't get in."

"No, cos yer a liar that's why" she had taunted me. "Liar, liar, pissy coat liar…"

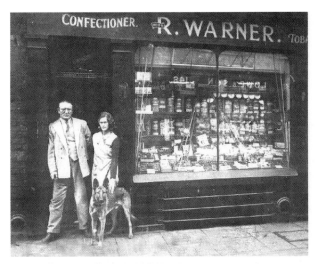

My Grandfather and his Stepdaughter Rose
later to be his Wife

My Grandmother Polly

My Mother and I on a visit to London

Joy aged 4

Joy aged 2

My Mother Vera in her
early 20's

Joy on location in Bolsover with
BBC TV in 1981 for 'Sons
and Lovers'.

Joy in New Years Eve Cabaret 1969.

'The Barchester Chronicles' filmed in
Peterborough by BBC TV. Joy poised
between Susie Birch and Sally treble.

Joy with Charlie Bartle at
Rockingham Castle in 1983
for the BBC's 'By the sword
Divided'.

Joy (right) with Sally Treble in 'Oliver' at Lincoln for BBC TV.

Joy in 'Make up' for 'Oliver' at Lincoln Castle.

Joy as a School teacher in Derby for BBC TV's 'Nania Chronicles' in 1990.

LEFT: Joy with Leslie Crowther at Central TV Studios for 'The Price is Right'.

RIGHT: Joy in 'Bleak House' for BBC TV at Thorpe Hall, Peterborough. It starred Diana Rigg and Denholm Elliott.

LEFT: Another photo of Joy in 'Bleak House' for the BBC dated Sunday 5th August 1984.

Joy on the set of 'Yesterdays Dreams' for ITV with Judy Loe (wife of Richard Beckinsale).

Joy backstage with Shareena during the 'Danny LaRue Show' in 1989.

CHAPTER 7

THE PLEASURE OF ILLNESS.

With Carols accusing words ringing in my ears, I worried about how I might show her the pipes and prove her wrong and me right. But first was to come one of the happier interludes of my young life. I'd woken a day or so later with a sore throat and a high fever which made me light headed and unsteady on my feet. Childhood illness in our house was a blessing in disguise and to be welcomed, for mam was unusually kind and caring and more, you got to sleep in her bed. But there was an even bigger reason to be thankful now. It got me a bit of respite from Carol's nagging. I got out of bed that morning and shakily staggered down the first flight of stairs into mam's room. Our mam, bless her, was bad tempered at the best of times, but *wake* her up and brother did you ever hit the jackpot. I tried to diffuse her wrath by stroking her face very gently.

"Mam, mam?" I said as quietly as I dared, "ah'm really badly. Me throat 'urts bad an' I'm on fire."

197

Mam struggled through the last vestiges of blissful sleep, opened then quickly closed her eyes again as the daylight pierced through a chink in the curtains and seared into her. A second or so later, she opened them fully and stared blearily up at me.

"Come 'ere'" she mumbled. I moved closer to the bed and she reached up and felt my forehead. The heat made her completely wake up.

"Aww, sheeit, you're on fire. Ya can't go to school."

She struggled onto one elbow, reached for her cigarettes, took one out, lit it, fell back on her pillows and drew deeply on it. She 'phewed' a sort of half sigh and half smoke exhalation.

"…yo'd better stay off, tell our Mickey I wants 'im."

She began to cough and struggled to sit upright. I moved to the top of the stairs to do her bidding and called his name as loud as my sore throat would permit.

"Mickey? MICKEY? Mam wants ya." He came running.

"Nip dahn the doctors on your way to school and ast 'im to come an' see 'er will yer? Tell 'im she's burnin' up and she's gorra sore throat. An' tell 'er teacher she's badly annall….an' make us a cuppa tea afore you go."

Two spots of high colour burned in his cheeks. I knew him

and knew it to be a sign of anger. I followed him downstairs.

"Thanks a lot yo'," he barked at me, "Now ah'm goin' to gerrin trouble at school cos ah'm late on account o' yo' skivin'. All the way to the bleddy doctors an' all that way back again."

"I'm not skivin' our Mickey, look at me sore throat."

I opened my mouth to show him but he angrily pushed me out of the way and barged into the scullery.

Dr Lynd's surgery was on Alfred Street South and was a fair old walk away. Before I could sympathise with him, mam called me back upstairs. She was up and pulling on her frock. "Get yerssen washed – PROPER MIND - then gerrin this bed an' wait fo' the doctor to come."

I needed no telling and ran back downstairs. As I did so, I heard the back door slam. A cup of freshly made, steaming tea was on the kitchen table and Mickey had gone. I washed sparingly in the icy cold water at the scullery sink and, subsequently frozen to the bone, went back up to mam's room. She was now fully dressed and she opened the curtains, picked up her nightgown off the floor, used it as a duster to wipe down the surfaces of the bedside and dressing tables, pulled the bed clothes into shape, pushed the pot further under the bed out of sight, told me to get in bed and clumped heavily downstairs. I needed no second telling.

Mam's room was sumptuous. It had a big bouncy soft bed, covered with white soapy smelling sheets; prettily hued ribbon bound blankets, a blue satin eiderdown with matching counterpane and wonderfully soft downy pillows. A large old fashioned brown wardrobe stood in one corner and held the entire families day to day and Sunday best clothes, there not being much, if any difference. There were a couple of musty, fusty suits of dad's and an old moth eaten, fur trimmed coat of Mam's. I had never known either of them wear these things. A pair of 'best' shoes of dad's and precious little else. Our day clothes and underwear were laid in the two drawers at the bottom of the wardrobe.

She had a rickety dressing table with three drawers which held her underwear – dad didn't wear any - and three mirrors which she could move this way and that to see the back of her hair. Laid out on its top was a decorative set of green glassware, comprising candlesticks, powder pots and a trinket tray on which sat a beautiful cut glass scent bottle, still with the haunting whiff of Evening in Paris or Californian Poppies perfume. A green silk backed set of hair and clothes brushes with matching mirror and comb posed prettily in front of the glass tray.

The floor had green lino polished to a high gloss and two small wicker tables sat either side of the wooden bed head. Above the bed was a picture of a little girl blowing the seeds off a dandelion, below it the caption "One o'clock, two o'clock..." Like every room in the house, this room had a fireplace and quite often in the coldest winter, fuel allowance permitting, a fire would be lit in it. If illness necessitated a home visit from the doctor, this is the only room he would see, the opposite bedroom door being tightly closed to his sight. I leapt into the bed and found it still warm, exquisitely cosy and with the strong sweaty smell of mam. With my head almost floating on the downy soft pillows, I caressed the satin eiderdown and counterpane.

The cold morning sun shone gently through the window onto my face. There were no bogeymen, mice or darkness in this magic place. Bliss. Within seconds, I was soundly and safely asleep. Some time later, I was woken by Dr Lynd's booming voice coming into the room, followed by mam.

"And what's the matter with you today Missy?" he was asking as I strained to sit up.

"Me throat 'urts and me 'eads 'ot." I told him still struggling out of sleep and suddenly keenly aware of the excruciating pain in my head and throat. In one move, he lifted my hand, felt my pulse and checked his watch at one and the same time. Now he put his fingers on either side of my throat, gently pressing whilst looking at a spot somewhere over my head. He bid me open my mouth and inserted a spatula on my tongue.

"Say ahhhh…"

"Ahhhhhh…."

Peering into my throat, he studied it through a deep frown and slipped a thermometer under my tongue.

"Don't bite on it," he warned.

"It's nothing to worry about, just a throat infection Mrs King, there's a lot of it about at the moment. Keep her in bed for a couple of days and I'll give you some medicine for her – and mind you take it -" he admonished me.

"Ah'll mek sure she does annall docter."

"I'm sure you will. And how's the rest of the family? Baby
ok? Albert?"

"Oh yeah, doctor, ah can't complain"

"Good… good".

He turned to me, ruffled my hair and said:

"I know it hurts, but you be a good girl and stay in bed and it
will be all gone in a couple of days. I'll not need to see you
again. I'll be off Mrs King. No, there's no need to see me out,
I know the way."

His ruffling of my hair was a kindness in itself and bought
tears to my eyes. I didn't have much skin on skin contact with
adults.

"Now you're sure you don't want a hot cuppa tea before you
go? Its bleddy cowd out there. Its no trouble you know."

"No, thank you, no…I have a good many calls to make today
and must get on. Good day to you."

He picked up his bag and left.

"Stay in bed and keep yourself warm while ah goo an' get this
medicine from the chemists," mam said. I needed no telling
and snuggled down as she left. The last coherent thought I
had before I fell deliriously into the most beautiful of dreams

was; 'does Dr Lynd *really* think we all sleep together in here?'

At some time, mam came back and gave me a spoonful of yucky bright pink, cloudy medicine, with a drink of warm milk and a digestive biscuit to wash it down. There was also a treat of The Beano comic but I left it unread and soon fell easily into sleep again. The sound of the kids coming home from school woke me and I smiled at where I was. Remembering the comic I reached for it and read it cover to cover. A little later Mickey came up and bought me my tea of a plate of sausage and chips, two pieces of triangular cut bread and margarine and a drink of milky tea. Seemingly he was over his pique and he asked me was I any better, talked about his school day as he put the food on my lap, and then went down to his own tea. I was hungry, more, having had only a biscuit that day, I was ravenous and this was to cause me a dilemma. The chips were home made, crisp and browned just so. The cut up sausage had the tell tale tinge of red, meaning they were my absolute favourite tomato kind. *But, mam had a saying*; 'Yo' aren't really poorly, not proper poorly, if yo' c'n eat'.

If I ate it all, mam would most likely consider me to be well and make me resume a normal day to day routine, even go back to school as early as tomorrow. Hunger struggled to outweigh the pain in my throat but hungry as I was, I had to leave some. I ate some of the chips – the crispiest and biggest ones - had one piece of bread and a little more than half the sausage. If truth be told, I could have eaten the lot twice over, but it simply wouldn't do. Slowly the remaining food went cold and congealed back into the beef dripping in which it had been cooked. A little later, Mickey came up for the tray. He grabbed the bread, stuffed the chips and sausage on it, wiped it in the hardened grease and wolfed it down, leaving a nice clean plate. I could cheerfully have killed him.

I drifted in and out of sleep for the remains of the day and was woken when dad lifted me out of bed and carried me up into the attic. He laid me down alongside Mickey. "There you go, back to sleep," he said, pulling the overcoat snugly around me.
But I lay awake for hours; all the old fears of the cold stark room came rushing back as I tried in vain to escape into sleep. The next day I was back in the womb like wonder of mam's

bed. And again, once my parent's bedtime came, dad lifted me and carried me up to the attic. I was thus molly coddled for a few days until one night dad's words sent a shiver down my spine. He tucked the coats around me and, laying a hand on my brow, he said;

"There ya go, ya lookin' better nah, an' yo're not nearly so 'ot …bet yo'll be well again tomorrow…."

With that he left. I put my hand to my forehead and he was right. I was cool to the touch. I swallowed and my throat, whilst still vaguely sore, was much better than it had been. Tears welled as I realised I would not get to spend another day in mam's room. I lay there wallowing in self pity, prickling with fear at the coming confrontation with Carol and frantically trying to think of a way to stay in mam's bed. And then the answer came to me in a flash! *I simply had to stay ill.*

Softly I got out of bed and removed my vest and knickers. The cold went instantly to my bones and I shivered. I got back on the bed and lay on top of the bedclothes until, numbed with cold, I finally fell asleep. The next morning, I was well! My temperature was normal as was my throat and chest. I spent the day running hither and thither doing errands for mam and the street aunts. But despite my telling mam over and over I still felt ill, I was sent back to school the following day. If I had dared entertain the idea that Carol would have forgotten all about the pipes, I was quickly proved wrong. As soon as I got in the school gates, she made a beeline for me.

As the youngest of a large family, all mainly grown and flown, Carol, the baby of the family, had the best of everything. When Santa came to her house he bought her everything she put down on her list and more. She asked for a double jointed china doll, she got the doll *and* a pram. She asked for a dolls house and got the house with every room filled with exquisite miniature furniture and even a miniscule family to live in it. But somehow, no matter how modest my requests, it was apparent Santa never read my list. My hair was cut with the aid of a basin, her mam took her to Madame Maison's and had her flaming red, naturally curly hair cut properly and it was always neatly dressed in the prettiest of coloured satin ribbons. Resplendent in smart daily clean clothes and with new shoes every few weeks or so it seemed, she was confident and attracted a lot of friends. I envied her.

"So when ya goin' ter show us them pipes then eh?" She said

catching me as soon as I got into the school playground.

"I can't. They're in Ben's room an' I just can't go in there when our mam's in."

"Yeah course you can't. They aint there, that's why?"

"Carol cross my heart and hope to die, thi' are. Ask our Mickey he will tell you."

"Liar…liar." She chanted.

Miss blew the whistle and we all stood still. On the second whistle we trooped two by two into the hall for school assembly and sat down on the hard wooden floor. Carol got behind me and whispered 'liar liar'. My face flared and I could have cheerfully hit her.

I worried about it all through the class but by playtime when she sought me out yet again, I had formed a plan. After school when I went in to make Uncle Ben's bed and empty his piss pot that night, I would close the door firmly and should be able to hurry the jobs up and rush to show her the pipes. Mam never checked how well I did these jobs as she couldn't stand the smell and look of her once proud room. Uncle Ben never noticed whether I did a good job or not. Better yet, now that there was no-one ill in the house, there was a good chance mam may well be at aunty Bet's gossiping.

"Ok, then, come to our 'ause after school. Don't knock on the door an' don't mek a noise or our mam'll hear ya an' she'll skin yer alive. I'll show ya the pipes through our front window."

Luck was on my side for once. The house was empty, mam was nattering at Bet's and it was easy to slip into Ben's room. I emptied the pot down the drain outside the scullery window, pulled at the bed sheets, tidied them up and was done in seconds. I looked through the slit between the chests and peered out of the window. Carol was walking up the hill with the same group of friends. They came to stop under the window. So afraid was I that mam might come back at any minute, I held my breath but for once, not because of the stink. I dragged the chair over to the window and placed it in front of the chests. Stepping up, I stood on tiptoes on the very lip of the bottom chest and managed to open the top one, it just about covered the whole of the window and blocked out much of the light. Carefully I lifted the long thin pipe, took it out of the wrapper and with one hand precariously holding onto the pipe, gently closed the chest with the other and held the pipe close to the window pane. They, like me, were unimpressed.

"Show us the black 'un, an' the lion's 'ead," Carol shouted. Nervously I looked over my shoulder towards the kitchen but all was quiet. I shushed her and tucking the clay one under my arm, opened the chest again and sought the Negroid one.

I repeated the process and held that one close to the window. Carol begged me to take it outside but I daren't. Then I froze as I heard the scullery door open and mam come bustling in. Hastily I shoved the black mamma doll pipe back in the chest and as I tried to take the long one from under my arm my foot slipped and I fell heavily. As I landed, I heard a nasty crack, loud enough for the very devil himself to hear.

"What are yo' doin' in there?"

"Just making Uncle Bens bed mam." I called.

"Well be quick about it, I want ya to fetch me some fags."

The audience outside heard mam's voice and noisily took off down the hill. With my heart misplaced somewhere in my throat, I hastily crammed the two halves back into the chest and quietly closed the lid.

For several days, expecting my misdeed to be uncovered at any minute, I walked on egg shells and slept even worse than usual. I was wracked with guilt and worried sick of mam's reaction once she found out what I had done and she *would* find out. It was surely just a matter of time. The only good thing was, I was back in Carol's comparative good books. She was satisfied, though she went on a bit about wanting to see the lion's head but she'd seen enough to satisfy herself and it all went quiet. Then I started itching.....

I'd kept our Mickey awake all night, scratching away at the backs of my hands, clawing at my arms and legs. I went to school that morning and was no sooner through the school gates than I was pounced on by Mr Martin the headmaster, who took me to one side and studied my rash and bloodied scratch marks. He sent me home and told me to get mam to take me to the doctors at once and not to come back to school till the spots had gone. I ran back home, went upstairs to mam and woke her as gently as I could. I fearfully explained why I had been sent home. She sat bolt upright, snatched at my hands, turned them over, spotted the red marks and glared at them.

"Bet you've got bleedin' dicks again entcha… Aww, if it ent one thing it's a – bleddy – nother."

She roughly pushed me away, reached for the nub end in the ashtray.

"Get downstairs and mek me a cuppa."

A few minutes later, I heard her heavy footfall descend the stairs. She threw herself heavily in her chair, lit up the first full cigarette of the day and went into a frighteningly severe coughing fit as I set her tea before her. I had made it to perfection, just the way she liked it, nice and dark, coloured with the cream off the top of the milk and sweetened with two generous spoonfuls of real sugar, for she would not touch the saccharin we had to use. I realised I was in trouble again and wanted to avoid another belt with the cane that seemed to have its beady eye on me. She finally stopped coughing and made me kneel in front of her as she 'walked' her fingers through my hair thinking it might be head lice, but for once, I was clean. She pushed me roughly away and asked me to pass her the doctor's book from the cupboard. Scanning the dog eared pages she found nothing to explain my symptoms so I was sent across the road to fetch Aunty Pat.

Pat, an extra large lady, with an extra large family and her husband Wally, an unbelievably tiny little man, lived directly opposite us on the corner of Upper Beacon Street and Moffat Street. Adult or child, when mam called you came running, there was no 'just a minute', you dropped everything and came hot foot. Aunty Pat was out of breath by the time she reached our door.

"What do these spots look like to yo' Pat? Measles?"

Pat peered at them without touching me.

"Hmmm," pondered Pat, staring at them intently and taking a tentative step back. This was one thing she did not intend to borrow.

"….well they're not measles that's fer sure, measles doan itch."

"There's them foreign measles goin' round on Turner street. 'appen they different."

"No, them's not German measles neither, I knows abaht German measles, our Joanie 'ad 'em. Yo'd be best tekkin' 'er ter the doctors."

"Aww, pissin' 'ell, that's all ah need. Its allus 'er that brings these bleddy things in." she glared at me. Aunty Pat jumped to my defence.

"Its not 'er fault yer daft mare. She can't 'elp it."

"It's alright for yo', your kids never ail a day. She's only just over that bleddy bad throat an' now she's bought this bogger in."

"Now you're just talking silly Vera. She is just a little gel."

"Don't matter how little she is, she can keep herself clean, just look at the bleddy muck on 'er 'ands, she's gone to school like that this mornin', Not even ad' a wash…… whatever she's scrattin' at its not off the bleddy soap she's used, the safest place to hide money from her in this 'ouse, is to put it *under* the bleddy soap. Gerrem washed yer dutty mare yo' fer yer nowt else."

Mam whacked the side of my head with such force that I staggered forwards almost falling into the scullery, where I scrubbed them clean with carbolic soap and Vim, as my ears rung. Aunty Pat was still defending me and not for the first time.

"I keep tellin' yer Vera, one of these days, yo'll hit her too hard. Yo're too heavy handed and that's a fact. Yo'll land 'er such an unlucky blow an' yo'll kill 'er…"

I have only to close my eyes and Aunty Pat's words echo through my head…

"One of these days Vera, yo'll land her such an unlucky blow an' yo'll kill 'er."

"'it her? I'll bleddy swing for 'er. She's bin towd over an' over an' over", mam emphasised each word with a hard slap across my legs, one slap per word.

"Aint I towd you, over an' over? Ent I? ent I? ent I?"

"Yes mam", I sobbed.

"Whorr 'ave I towd yer eh? What?"

"Not to let nobody touch me down there."

I answered through my terrified tears.

"See, the little bleeder knows full well it were wrong."

She ripped into me again and I had all on to stay upright on the newspaper covered table. Aunty Pat pulled me off her but it was a red rag to a bull and mam yanked me back and lit into me yet again with the wet flannel. When mam was in full flow, there was no stopping her, no reasoning with her, no adults plea's, children's tears or even their bloodcurdling screams could penetrate the red mist that descended into her eyes. But Aunty Pat went on trying.

"Vera she is only five. Even if she had told him not to touch her, do you think he would have listened? For God's sake, leave 'er alone."

A few days earlier, mam and Aunty Pat had gone to the rag
market. As was normal in those days, we kids were left to fend
for ourselves. Our houses were as open to us children as they
were to the adults and a lot of us street kids were sat in Aunty
Pat's. She took lodgers from time to time and her latest
lodger Paddy, was entertaining us. We were laughing at the
way he talked and at his silly jokes. Then he pulled out a
pocket full of loose change, threw it on the table and told the
kids to go and spend it on sweets and we were to go to the
park and share them out equally. We all made for the door.
"Oh not you Joy, I want you to help me cook some breakfast.
You stop here with me and I shall give you an egg."
I had never had a whole egg all to myself.

I can see, smell and hear that room. I can see the pan –
small, dark blue enamel with white chipped enamelled
interior and the three brown eggs within – the table, the fire
and the two windows, the brown drop ended leather couch on
which I sat, the clothes I was wearing; my winter coat and
dark maroon knitted hat. I have honestly blocked out what
actually happened. I only remember running and crying down
the street with my knickers in my hands to find mam. She

216

turned the corner with Aunty Pat...

Now here I was, a few days later, going through the painful ordeal of getting ready to go and see a doctor. Not kindly Dr Lynd, Dr Lynd ruffled my hair, I was not afraid of him. I was afraid of this new unknown doctor, but more, I was so deathly afraid of my mother. She dragged me still sobbing softly all the way into town to the doctor's office. I was taken into a room and mam and he talked awhile, then he lifted me onto a couch and started to take off my knickers. I fought him and I , screamed the place down. Eventually mam slapped me and held me down whilst he took off my knickers and examined me. She then shoved me, still sobbing, out of the room into the empty corridor. It was clinical and the walls were covered in white tiles with a frieze of patterned green smaller tiles and I traced the Greek key design with my fingers as my sobs subsided. I would like to be able to say this incident was never mentioned again but I can't. It is odd that I recall nothing of the actual sexual assault and every single nuance of the following viciously cruel incident.

It took place a few months later and must have been Easter or Whitsun for we were sat at the table eating a very special

*tea. It was special enough for mam to set it out on a snowy
white cloth and her Willow patterned tea set that only came
out once or twice a year, took pride of place. Her best tea set,
sadly her only tea set.*

*I remember the room better than any one I have ever
remembered in my whole life. The way the sun light caught
the blackleaded fireplace, the green wrap around floral
pinafore mam was wearing, the snowy white tablecloth,
Mickey to my right Eileen to my left, mam and dad on the
opposite side of the table. I took a drink from the tiny china
cup and placed it oh so very carefully back into the saucer.
We usually had old enamelled or tin cups or even the jam jars
deliberately and sensibly made to look like drinking glasses to
drink from, so this delicate and fragile China cup was a real
treat. I picked up the cup again and took another sip of the
condensed milk sweetened tea and went to put it back. It
slipped from my fingers and dropped onto the saucer
snapping the handle clean off. Tea spread in a damning
circle, soaking through to the polished top table below. Very
quickly, dad lifted the cloth and shoved a plate under it to
keep the heat from damaging the table. The huge brown mark*

on the white cloth mocked me. Mam went berserk and lunged at me. I'd seen it coming and had fearfully pushed my chair right back from the table and she could not quite reach me. She stood up and again tried to whack me across the face but again could not quite reach. Then she turned, fumbled for her fags on the end of the high mantelpiece, pulling her coverall pinny out of the crease of her backside where it had stuck. Now she turned to face me with hatred the like of which I have never known before or since. "You're nothing but a lousy little bastard. My best tea set, my ONLY tea set and you've effin' smashed it."

She poured misery after misery onto me, cursed me again and again and ended the tirade with;

"I wish Paddy had ripped you right apart."

There has barely been a day in my life when those words haven't come back to haunt me and the years have not dimmed the shock I still feel.

There is talk today of mixed messages. Mam was champion at this. As our finances got better, our parents used to go out on Saturday nights having first put us to our beds with the direst warnings as to what would happen if we dared get out of bed and come downstairs. A warning we heeded. Outside in the street, our friends would be playing but we could only watch. Eventually we would fall sleep only to be woken up sometime later by mam calling us to come down and finish off the fish and chip supper they had bought in en route home. I used to dread this for I was only allowed to eat after I had shown dad my 'tuppence'. Mam would pull me screaming onto her lap, pull down my knickers, force open my legs and expose my private parts, much to everyone's amusement. I would sob and cry and try to stop her but she would end up slapping me.

"One of these days you will hit her too hard. You'll land her such an unlucky blow you will kill her."

I could have recovered from another good hiding aunty Pat...

CHAPTER 8

SCABIES! MY HERO'S.

By the time Pat had given up on the mysterious spots and returned home, mam had calmed down some. She plastered me liberally, and considering her earlier temper, reasonably gently with Calamine lotion, warned me darkly not to scratch and said she'd wait and see if that worked before seeking Dr Lynd's advice the next day. The itching eased not at all and I spent the day running errands, making tea, doing her bidding and, once out of her sight, scratching like mad. But when Mickey came home at the end of the school day, he too was itching...

"Aww bleddy 'ell, not yo' annall".

Despite telling mam we weren't ill, she sent the two of us to an early bed covered in the lotion which had dried to a white powder and we spent a pleasant hour playing ghosts in the darkening attic. The next morning we came down to a rare sight. Mam and Sandra were up first. The baby seemed to be ok, but mam's hands and arms were covered in pimples with angry red welts and her skin was broken where she had clawed them to assuage the itch. Now Eileen toddled downstairs and she too was like affected. Mam hastily washed and dressed us and we itched our way to the doctor's surgery. Dr Nelson examined us and then looked closely at mam over the top of his horn rimmed glasses.

"Mrs King, have you been buying second hand clothes off the market and not washing them?" he boomed in his lilting Scottish accent.

"Yes, burr I allus washes 'em, I 'ave to buy second 'and clo'es n shoes – ah got no choice - burr ah do wesh 'em."

If we kids told porkies, we got belted, but I had learned a long time ago that adults were not governed by the same rules of truth as we children. Mam rarely if ever washed the clothing she bought us second hand from either Sneinton market or Pownalls rag shop. She would give them a cursory glance, sniff them and we would be allowed to wear them immediately. Indeed the cardigan I was wearing that very day had not been washed. I was with mam when she'd bought it for a few pennies off the rag market a few days before. The only one I owned and therefore had on that market day was a grey hand me down of a many times 'hand me downs.' It was as stiff as a board and made my arms itch. I had spotted this one on a market stall for 2d (1p) and begged her to buy it for me, which she did. It was a lovely sky blue colour, was down soft and I loved it so much I had implored her to let me wear it instantly. She had agreed and took the old one from me, folded it up and put it in her bag.

"It'll be a bit big yet, but she'll grow into it."

The board stiff one would, no doubt, be handed down yet again, this time to Eileen.

Dr Nelson delivered his verdict. It was more shocking than if he had issued a death warrant.

"Well you've all got scabies and that's the result of wearing the clothing of, or being in contact with someone else who has them."

Odd then, that this wonderful soft garment I was wearing, even as the doctor examined the suspect spots, seemed the likely source of what ailed us all.

"Scabies?" mam's voice trembled and her face whitened, then reddened. I thought she was about to cry.

"We can't ave' scabies, ah'm too clean me, ah keep my place good, ya know that doctor."

"I know you do your best Mrs King," he replied
diplomatically, "but nevertheless, that is what you have. It
needs to be cleared up at the skin clinic and quickly."

I found my voice and asked curiously,

"What's scabies eh docter?"

"They are tiny little mites – insects - that burrow under the
skin and live there. Look, can you see those little wavy lines
like pen marks? That's where they are, under your skin."

I looked down in horror and fancied I could see whole armies
of them marching about their daily business along these tiny
blue corridors.

"You mean ah got beetles running up and down under me
skin?"

I howled.

"Shush child, they don't do you much harm, just make you
itch and we can soon be rid of them. You'll all have to go to
the skin clinic and I do mean all of you, including Albert, and
it's really best to burn all the clothing you have worn since
you started scratching."

I will never forget the look on mam's face at that suggestion.
It was lost though as the doctor busied himself writing out a
letter for mam to take to the skin clinic as soon as possible.

He also gave her a pamphlet that explained the procedure. "We'll be there tomorrow" said mam, rawking at her arms, "you can count on it."

What a kerfuffle that turned out to be. But in the meantime, she had a few things to do before she broke the news to dad……she headed straight for Aunty Pat's, leaving us to ponder what tomorrow had in store.

Mam's news about the identity of the spots meant that she wasn't quite so welcome at Pat's and she was back within a couple of minutes, hugging their bath which Aunty Pat had reluctantly loaned. Mam lugged it into the kitchen and placed it in front of the fire on the hearth rug. Almost before she had got through the door she had stripped us naked, emptied the hot water tank at the side of the fire into the bath, boiled up a few pans and, one by one, had us dunked in the water. It wasn't really warm unless your leg touched the side nearest the fire, then it burned! This was exciting. It was the first ever time we had been bathed in a proper bath. Usually we got dunked in the copper!

Even allowing for the new Sunday school regime which took all the pleasure out of Sundays, I still hated Mondays the most and would dawdle home, not wanting the ordeal of bath day. Mam grabbed us as we came in from school, stood us up and 'bathed' us in the scullery copper in the left over soapy, laundry water. It wasn't big enough to sit in and its bottom was shaped like a modern day wok, making it extremely difficult to even stand in, much less stand *steady* in. Mickey would race home to get it over with, me, I'd rather dawdle and put off doing something I hated until the last possible moment, time has not changed me one iota. By now, after a doing a full day of hard physical graft, mam, never blessed with a tender side at the best of times, was dog tired and in no fit state to be troubled by my moans as I was being roughly scrubbed in the slippy lukewarm dirty water. It stank of Oxydol and bleach and stung my skin. Getting carbolic soap sloshed into our eyes as she washed our hair was something to be borne bravely, for any loud yells or cries would result in a hard slap, which delivered by wet hands on wet skin, was twice as painful. She'd wring out our hair much like she'd wring out the floor cloth, raising our eyebrows by several inches in the process. Thus she got us clean. Then, wrapped up in paper thin, rough towels, she'd bid us sit our shivering bodies closer to the fire. But since there was a huge clothes horse full of drying washing in front of it, trying to find a glimmer of warmth was a useless exercise. Bath time was not fun time, it was an ordeal to be endured. As I have already told you, there was a large metal hook on the wall, alongside the back window, where a galvanised coffin shaped bath would one day hang, but until that day came, we kids got the kitchen copper dunking, whilst mam and dad either went to the public baths or, after we had been put to bed early on a Sunday night, borrowed Aunty Pat's and bathed in the comfort of a warm room in front of a glowing fire. Now here we were, experiencing a proper bath for the first time ever.

After the dunking, she roughly towelled each of us semi dry and dressed us for bed. Now she turned her attention to the scabied clothes we had taken off. They were to be washed and dried overnight ready to get into the next morning and accordingly, were put into the copper and the bath water was emptied, pan by laborious pan, on top of them.
"Throw 'em away indeed, the man's a bleddy idiot. The likes o' 'im, don't live in the same bleddy world as the rest of us

poor sods. 'ow the blazes am I supposed to afford new clo'se fer all yo' lot at the drop of a 'at? I'll gi' 'im burn 'em. Scabies livin' under us skin eh? Let's see the boggers live through this…."

Grimly she added a whole bottle of Chlorus bleach into the water and as I watched the colour drained out of my wonderful cardigan, so it drained out of my face. Right before my eyes, mam pressed down hard on it with the copper ponch again and again and soon its scabied flawed beauty was no more than a memory. The next time I wore my lovely soft pale blue cardigan it was grey, felted, stiff as a board and it made me itch!

On hearing his footsteps down the entry this night, dad was surprised there was no race to meet him and raid his saddle bag for the left over sandwiches he always bought home. When he got in, he threw back his head and laughed at the sight of us. I was comically attired in an old moth eaten cardigan of mam's and Mickey in one of dad's old shirts which she had fished out of the rag bag. Mam told dad about the days events and handed him the pamphlet. He glanced at it as he took off his jacket and sat down to read it properly.

"Did you read this when he gen it ya?"

"Read? READ? What bleddy time 'ave I 'ad for reading, I ent stopped all day."

"Well read it now then."

He handed it back to her. Only now did she read the pamphlet and learn she had to take fresh clothes for all of us to use *after* the treatment, which consisted of being *bathed* in chemicals. "Aw shee-it! We all got to be bathed again tomorrow. Wish I'd ave bleddy known before, ah could 'ave saved messen all this trouble." *And folk wonder where I get it from!*

That night we kids ate a hasty meal of dry bread dunked in warm saccharin sweetened milk and went to an early bed. She put out a complete set of clean undies for all of us, with sets of fresh outer clothes. The next morning, mam stood us on the table and gave us a rough wash down with a flannel and only then could we get dressed. Now scrubbed and clean beyond belief but somewhat shamed and subdued, we made our way to the clinic in the middle of town slap bang next to a cinema that showed only cartoons. I knew where I would sooner be going. Mam gave the doctors letter to the nurse and it all went a bit mad from there. We kids, Mickey Eileen and myself were fetched by a team of nurses, stripped of our clothes, stood in a bath of hot water and painfully scrubbed down with a hard bristled brush. The water was pleasantly warm, had a greenish tinge to it, stank of disinfectant and we were given flannels to keep pressed to our eyes lest they sting as they very carefully washed our hair. Then the three of us were put into another, gentler bath that smelled sweetly of scent and were washed again, even baby Sandra was dunked too! We looked like drowned rats and when we were all wrapped up in large white towels, they sat us down beneath a huge clothes airer full of drying towels high on the ceiling. The room had a roaring fire and after a while mam and dad joined us every bit as bedraggled and we sat there enjoying the warmth of the fire. Someone came in and gave us kids a drink of warm milk and a biscuit and my parents enjoyed a cup of hot sweet tea. The nurse then told us to all to get dressed and go along the corridor to the office. A few minutes later, we all trooped in and mam and dad took the two chairs as we quietly stood behind them.

"My name is Mrs Beale and I am the head nurse. I need some information from you Mrs King," said the officious woman whom mam later described to the street aunts as being 'Hoity Toity'! She sat down at her desk and bid mam sit.

"Name?"

"Florence Vera King."

"Address?"

"80 Moffat Street St Ann's."

"Married?"

"Yes"

Mrs Beale looked up sharply. Mam glared at her defying her to argue mam's marital status. She dropped her eyes and methodically took down all the details mam gave of our family.

"How many bedrooms do you have?"

"Three."

"Is that three bedrooms or two and an attic?"

"Two and an attic."

"Bathroom?"

"No"

There was only one bathroom in our entire street and it belonged to Aunty Bet's. But it was used as a bedroom with a board on top of the tub, a mattress on top of that and her son Colin slept on it.

"Toilet?"

"Yes, well, no not really, we used to share wi' them next door, but they gen it to us and they share now."

She gave mam another funny look and tutted. Mam scowled.

"That's all Mrs King, you can go now. You have been washed down with a special chemical which will totally destroy the scabies. I know it's difficult but may I suggest you try and keep your family a little cleaner, then this won't happen again."

Mam went red to her wet roots and instantly lunged at the woman across the desk. Dad tried to hold her back but it was an effort, so riled was she. The woman dodged backwards. Dad hurriedly pulled at mam and managed to sit her down with a thump. The woman regained her posture and without further comment left with mam's words ringing in her ear.

"Yo' cheeky get yo' fo' yer nowt else, I'll swing fo' ya. I'll report ya, ya leery mare yo'....an' what are yo' lot gawpin' at?" she turned her fury onto us kids, as the door closed. On the way out, mam crossly asked the receptionist for the return of our pillow slip and our other clothes. They had all been burnt. I learned a few new swear words that day.

Mam made a beeline for Aunty Pat's on our return and bought

her abreast with the days events.

"Ah've been thinking Vera, ah don't think as Joy bought them scabies in ya know, ah think I know as 'ow yo' got 'em.'"

"From wearing Pownalls second hand clothes that's how we got it. Dr Lynd said so."

"Yes, but there's more second hand clothes in your house these days in't there?"

"What d'you mean?"

"Ben."

Mam's face was a blank for a second or two then showed horror as the penny finally dropped.

"BEN! Oh Jesus, of course. That meks sense."

The thought that Ben was responsible for bringing scabies into the house was too much. Mam jumped up and headed home with a face as black as thunder.

Uncle Ben was gone by morning. In one fell swoop I was saved from a certain beating for the broken pipe and a ton of guilt slipped from my shoulders. Over the next couple of days or so, there then followed the most top to bottom thorough clean I have ever known. Boxes of DDT and soap powder, bottles of Chloros bleach, gallons of boiling water was sloshed through every room until the whole place was fettled to mam's total satisfaction. Day after day we came home to a house stinking of a cleanlinesss that stung our eyes and made us gasp for breath. Out went all Ben's stuff, his bedding was doubly ponched and boiled, the mattress burned and the bed base stored in the back bedroom, a bed base I was one day to inherit. The front room gradually regained its previous elegance.

Now mam started to make sure we were as clean inside as we were out. She started dosing us with cod liver oil, malt and brimstone and treacle. If you have never tasted brimstone and treacle, man you are truly blessed! Liken it to eating a bucketful of Skegness sand, with a dollop of soda added, now mix the lot up with treacle and you are not far off. Ugh! I quite liked the malt and it helped keep down the cod liver oil which threatened to very quickly and dramatically return from whence it came!

Meanwhile, Uncle Ben along with his precious trunks went to a men's hostel in Sneinton, not a stones throw from where his beloved hero Bendigo had lived and fought. Very soon after he left us, Ben died. Mind, he was in his eighties. Many years later, I recounted the broken pipe incident to dad. I was wrong. That pipe wasn't clay it was ivory. To this day, I can still hear that 'snap'....Oh and one more thing; Ben bless his holed socks, could not have been at the Bendigo fight! He wasn't even born when Bendigo died.

We missed our Uncle Ben, but then something really exciting was about to happen that would push him to the back of our minds. We had a visit from the police and they came via those front doorsteps.

CHAPTER 9

THE OTHER MAN'S GRASS......

One of our daily bottles of milk began to disappear from our front doorstep. To begin with mam blamed Tom our milkman and told him he'd forgotten to leave it. Tom replaced it but when it happened again, as a favour to her he began to bring the milk round to the back and leave them on the door step but the theft of just the one went on. Tom was a personal friend who liked nothing better than to come to our house on a Sunday afternoon and play cards with my parents. Mam was well happy as nine times out of ten, she won the cost of her weekly milk bill anyway and so to keep the peace and his Sunday game, Tom replaced it over and over.

Our daily journey to school took us past the now little used air-raid shelter. It was a smelly, dark scary building that tramps and other odd night time creatures used and I wouldn't go in it for all the money in the world. One morning however, we were astonished to hear a 'psssst' as we passed. It came from the blacker than black gloom of the shelter. Mickey and I ignored the sound and quickened our steps.

"Mickey? Joy? It is you two isn't it?"

Out of the shadows appeared a tall scrawny young lad of about 14 with a thick mop of sandy hair. He looked dirty and dishevelled.

"Who are you? How do you know our names?" Mickey asked cautiously.

"It's me, Joey. I am your cousin from Kent. Your mam is my aunty Vera. I've run away from home and been sleeping in here all week."

I suddenly cottoned on to who he was and gasped.

"Oh ah know who yo' are, yer Uncle Joe's lad aren't ya?"

I remember mam talking about him when she was telling us all about her eldest brother. He also had two daughters and a wife, aunty Doll. Mam didn't ever see her relatives at the Kent seaside but they exchanged Christmas cards and wrote to each other from time to time.

"Yes, I am your cousin, but don't you dare tell on me. My dad will skin me alive if he finds out and if Aunty Vera knows she'll tell him, she will have to. Promise me you won't tell on me?"

"I promise." I said fervently. I nudged Mickey and he too gave his oath.

"I've been sleepin' in here and it isn't half cold at night."

"IN THERE?" I asked, shocked at his bravery.

"Yes, in there."

"Ohh, I don't know 'ow you dare. Aren't ya scared?"

I looked past him to the gloom beyond. I shiver ran through me just looking into the dark interior. I would not go in there even in broad daylight, apart from anything else, it smelled horrible.

"Course not, what's to be scared of? I tell you what though, I am that bloody hungry, I could eat a scabby dog. All I've had all week is bottles of milk off Aunty Vera's doorsteps."

"Oh *that's* where it's been going. *You've* been nicking it." Mickey gleaned.

"I only took the one bottle and it's either that or drink out of the puddles. Can you get me some money and get me something to eat?"

"Money?" Mickey laughed, "…in our 'ouse? Yo' must be jokin."

"I can run back 'ome and get ya some bread and jam." I offered. "Mam's still asleep in bed."

"Jam? Is that all you've got? Haven't you got a bit of chicken or bacon?"

I left Mickey doubled up with laughter as he tried to get his breath long enough to tell Joey just how well we *didn't* eat in our family.

Racing down the jitty as quietly as I could, I leapt the three steps in one bound and gingerly opened the backdoor. I fully expected mam to jump out at me but all was quiet as I crept back in. Quickly I set about hacking two chunks off the stale loaf of bread on the table. I spread it with the half frozen suet like margarine and scraped a little jam on it before silently closing the door behind me and racing off on tip toes down the entry to Mickey's side. I gave Joey the unwrapped doorsteps and he viewed them with suspicion.

"It's all I could get ya'." I explained.

"We gotta go to school else we'll be in trouble. Come on our Joy, mek 'aste."

We began to walk quickly away as he wolfed the food down.

"Can you get me some more to eat tonight?" he all but whispered.

"We'll see what we can do." Mickey replied as we turned the

corner and tore up the steep hill to school, Mickey still laughing at the idea Joey thought there to be chicken casually lying around on our table.

After dinner that night, as the two of us washed the mountain of pots and pans, Mickey managed to stuff a few potatoes and left over cabbage into an empty processed peas tin and under the pretence of going to the lavvie, smuggled it out to Joey. Later, in our bed, he told me in whispered tones of how Joey had stood under the street lamp peering into the tin, vainly looking for meat! He chuckled quietly. We had almost dropped into pre-sleep mode when suddenly he jerked wide awake and began laughing hysterically. Despite myself his laughter affected me and I too began to giggle.
"What, what?" I finally managed to ask, my ribs aching from the laughing fit.
"Bleedin' chicken and bacon…he must be mad to come 'ere if he lives that bleddy well at home. I dunno about him leaving 'ome, if they eat that well dahn there, 'appen we ought to run away to 'is 'ouse."
His words caused us another giggling fit.

We managed to keep Joey's secret for a few more hazardous days and if we pushed our fears of mam finding out about our involvement in his disappearance to the back of our minds, it was quite fun knowing something she didn't. But a couple of days later all that was about to alter as the police knocked on our front door. In those days, a visit from the coppers was a matter of suspicion, shame and fear. There followed a long question and answer session over cups of steaming tea and Park Drive cigarettes as mam learned all about Joey being missing. When they had gone, mam put two and two together, came up 'missing milk off the doorstep' and asked us did we know. She glared so hard at us, I was sure she had guessed and told mam where he was. Whilst dad went down the hill to the public phone box to tell the police and Joey's dad, mam fetched her nephew, half frozen and desperately hungry, back to our house. Early the very next day, his father fetched him in his big swish black car. He was a big brute of a man and I feared for my cousin's life. Mam pleaded with him not to hit Joey. I saw this as us being off the hook for keeping Joey's secret and relaxed visibly. Wrong. We were both soundly beaten and sent to a supperless bed.

I had a period where I did not sleep well yet again, feeling guilty at my betrayal of my cousin and worrying about him. But a few weeks later, a large parcel of books and comics arrived for me and Mickey as a thank you from young Joey. I never heard from him again. But mam was now reunited with at least one member of her family and promised to go down to Kent for a visit in the summer. This was to be a frenzy of a time for mam, but to our chagrin, just her and Sandra were invited and we were to stay home with dad. Mam began to make her preparations and managed to get a new dress and shoes from the Co-op and also another second hand dress and coat from Sneinton rag market. She found the time over the next few weeks to knit herself a cardigan and she made Sandra a lot of hand knitted cardigans. We watched the preparations with growing excitement tinged with more than a little disappointment that we could not go, for we had never seen the sea.

The day before she was to go, we came running in from school to hear mam happily singing along to the radio, open on the table was the suitcase borrowed from one of the neighbours which she was beginning to pack. All Sandra's things were carefully folded and put in first. Then came her own clothes and now she held up something really funny for us to see. Someone had loaned her an elasticated swimsuit that would stretch through to the middle of next week and we thought the idea of mam in a swimsuit so comical we howled. Full of the excitement of the coming journey, she showed us a side to her we seldom got to see, as she told us of the time when she was very young and had entered a beauty competition. She told of having to wear a swimsuit and parade up and down with a lot of other girls.

"I 'ed ter walk raund the room like this".

She walked across the room on tiptoe, with one hand on her hip and the other on the back of her head and waddled her bottom from side to side making us giggle.

"Oh our mam, you look essa funny."

"Well ah din't then, ah was a lot slimmer, an' ah won!"

"What did ya win eh mam?" I asked goggle eyed.

"I won an 'undred quid. It were a LOT o' money in them days, 'undred quid woulda bought a row o' 'ouses like this."

"Cor mam, what did ya buy wi' it then?"

"Ah shoulda 'ad more sense an' bought an 'ouse, burr ah was young then, ah were nowt burr a daft kid in them days and ah

got some real crocodile skin high heeled shoes and matchin'
'andbag."

We looked one to another. I had never known mam have
anything remotely like that.

"Where are they now mam?" I asked puzzled.

Her eyes took on a distant misty look and she said

"Ee, ah'm boggered if ah know, ah musta gen 'em away
sometime, shunta done though, wish ah'd still gorrem…"

For the briefest moment her eyes fell again on those
glamorous long gone shoes, that lovely matching bag, that
glorious winning time of those far away days but the moment
passed and she sighed and got on with her packing. She
picked up the swimming costume once again and held it at
arms length looking at it and stretching it, then she threw it on
the back of the chair and closed the suitcase.

The following morning she was gone and we were left to the
mercy of dad and his cooking. It was the first day and at
lunchtime we tore down the street from school and headed
home. As we opened the back door, we got a whiff of food!
HOT FOOD! It was astonishing. The house was as neat as a
new pin, the hearth was devoid of fag ash and shone brightly,

the table set with plates and cutlery on a *tablecloth* mind and a huge home made meat and potato pie took centre stage. Oh wow. We sat down and dug in with gusto. I pushed my knife into pastry normally as light as a feather but this was rock hard and it shot off the plate, zoomed across the table and fell into the hearth. We had a fit of giggles and there was no mam to admonish us for making the noise at the table. Nobody had told dad that pastry had to be made with flour and *lard*! Flour and water worked just as well for him. But the meat and potatoes were heaven. We chattered and giggled on in delight much like we did at the Christmas table.

"Anybody'd think you lot ad never had a 'ot dinner." Dad laughed.

"We don't," I said, through a mouthful of hot potatoes.

"What do you mean you don't? What do you 'ave fer dinner then?"

"A bit o' bread and lard, or marge."

Eileen answered, speaking with her mouth full.

"What every day?"

"Oh yeah."

"We 'ad chips one time," Mickey offered.

Talking with ones mouth full was getting to be infectious.

"Yeah but that was a long time ago." I mumbled.

"Who gets ya dinner then?" dad seemed curious.

"We do."

We all said in unison.

"You do? Well where's yer mam?"

"Oh she's at aunty Bet's or aunty Pat's…" Mickey began.

"….or still in bed sometimes." I finished.

As we mopped up the gravy on our plates with a thick slice of fresh crusty bread, dad got up and went into the kitchen carrying the dirty dishes. We had stood up and put our chairs back under the table without scraping them as we had been taught when, to our astonishment he came back bearing a huge steaming rice pudding. This was utter bliss and we left for school fit to burst.

But the bounteous food didn't end there, when we got in from school at teatime, we had hot buttered pikelets and jam and sweet milky tea. It had been a day to remember. That night, he took us up and put us in a bed he had somehow managed to dry out and he tucked us up and gave each of the three of us a kiss. After he had gone downstairs, we called to him and asked for a drink. He obligingly came up both flights of stairs bearing a cup of water for us but when we tried to do it again, he came up with a cupful of warm water and it stopped us.

We ate like royalty for the whole two weeks and his cooking skills improved greatly. We went to school hardly recognisable in clean clothes and polished shoes, with our necks and knees well scrubbed and our hair neatly brushed. The house meanwhile took on a new identity of sweet smelling, shiny cleanliness. If mam had had a holiday then so had we. This oh so brief two weeks had to have been one of the happiest times of our childhood.

All too soon, mam came home and we were glad to see her. Dad reported we had been angels and she gave us our rewards of little mementoes of her trip and told us many stories of how the sea sparkled and how the sand looked and felt. I was astonished to see how Sandra had grown in just two weeks and how brown her beautiful skin was, save for the white outline of a swimsuit she had acquired from one of the aunts down there. And oh how the sun had bleached the scarce, downy soft hair on her head, to an almost white blonde. That night we went to a late bed and were just happily drifting off to sleep when we heard raised voices, and one of them surprisingly, was dads. This was enough to make us sit bolt upright in bed, for it was most unusual. We could not work out what was being said, but we found out the gist of it when we came home for lunch the next day. As the previous two Mondays, we came home to a cooked meal and a side dish of a thrashing for telling tales on mam. We ate the food through throats choked with tears and it was not a happy meal. Fortunately she didn't bother cooking for us again at lunch time and in her absence we happily continued to grab a chunk of bread with a scrat of margarine.

CHAPTER 10

DAD BECOMES A SEAMSTRESS.

I have already made previous mention of our Singer treadle sewing machine sat elegantly once more under the window in the front room. Mam could just about thread it and sew a straight seam, beyond that she was stumped, so it was nothing more than a highly polished piece of furniture on which stood an ornament. But there came the day when our dad learned how to use it and to good effect. Very, very, good *financial* effect.

He became an agent selling football cards around his work place. The 3 inch square cards were made of a thick blotter like paper that had to be torn around the machine stitched edge, to get access. Inside there were printed rows of football clubs with imagined match day goal results. The ticket that had the most goals printed on the inside won varying amounts of money and, at only one penny each, they were very popular. There were set prizes of as little as say 2/- (10p) 5/-

(25p) and 10/- (50p); main prizes were £1, £2 and £3 but the one prize everyone dreamed of winning was the unheard of, fabled amount of £25. It was a dream of a fortune. Of course nobody had ever won it. Well, not up to then they hadn't!

Each Saturday night when the radio announcer read out the winning scores, we had to be dead quiet as dad checked the numbers against his own personal tickets bought with his commission. He occasionally won but not much more than 2 shillings. Then, one day, instead of tearing off the edge of the card, he idly unpicked it with a nappy pin. Noting it was a loser, he went into the front room, set the old machine up and practiced getting the stitch size as close as he could on a piece of newspaper and then carefully sewed that ticket back up again. He gave it to mam to examine and she said she could see where it had been stitched over and that the cotton wasn't quite the same shade as the one they had used. She was sure he would be found out and even dad wasn't confident he could get away with it. But as he so rightly said, who's to say he'd done it? Anyone could have, they would never know it was him. Every week he had to go into the office, take back any unused, unopened cards and collect the next week's batch. He secreted the doctored one in the centre of the returned bundle, secured them with an elastic band as was the way and waited with bated breath for them to notice the odd stitching. But the man counted them without removing the elastic band and satisfied, just threw them unopened in a bin containing hundreds of other such bundles and that was the end of it.

That reinforced his idea. In deep concentration, his tongue comically sticking out to aid him, he practised on the sewing machine for the whole week until he got the stitching *exactly* the right length and by the time the announcer began to read out the scores after tea that Saturday night, dad had carefully unpicked every unsold card he had left. At that very first attempt he won 5/-, the next week 10/-. Not exactly a fortune, but to put it in context, 10/- was probably a fortnights rent! Over the following weeks he won several small amounts which were given back to him to pay out to his lucky winners without question, the winner of course invariably being my dad. Now every Saturday night he was to be found in the front room pedalling away, re-sewing the cards back up again!

The money came in regularly enough to seriously help our family and one of the first things dad did was to restore deliveries of our daily paper, with another newsagent naturally. Mam thankfully threw away her nasty tobacco tin and smoked 'tailor mades' and to aunt Pat's relief, we finally got a bath, which mam proudly hung on the hook outside the backdoor. After several months, the impossible happened. Dad's sewing skills won him the jackpot! He opened up a winning ticket of £25! His face paled as he checked it and re-checked it, delighted and shocked in equal amounts.

"Bloody Nora, ah've only gone an' done it, ah gorrit!" he yelled. He checked it again and again. Then mam did the same. There was no mistake, it was a THE jackpot winner. It was an absolute fortune. Our kitchen was electric with excitement. Then mam started to have misgivings.

"Aw but Al, suppose thi' want ter know who won it…mek a presentation or summat?"

"They'll be lookin' at the winner won't thi'? Me."

"But worrif they find out?"

"Find out what? I ent stole it, I won it wi' a ticket I bought fair and square. Whose to prove otherwise?"

"But…"

"But nowt, I'd like to see 'em try an' not pay me. I won it fair an' square."

Dad's voice sounded like steel. Mam warned us not to tell anyone, not even our school friends, or even aunty Bet's and indicated the cane stood by the hearth. Just the look of it was enough.

"And don't you be telling Bet's neither," dad admonished mam. Mam nodded and this was one time she had to obey dad and keep her mouth firmly shut.

Even though dad knew there could be no possible proof of his embezzlement, the following week he was in agony. Would they pay him? Could something possibly go wrong? Mam daily took up the cane from the side of the fire and held it aloft as a warning to us kids of the direst consequences of saying anything to anyone. Though we ached to tell our friends of our coming fortune, we didn't need telling twice. The Thursday he was to be paid out was the longest of days. But at last his squeaking bike wheels echoed down the jitty heralding the hero's return and mam, followed by us kids, rushed out into the yard to meet him.

"Eya gorrit?"

"Did yer gerrit?"

"Show us the money dad…"

"Get in will ya, shuuuuush… think on woman…gerrin doors…the bleddy neighbours'll 'ear…" he loudly whispered. When we were all inside, dad firmly closed and locked the door, pulled the curtains against prying eyes and only then did he sit down. No sooner had he sat though than he jumped up again and went to the door.

"Nah what ya doin'?" mam said curiously and irritably.

"I forgot summat…" he softly called out from the scullery. He unlocked and unbolted the door and went into the yard and, just as soon, was back. The key grated in the lock and the bolts slid home once more and he came back into the kitchen carrying his snap tin.

"What ya doin'?"

"What ah do every night, getting' me snap tin in fer the kids. Leave it out there and somebody'll nick it an' there's summat in 'ere as yer've all been waitin' for, encha?" he asked .

He reverently put the tin on the table and stroked its battered and dinted green painted top. Sitting down, he turned again to the snap tin, winked at us and began slowly, oh so very slowly to open it. Every eye was pinned on his gnarled, work dirty hands. The lid creaked and fell back. With the lid finally raised, he took out a crumpled up piece of newspaper and opened it exposing the remains of his lunch a whole round of dried, curly edged sandwiches.

"Eh, I were that excited I couldn't eat a bleddy thing all day. Here kids, some grub fo' ya."

We all slumped. For once, those sandwiches were not the most important item on the agenda and they went uneaten.

"DAD? Did you or didn't you get it?" mam snapped.

Tortuously slowly, he began to look in first this pocket and came up empty handed. Then he tried another one with the same result. Now he patted his breast pocket and his back one. Looking puzzled, he pushed his cap onto the back of his head. Mam exploded.

"Gi' over dad, stop pissin' abaht. Eya Gorrit? Did thi gi' it ya?" He laughed, he meant having his fun that night.

"Gimme what?" he grinned.

"Oh you bastard for yer nowt else. You're getting on my effin' nerves."

Mam raised her voice to a scream.

(And while we're at it, there's another thing about my mam. If I was to say something had 'got on my nerves', mam told me I wasn't old enough to have nerves! But she had plenty. I didn't know where she kept them, but I did know that we were expert at getting on them.)

Dad grinned mischievously and would have continued to play with us all night but mam's faced warned him he had gone a tad too far. He finally stood up and pulled a small sheaf of thin white paper out of his inside pocket of his work jacket.

"This what yer want?"

He held up the precious bundle. I don't know what I was expecting but I was disappointed.

"Ah wish yo'd mek as much fuss o' me when ah come's 'ome from wok as yer do fo' this."

There didn't seem to me to be that much to make all this commotion about, just five pieces of a sort of tissue paper about the size of a flattened chip packet. Dad peeled one off and threw the rest on the table. He pretended to wipe his nose on it. Mam glared and snatched it from him, reverently ironing out the imagined creases with the flat of her hand. Sensing their importance, nobody moved. Spread out on the table was five, five pound notes. Nobody spoke. Haltingly, lovingly even, mam picked them up as if they the finest china. She had never held so much money in her entire life, only ever seen them in the cinema. One by one, she held them up to the light admiring them. She smelled them, she laid them on the table and carefully, humbly even, touched each and every one of them tracing the elegant words *'Five Pounds'* with gentle fingers as her bottom lip began to tremble. She sat down heavily in her chair and cried. A minute or so later, wiping her eyes on her pinny, she nervously snatched at her cigarettes and lit one with unsteady shaking hands, utterly unaware of the almost full one left smouldering in the ash tray.

"What we goin' to do wi' it eh?" she asked, her voice still quivering.

"Well, fust off, you know Ernie at wok? ...e's sellin' tharr allotment o' 'is in the 'ungerhills and I think as 'ow we ought to buy it. What do ya think? I'd love it messen."

"How much moneh does 'e want forrit?"

Her words came out on the back of her receding sobs.

"A fiver, but I reckon as I can gerrit for two quid nah an' pay 'im the rest at half a crown a week. Ah'll ast 'im at wok tomorrow. If I gi' it 'im all at once, 'e might just start to wonder where I got all that money from".

"Eee Al, I wunta thought o' that."

Mam looked at dad with something approaching awe.

"Ah well, it pays ter think these things through. Oh, just imagine mam, we can grow all us own food, sell some annall no doubt. I've seen it ya know. He took me up one day last summer; can you remember when I bought you that big bunch of marigolds an' daisy's back?" Mam nodded.

"I thought then worra lucky bogger he was and now its my turn an' ah'm gunna be the lucky bogger."

He got out of his chair and did a little jig on the hearth rug as we kids looked on through surprised and laughter filled eyes. Breathlessly, he sat down with a thump.

"There's a hut up there an' it be like we gorra caravan at Skeggy… There's a little stream an' yo' kids can paddle n fish in to yer 'earts content an' ya can eat as many apples an' plums an' pears as yer want, eat 'em all day if ya want. …ahh it'll be lovely, just you wait, a little 'ome from 'ome."

Mam's bottom lip let her down again and she howled afresh

burying her flushed face in her apron.

"Oh dad, we rich, I can't believe it….," she mumbled from the depths of the scrunched up soggy apron.

"….as for the rest", dad went on, "yo' c'n do what yo' want wi' it, we'll go to the Co-op Sat'dy and' spend the bleddy lot for all I care. I don't want nowt else fo' messen."

Mam' lifted her blotchy face. Still sniffing, she wiped her eyes and her nose and looked at dad in a way I had never seen her look at him before. The look was not wasted on dad.

"An' if Bet's or Pat asks where we gorrus new stuff from, you can tell 'er we've 'ad some cheques from the Co-op."

Dad really had thought of everything. Even the best of friends would be curious enough to ask where this sudden wealth had come from. Mam jumped up out of her chair and threw herself heavily into his lap, gave his a smacker of a kiss and laughing gleefully, got up and did a similar jig on the rug.

"We're goin' shoppin' an' yo'll all ev some new close at the weekend…." she sang, then "..oh, where we gunna 'ide 'em till then? Worrif we get burgled?" Alarm changed her facial expression.

"We'll not get burgled. I'll purrem in the cellar, no burglar would think o' 'em down there." dad said. And so they did.

Being a light sleeper, I heard someone get up at least half a dozen times throughout those two nights checking that the money was still there.

We were all up nice and early on the Saturday morning. We got washed without being told, neck, ears AND knee's in readiness for the great day ahead. So excited were we, we went without our usual Saturday morning fry up of bread and tomato puree and excitedly made our way on foot into town, dad and mam side by side, pushing the pram with us three straggling and struggling to keep up, for mam was in an almighty hurry.

We were heading for the Co-op. In common with most folk, mam had an eye on the divi paid out at the year end and meant spending as much of the sudden wealth there as she could. Our number was 103934. It was drilled into us and we knew it better than our own address. Mam wanted a new coat and went straight to the women's fashion department, almost running the last few yards. Within seconds she was rifling through the rails and pulling out first this one and then that. The assistant came to help. Mam told her she wanted a coat

and the young girl, straightening the rails as she did so, pulled
one out. Mam looked at the first offering. It was bright red.
She slipped it on, studied herself carefully in the mirror and
said through pursed lips,

"Nah, I look like a bleddy post box. Don't I Al?"

"No yer don't, ave it if ya want it. I like it."

"No, it's not me duckie," she said to the assistant, "ave ya
gorra a dark 'un, a navy 'un?"

"I am sure I have madam……Oh no, look, I have the very one
for you. It's not navy but it is a copy of the one designed by
Dior last year for Mrs Simpson. He called it the New Look."
She pulled out a very long black coat with a velvet collar.
Mam gave a little gasp and tried it on. Her face glowed. So
did dads.

"Oh look Al, just like Mrs Simpson's… I've seen 'er in it on
the Pathe news at the Cavo. Does it mek me bum look fat?"

"Does it boggery, yo' look lovely in it, just like a queen."

And she did. (Little did I know that some years hence,
this coat was to be a thrashing in the waiting for me!) Mam
preened this way and that, looking at the coat in every mirror
in every direction, stroking its collar like the velvet was some

rare exotic animal skin. Happy with her purchase, she gave it to the assistant to wrap and made for the hat department. Here she bought a small half moon hat of bluish black feathers and put it on for dad to admire. Next she found a navy and white spotted dress and a pair of black suede flat shoes. I don't recall her ever smiling as much as she did that day. Now she turned her attention to us kids. I got a green floral print dress, knickers and vests, socks and plimsolls, Eileen a matching blue dress, shoes and underwear, Mick got two new shirts, trousers, shoes and socks and baby Sandra got a purple coat. Dad got his customary nothing, except perhaps an extra Mars bar he didn't have to share and the sheer pleasure of opening his wallet, taking out the necessary legal tender to the astonishment of the cashier, and paying for it all. His pleasure was in watching the faces of his beloved family as he treated us all like the royalty he believed us to be.

"Anyway up…" I heard him say to mam later, "…if ah've won it once, who's ter say ah can't win it again."

"Oh dad, I don't think I could stand this much excitement twice."

She needn't have worried, he never won that much again.

CHAPTER 11

OUR SECOND HOME.

By now dad was officially registered by the council as an allotment holder and had put in a lot of work. He had it sorted, planted and well organised. I had never known him as happy as he was at that time. As a family we spent every waking moment at the Hungerhills. Our garden, for that's what we collectively called it, was in a lovely little spot and had several mature fruit trees and bushes that promised and later delivered much. Dad was true to his word; we could eat as many apples, plums and pears as we could as long as they were windfalls, those on the trees having to be left alone. The garden was remarkably private having thick, high, dark privet hedges marking our boundary on three sides and there was, as dad had said, a crystal clear, magic little stream that ran along the bottom in which, we'd paddle and fish for hours with penny fishing nets.

Just inside and to the right of the high, stout wooden gate was a large shed with a tiny stove and a sizeable table in the centre. Mam quickly turned this hut into an extension of home. She shopped at the Sneinton market and bought second hand chairs, stools, curtains, cushions, a kettle and pots and pans. These she took to the garden and turned the shed into a room of some considerable comfort. We stored jig saws and games like Ludo, cards, snakes and ladders, and when it rained we headed for the shed. But it didn't seem to rain much at all and mam took advantage of the privacy the high hedges afforded her and sunbathed for hours, pulling her dress down to her waist and exposing her huge pink bra as she contentedly knitted. Ernie had graciously included all his gardening tools, so dad was spared that expense. The rag and bone man, milkman, coalman or other such trades mostly delivered via horse and cart on our street and dad was out like greased lightning, lovingly picking up the horse shit for his garden with his bare hands, much to us kids' horror and the neighbours amusement.

After a couple of months, Ernie suggested that dad keep some chickens on the allotment and so get fresh eggs. Dad thought it a great idea, couldn't think why he had not thought of it himself and set out to buy a couple of hens. He bought them home, indignant heads hanging, beaks and wings secured and with their feet tied on the handlebars of his bike. Only when he got them home did he give any thought as to how he would keep them until he could get them up to the garden. He shoved them down the cellar until his next visit.

At work the next day Jack, another colleague told him he was daft to leave live chickens at the allotment, and, tapping the side of his nose knowingly, pointed out it was not just foxes that liked a bit of chicken for their dinner now and again. Dad cottoned on and decided the safest place to keep them would have to be at home in the cellar which was already conveniently divided into two rooms, one wherein the coal was tipped and a second, much darker one separated by a wall. I had never set foot in the second one as I knew all the bogeymen in the world lived there. Dad put them in the dark second cellar with a lean to door propped up against the opening. It took them two seconds to get out and they seemed to settle not at all unhappily among the coals close to the grating where the light streamed in.

All day long they clucked and called to the passing ankles in the street. Dad told mam he was worried he would not be able to find the eggs in all that coal. He needn't have bothered; laying eggs were not on the chickens agenda! Up till then the only chickens I had any knowledge of were the kindly animated ones I saw in the Disney cartoons at the threp'ney rush Saturday cinema, or the colourful cuddly ones in my school books. These buggers were neither colourful nor kindly but boy, were they animated.

Being 'invited' to fetch a bucket full of coal up from the cellar now held a new threat. As soon as the chickens heard the sound of the latch going on the cellar door, they were waiting to meet us as it opened, dashing through our legs and into the kitchen. They then had a high old time trying to avoid capture by jumping on and clawing at the table, curtains, and chairs. Indeed in order to avoid being caught, they dashed anywhere and everywhere they could as we vainly tried to catch them. And when we did catch them, they clawed us with their talons and pecked us viciously with their razor sharp beaks, as well as covering us and the kitchen liberally in coal dirt and chicken shit, much to mam's annoyance. And though we daily went on the hunt, there were never any eggs.

Dad reported the egg famine to Ernie who asked him what he was feeding them on. Dad told him left overs. Ernie pointed out that at our house, they were being fed 'left over' left overs, and it was no wonder they weren't laying. The birds needed grit and stuff in their diet and the only way to get them to do their job and lay eggs for us was to treat them properly and buy them proper food. The following day dad came home with a big bag of 'grit and stuff' and fed it to the birds. They loved it but laid not one single egg.

Ernie suggested he buy six china eggs; lay those around the cellar and it would give them the idea of laying themselves. Dad bought six china eggs. The next few days saw the egg count rise to six...all china! Ernie told dad he should get a cockerel as they would settle better with a cock crowing. Dad would have bought one too until Jack told him Ernie was pulling his leg. Then, one 'fetch us some coal up will you duck?' moment, the chickens sealed their own fate. It was a Friday, top to bottom cleaning day and as Mickey opened the cellar door, the chickens shot out like a bullet from a gun and the chase was on. They ran hither and thither, over the table, under the table, knocking the milk bottle flying and smashing it onto the nice clean floor, up the curtains, under dad's chair and when just about caught, dodged out and went under mam's chair. Round and round, on and on they went and Sandra, a sturdy toddler by now, added to the commotion by screaming her terrified head off. Then one of them tried to jump on the high mantle shelf and fell into the fire, just as quickly he squawked and fell into the hearth and was up and running again. But he had knocked over some hot coals and they set fire to the rug. It was utter bedlam. We finally caught them and having stowed them back down the cellar, mam surveyed the carnage they had wrought while we nursed our bloodied injuries. It was a steely eyed woman that awaited dad's return that night.

Almost before he had got through the door, mam gave him a blow by blow account of the evenings happening and told him in no uncertain terms he had to 'neck 'em'. We sobbed. No matter the birds had treated us so cruelly; we did not want to see them dead. We howled pitifully, until finally he gave in and said he would take them to the garden and they could live there always. The next night he trussed them up, hung them over the handlebars and headed up the jitty en route to the garden. Mickey and I begged to be allowed to go with him but he said he hadn't got the time and would be back in half an hour. And so he was.

He told us the chickens had gone straight for the stream, splashed about and washed all the soot off themselves till their feathers showed all their true colours and looked absolutely beautiful. The last time he saw them, they were paddled downstream and though he called to them to try and fetch them back, he lost sight of them. Every time we went to the garden after that we looked and called for them but never saw them again and I don't know at what point in my life I realised that chickens cannot swim, but I swear it only occurred to me in my later years. Mind, mam did make some tasty soups with home grown vegetables about that time if my memory serves me right!

I vividly remember that first year, the digging, planting and weeding, the long anticipatory walk there and as the sun was setting, the even longer, dog tired walk back, pushing our pram laden down with fresh fruit and vegetables, whilst Sandra, deeply browned by the sun, rode high on dad's shoulders. Though the actual war was all over bar the shouting, the effects of it were long lasting and food of every sort was still in short supply. What dad grew he gave away more than he sold and the street aunts benefited from his hard labour and good heart. We ate well and often. When the apples came to full fruition, mam and dad greased them with Vaseline, wrapped them in the daily mirror and laid them in boxes in the cellar alongside the barrels of potatoes. She also salted and bottled kidney beans, pickled baby beetroots, red cabbage and shallots ready for the winter and as we edged nearer to the first frosts, dad closed the garden down for the last time that year. It was to be another hard cold winter.

But for now, mam came into her own and began to make a bob or two here and there on the so called 'black market'. Behind the two easy chairs in the front room, two huge bags of men's interlock vests and pants were secreted. I don't know where they came from, they just appeared. Being cheap and coupon free, they sold like hot cakes. Everything we needed or used, food, clothes, sweets and even petrol were still rationed, not that that bothered anyone on our street as no-one owned a motor and the only cars that ever came down the road was the doctors, tally man's, those belonging the G.I's who were courting the local lasses, or the odd black mournful funeral car.

Word soon spread about the underwear and a steady stream of folks found their way to our back door. The trade was done behind closed curtains, after mam had a quick look up and down the street lest they were being watched. At first she was afraid of getting caught, but when nothing happened she became bolder and her stock grew to include tea and sugar provided by a local grocer. This line didn't last long though. By the time it was all sold and the man wanted paying, mam had somehow spent the money and he too was added to the "Shintin" list. But with mam, as one door resoundingly slammed shut, another, often more lucrative, usually opened…

Aunty Bet's eldest daughter Nora had been doing a spot of additional courting with Joe, a young American soldier stationed just outside the city. But there was also a certain dashing young local lad, Jimmy Weatherall who only had eyes for her too. He began to suspect she washed her hair rather a little too often and started to watch her every move. As is the way of these things, someone whispered a certain something into his shell like and he followed her one night and noticed how remarkably dry her newly washed hair seemed to be and how stunningly beautiful she looked in the real musquash fur coat he had bought her a few weeks previously. He watched as she went into the Astoria Ballroom, meeting up with and lovingly embracing an American serviceman.

He watched through the crack in the door as she handed in her coat and then discreetly went in himself. Once inside, he raced upstairs to the balcony and hid covertly behind one of the marble pillars. Here he was able to see without being seen and watched as she danced, jived and jitterbugged her way through the night, dancing with and having eyes only for the G.I. It took awhile for his dander to rise but it finally hit him hard when the band went into a slow number and she smooched cheek to cheek with him. He waited until the last note died and the band ceased and then shouted down to her as the floor slowly cleared.

"Oi! Nora? Ah thought yo' was supposed to be weshin' yer bleedin' 'air ternight?"

The two of them jerked their heads upward, spotted him and Nora visibly paled. They stood stock still in shock, unsure what to do. The other dancers had moved to the sides and Nora and her Joe were about the only ones left on the dance floor. The room began to quieten down as the other dancers, realising something was afoot, swung their heads from balcony to floor and back again as if they were watching a lopsided tennis match. Nora opened her mouth to speak and then quickly closed it again.

"Ah'll ev me coat back if it's all the same ter yo'." Jimmy yelled loudly. Embarrassed, Nora began to move off the floor and in one of those unusual 'hear a pin drop' silences that sometimes happen in the noisiest of places, his voice reached everyone in the whole room as he boomed;

"An' them bleddy false teeth yo' gorr in yer gob, ah paid fo' them boggers annall an' ah want the bleddy things back."

With that unaware and uncaring that all eyes were following

him, he ran down the stairs, raced into the cloakroom, took the coat and stormed out. Nora went on seeing her Joe and was soon sporting an even nicer fur coat. Joe proved to be a pleasant young man who kept the street kids in chewing gum, his girl friend and her sisters in nylon stockings and the street aunts in whatever he could wangle from the NAFFI.

The sugar shortage was quite acute and he it was who bought mam a couple of huge tins of molasses. She quickly learned how to use it and made a wonderful gloopy toffee which dried to a crisp crunch. She coated our home grown apples with it and sold them for tuppence each from our doorstep. Mickey and me were put to work chopping down bundles of crude firewood into lolly sticks, or even played shopkeeper and sold them from a tray on our front doorstep. She did brisk business because, of course, there were no coupons needed. By the evening, mam would have us run around the streets picking up all the discarded sticks and she would use them again the following day. By the morning, the toffee on any left over apples would be sticky and runny, she'd simply re-dip them and sell them on as fresh.

The biggest trade came after the cinema turned out on a Saturday night. Even as late as 10pm, we often had sizeable queues waiting for the fresh batch mam was just making. And what did mam do with all this new found wealth? Well, the one thing she was really good at was not managing money. As fast as it came in, mam would find some way to spend it. Her fags now came in packs of 20 instead of her more normal 5 or 10, and oh, she did love to gamble. Her once weekly indulgent trip to the St Catherine's whist drive, was now almost nightly. The card game at the church hall on St Ann's Well Road was run by the most innocent of vicars. But once the drive was over and he had retired for the evening, the night watchman turned a blind eye to money passing over the tables and even joined in the illegal gaming. Admittedly her purse would often bulge with pennies from her gambling but there must have been times when she lost too.

All those pennies in mam's purse were so tempting. Early one morning I decided to chance nicking a couple of them and entered mam's bedroom whilst she slept. I knew how to open her door without it making a sound. The latch had a certain way to it and it was easy to open it silently once you knew how to grasp the door handle firmly, tilt it slightly forward and then turn it. There then came the choice of floorboards. The one nearest the door to the left had a certain squeak to it but the one to the right was safe. Her purse lay on her bedside table just a few steps away from me and it was crammed fit to burst. Oh so very quietly and not daring to breathe, I crept round the bed and stood alongside mam. She had one arm flung over the side of the bed, the other tucked under her head and was snoring loudly, her mouth agape and deep frown lines creased her forehead. I was standing in a veritable lions den and stood for an age frozen with fear, hardly daring to breathe.

Avoiding the outstretched arm, gingerly I picked up her purse and softly pulled at the press stud fastener. It gave way in an explosion of sound and a river of shock ran through me. She slumbered on. Stealthily I withdrew three pennies, causing the rest of the coins to settle with a loud clink that made me flinch. I rode again on the river of shock as I watched and waited for her to hear this unbelievably loud noise. Still the lion slumbered on. Oh so agonisingly slowly and softly I pushed home the press stud and again came that same atomic bomb sound. Now I was in a hurry to get out. If she woke and I was caught…it didn't bear thinking about. Little by little and oh so gently, I inched my way to and through the door closing it behind me with the utmost care. On the safety of the landing I breathed a deep sigh of relief, the first real breath I had taken since I had embarked on this dangerous venture.

It was inevitable I would be found out and deservedly punished. I didn't get caught in the act but my purchase of sweets en route to school that day did not go unnoticed and the corner shop owner wherein I had spent the pennies, told mam I had been in buying that morning. I came home to the most enormous row and was made to tell her where I had got the money from. I had to tell her the truth. The only trouble was, I was not believed that it had happened only the once and as the stick crashed down on me again and again, I readily admitted falsely to her that I had been doing this for months and had had several pounds. Beaten black and blue, bruised, and hungry, I was sent to an early, dinnerless bed for a solid week. I learned a lesson from this - never get caught!

Mam hid her purse from then on, though even I was not brave enough to ever try the exercise again.

Then mam's money making bubble burst over remarks she made to dad at the dinner table one night.

"Yo'll never guess who bought toffee apples off me terday!" she said.

"Ooo?"

"On'y two coppers."

"Coppers?" dad dropped his fork with a clatter, his voice unusually sharp, "what bleddy coppers?"

"Oh that new lodger of Pat's 'as done a runner an' nicked 'er ration books."

"When wa' that?"

"Last week, I did tell ya….ya never listen to me do ya? Always got your bleddy 'ead stuck in ya bleddy Handicap books".

Dad studied the horses and to this end, bought this almost bible of a weekly magazine to assist him with the odds when he had the odd penny flutter and believe me it was the odd penny. The book did nothing to enlighten or enrich him.

"You do realise don't you, sellin' them apples is against the law?"

"Don't be daft. How can it be wrong to sell summat I made messen?"

"It's not legal to sell owt wi'out a licence an' suppose they ask where you got the sugar from to make them tuffee apples, Eyya thought o' that?"

"Thi' were alright. Just a couple o' young lads ah tell ya. Anyway, if they do ask, I can tell 'em I used me own sugar to mek 'em. "

"Vera, I give up on yo'." he said, "…you ent got the sense o' these kids. The amount you sell, yo'd need a bleedin' shop full o' sugar, neh mind the odd half a pound."

"O' don't be s' daft. Thi' were all right I tell ya. Yo'd put the bleddy kibosh on owt yo' would," she snapped, pushing her plate away and snatching at her fags and matches. Only, in her bluster, she didn't sound quite so confident anymore.

"An 'ow do yo' know they weren't 'ere to watch what yo' were up to, ow do yo' know somebody ent snitched on ya already? You just want to watch it is all ah'm sayin'" he ended lamely.

"Worra yo' lot wiggin' at?" she snapped at Mickey and me, "worrave ah towd yer abaht listening in to adult conversations? Yo've allus got yer tabs open. ..get this bleddy table cleared, get the pots weshed an' make me a cuppa tea instead o' gawpin'. An' when you've done that, ya can get to bed. I'm fed up o' the lot on ya."

I think she included dad in that. I didn't need a second telling and having scarpered, I heard most of what she said from the safety of the scullery over the sound of cold water filling the kettle.

The constables reported back a day or so later and mam was sat in Aunty Pat's having a cuppa and a fag when they knocked on her door. They had found the lodger but the ration books were gone. She would have to apply for new ones. They had a cup of tea, handed their fags round and spent a pleasant hour chatting. The conversation turned inevitably to the shortages bought about by the effects of the war. Mam told them she knew where she could lay her hands on a couple of sets of interlock underwear. They had never been worn she explained and had been found in an old man's house after he died. His widow wanted 2/6d per set. The lads said they were interested. It was proving to be a cold winter and long johns on a cold night shift were to be welcomed. It was left that they would come round the next day for them. She could not resist telling dad when he sat down to his mound of mash, mushy peas and his beloved steamed plaice smothered in parsley sauce.

"Them coppers come back today. Pat's got to apply for more coupons."

"O-ay?"

"Ay, an' they sat there above an hour chattin' to us, an' we smoked their fags…nice lads. I told 'em I knew where there were a couple o' sets o' new underwear an old man who died ad left an' 'is widow wants ter sell 'em."

Dad picked a bone out of his mouth and laid it carefully on the edge of his plate. He stopped and looked at her through lowered lids.

"One on 'em went to Bluebell 'ill school," mam chattered on.

"Oh that's alright then. You can do owt as long as you went to Bluebell 'ill school. Sounds very cosy, I 'ope you know what you're doin' is all I'm sayin'."

His voice rose in warning.

"Oh there you go again, you are a mardy arse."

She snapped at him, clattered her knife and fork down and pushed her near empty plate away.

"They're alright I tell you. They're coming back tomorrow. They want to buy 'em. See, I'm not such a dozy sod as you think."

"Ah didn't say as you were dozy, I just said yo'd to watch it." She jumped up, went up stairs and got ready to go out to the club for the night. A few minutes later, she clumped back downstairs, put her coat on and went out without another word to dad and without giving him the customary kiss on his cheek. He ate the rest of his dinner in contemplative silence. When he had finished, Mick and me cleared the table and washed the dishes as was our wont.

Instead of settling down with his Handicap book he sat for quite a while staring into the fire twiddling his thumbs, his usually calm face creased with worry lines. Now he stood up, went into the front room and hauled out the two bags of underwear. We watched in astonishment as he methodically, pushed the garments a few at a time into the hot coals with the long brass handled poker. The flames caught hold of the cotton and the chimney roared. It took a couple of hours to burn the lot, but burn it he did, even the bags they came in.

Now he brought up from the cellar the remaining large tin of molasses. He went out of the backdoor and made for the toilet where he spent some considerable time tipping it down the lavatory. The row that ensued when mam got home woke us up right at the top of the house. I clearly heard him shout that if the coppers did come snooping, they would find nothing in this house that didn't belong to us. The next day the two policemen came to our door and we called out; "Shintin". They went away and we heard no more. Mam reminded dad daily that he had been wrong. Shortly afterwards, mam stopped making the toffee apples, although I don't know how much this was due to dad disposing of her molasses and warning her off or to the fact the mice had found the apples in the cellar.

CHAPTER 12

THE FLICKS.

A group of us were sat glumly on the roadside edge late one Friday afternoon. It was the last day of the school holiday and we'd all be back there on Monday so we hadn't got a lot to smile about and when mam came back from her gossiping session with aunty Bet's, found out what we'd done, called us in and meted out the unusually excessive punishment, we were even more down in the mouth. The other kids were avidly listening as Mickey verbally set about me.

"What's she done to ya?" enquired Carol.

"Mam's belted me wi' the stick and it were all 'er fault, she towd on me to our mam."

Carol looked at me through slitted green eyes.

"What's it got to do wi' yo' yer nosy cah." I said, giving her the evil eye. I turned to Mickey,

"I didn't mean to our Mickey, but she was 'ittin' me really 'ard wi' the cane. An' anyway, we shunta nicked it, we knew we'd cop it."

"Bit late to be sorry nah innit? …why should she hit me like this eh? yo' 'ad yer share an' she didn't 'it yo' half as hard cos yo' towd on me, yer nowt burr a bleddy tell tale tit.!" he accused me. Carol broke into the song.

"Tell tale tit, yer tongue will split, all the little bird'll come an' ev a bit."

"Aw shurrit yo'," I blustered at her. I keenly felt the shame of what I had done and didn't need her to remind me. Tears of both anger and guilt welled up in my eyes. Mickey saw them.

"It don't matter, it doan hurt," he snapped.

The weals on his legs said otherwise.

"I'm sorry our Mickey, I really am."

And I was for I adored him.

"She's a maniac. Just look at what she did to me!" He stuck his leg out in Chas and Jimmy's direction. Those all too familiar angry red spots highlighted Mickey's cheeks again. Vivid white ridged welts had formed where the punishment cane had crashed down on him again and again. The welts were even more pronounced on his arms and shoulders where he had tried to shield his head as he'd huddled, curled up in the foetal position, on the floor in the corner of the kitchen. He rubbed at his sore legs and then his shoulders then back to his legs, unsure what part of him hurt the most. I couldn't help but think, if we had waited to nick the cake till next week, he would have had some protection from the new thick socks mam had bought him today. Although I too had been given a few whacks of the cane myself, he had taken the brunt of her anger.

"Don't matter," he said again, turning his head away from me. Winnie stopped chewing on her cardigan sleeve momentarily and nudged up closer to Mickey. She 'tutted' and stroked his sore leg. Angrily he pulled himself away from her and had another go at me.

"Anyway, she's stopped both our pocket money so you can't go to the flicks either".

"Just wait till I 'ave kids, I won't ever stop my kids pocket money." I said passionately. *(I never did!)*

"Oh yes you will, just like our mam, as soon as the rent man or clubman wants paying' an' yo' got no money, ya will, yo'll see."

We fell silent.

The year or so difference in our ages made Mickey seem years more worldly wise than I and he understood grown ups far better. He had long ago sussed out that mam, short of a penny for the gas or electric meter or even for a packet of fags, sometimes blamed us for some tiny little misdeed or other just so she could stop our pocket money. Our dad had a saying to cover most of life's pitfalls and of poverty he used to say;

'Yo' broke if yo' ent gorra penny for two halfpenny's but yo' bleddy broke when yo' ent gorra halfpenny fer two pennies.' And in those far off days, a halfpenny was a fortune to even adults when you didn't have one.

When needs must and they often did, I had known mam decant the Chlorus into a worthless empty vinegar bottle just to get the penny deposit back on the bleach bottle. That was not good news for me since I loved vinegar. When I had a bag of chips, having extricated the last tasty morsel from the very corner of the brick shaped shallow greaseproof paper bag, I sucked the vinegar that was left with great relish. One day I had walked into the scullery and having seen mam hanging out of, and cleaning the attic windows, knew it to be safe to take a long swig out of the vinegar bottle that was sat invitingly on the scullery top. But it was decanted bleach and

I swallowed it down. It burned and I ran screaming to mam up two flights of stairs. How she held her grip on that narrow ledge I do not know. A free health service was still a long way off and mam, unable to pay the rent let alone a doctor's fee, ministered to me herself by making me drink salt water and forcing me to be sick. I must have been a trial to her.

"It's too daft to laugh at anyway," Chas broke the painful silence.

"Ah know ah saw Pauline tied to them railway lines, ah KNOW ah did, an' I saw that train was going to 'it 'er an' yet she still gorraway. Ah saw 'er, we all did. It's a dead swizz."

"Yeah, but remember, she's tied up dead good this time an' them injuns have lit a fire under 'er. We all saw them flames going up under 'er legs last week dint we? She's definitely 'ad it this time. She can't gerraway."

Winnie's voice rose excitedly as she explained the plot of the latest Perils of Pauline serial. We fell silent as our minds, fuelled by Win's recap, drew to mind the sickening flames creeping up her bare legs. She was a gonner this time for sure.

"Ah'm goin' to be a film star like Pauline when I grow up," Win said dreamily.

"Look Chas, I gorra beauty spot already."

She pushed her thin pointed chin out to show him.

"That's norra beauty spot Win, that's a mole an' it's got a bleddy gret hair stickin' out o' it."

Chas guffawed at his own joke and we all joined in the laughter, even Mickey. Stony faced, Win thumped Chas, bit a chunk out of her skirt hem and chewed thoughtfully on it.

Our only treat of the week was a trip to an early morning film show at the Cavendish cinema on the main St Ann's Well road. At sometime, someone had charmingly nick-named it the 'threp'ney rush' by reason of it being it being just three pence entry fee and as such, cheap enough to attract a lot of small but very noisy customers, who hadn't the faintest notion of the etiquette of queuing and charged en masse through the doors as soon as they opened, hence the 'rush'. Mine and my brother's visits were dependant on several factors. Good behaviour was paramount naturally and that covered a multitude of sins from doing our chores well to behaving in school but mostly it was reliant on mam giving us our pocket money in the first place and that in turn depended on her having the money and being in a sweet tempered mood. As I am sure you have learned by now, it didn't take much to fire mam's temper. But, whilst we didn't get to go every week, it has to be said in all fairness we managed a good few visits. The money wasn't always an issue either, running errands added a few pence to our pockets, unless mam needed it of course, but just having the money was no guarantee we would actually go. Mam could and would stop our cinema visit at the drop of a hat and all it took was one little misdeed by any one of us, (and it was usually me) and the treat was forfeited. But this day was to turn out better than we expected. We were to make that visit in affluent style and it was all down to the business like brain of one Teddy Alexander Bennett, known affectionately as Tab.

Mam still spent every Friday morning doing her top to bottom clean, spurred on to work twice as fast by the thought of dad's wages burning a hole in her pocket and by the afternoon, the house was spick and span so she took her justified reward and went into town and shopped. It was always a much loved glorious treat for her and since the going was all downhill, her step was light and she almost skipped as she boarded the bus. Occasionally she would wait until we got out of school and take one or the other of us with her to carry the bags, but largely she went alone whilst aunt Bet's looked after Sandra. I well remember coming down Pym Street one afternoon en route home from school – I was eight - and I spotted mam just turning the corner of Moffat Street on her way into town. She was really dressed up in her Mrs Simpson coat, feathered hat and smart shoes. I tore after her and begged to be allowed to go with her. She looked down at my dirty dress and face and said she would take me nowhere in such a filthy state. I pleaded with her to wait whilst I changed my dress and washed my face. She said I would be too long and she was late already. Still I pleaded my case, until she gave in and bid me hurry up and she would wait for me.

I raced up the hill, washed my face whilst struggling out of my dirty dress and into the clean one I had hastily snatched from the overhead pulley. It must have taken me mere seconds for I was only too aware of her impatience. I grabbed at the family hair brush and slicked my flyaway hair into something resembling tidy and in only a matter of a couple of minutes, flew on winged feet to join my mam. I gleefully ran round the corner but she had gone. I threw myself down the hill and made for the bus stop thinking her to be waiting there for me. But she was nowhere to be seen. I sobbed bitterly all the way home. She later told me she had waited for me, I had just not seen her. Oh adults could half fib.

Sometimes on her shopping trip, she would indulge herself by going into Woolworth's café and having a dinner she had not cooked herself. I had seen her attack this delicious fare with gusto and after having a cigarette, she would occasionally move to another table, sit awhile and then join the queue and have another repeat meal. Other times though, for a change, she might stop at the Lyon's corner house café in the old market square or even the rag market tea stall for a cup of tea and a slice of cake for a small fixed price.

But that Friday's afternoon's shopping treat had been different and as she was not looking forward to it this time, she was particularly bad tempered. Sandra was over two years old now but she sure as hell still screeched a lot. Aunty Bet's could not have her this day so mam had to take her in her pram screeching all the way and that did not make for a happy woman. Our return to school after the long summer holidays was imminent and mam had taken out credit cheques from the Co-op to clothe us. But she knew there was to be little pleasure in spending them for we were all desperately in need of something or other, especially Sandra who seemed to grow out of her stuff almost daily. But mam, who never had anything, badly needed a new dress. The one she now had on, previously her best navy blue spotted one from the Co-op, was indeed the only one she owned and had to be washed and dried on the range a couple of times a week, only to be worn again the following day. It had rotted away under her arms from this constant wear and tear and had been patched again and again until there was too much 'hole' to sew, so she gave up trying, cut out the remains of the sleeves and hemmed the edges.

Now it was beginning to get a bit cooler, she had bought a second hand jumper off the market, unpicked it and re-knitted herself a long sleeved cardigan wearing it over the ragged dress. Moving from department to department, not daring to look in 'Ladies Wear', she bought as cheaply and frugally as possible in order to get as much buying power as she could out of those cheques. Her spending power had swiftly dwindled and the thought of some little luxury like her much needed new dress, or new sheets, disappeared like a politicians promise. With the cheques finally spent to the very last penny and the precious purchases tucked out of sight under the blankets in the bottom of Sandra's pram, she dropped into her second favourite café on the way home and took her usual tea, cake and cigarette.

On her return we raced down the hill to greet her and helped her push the pram. It was the same every September. In time for the return to school and again in the spring - in time for Easter - we got two pairs each of socks and new footwear – a pair of plimsolls for the summer or shoes for the winter. Our Mickey always had the traditional long woolly grey socks and within a few days, the first hole would appear at his heel. Fearful of mam's reaction to this apparently wanton destruction, he would pull them down a little. It wouldn't take long before the socks would be folded up uncomfortably under his toes, there being several holes all the way down the back and he'd have to thread his way into them and would appear to be wearing, in effect, ankle socks.

Obediently we waited for mam to show us our new clothes. I looked at my new shoes, they were not at all like Carols; hers were black shiny patent with a pretty ankle strap that crossed at the front and had a pretty leather bow, mine were brown lace up brogues from the boys department. But I had new socks and a uniform of a navy blue gym slip and two warm winter jumpers, again from the boys department, Eileen had the same and ditto Mickey. Mam wagged her fingers at him and warned him not to dare hole these new socks. He had asked her could he have long trousers this year but his new ones, made of grey itchy wool, were just as short. Eventually all mam's purchases were laid carefully on the back of her chair and now she turned to the rest of the shopping and out came the slab of cake from the cafe...... It had lain there on the table haunting me, taunting me, three layers of pink white and yellow cake sandwiched with jam and cream. Mam grabbed her fags and shopping and took herself off to Aunty Bet's to show off the latest buys. Making sure she had gone, I had taken the thinnest of slices off the cake, Mickey too. But what he didn't know was my greed had overcome me and I had gone back for another piece. (*Sorry Mickey!*) Retribution had been both swift and brutal.

In the distance Tab, the son of the new owner of our chip shop, came striding up the street chewing on an apple After the shop shut of an afternoon, he would often bring us loads of lukewarm chips wrapped in newspaper or, better still, the crispy bits his dad raked out of the mammoth chip pans. Sometimes there were bonus bits of fish and lots of tiny crunchy chips, but mostly it was bits of deep fried batter. Soaked in vinegar and sprinkled with salt they were utterly delicious. We looked in vain for a newspaper parcel but he was carrying nothing today. At almost 13, he was a few years older than Mickey and his voice was on the verge of breaking. It was odd to hear him begin to speak in a normal voice only to have it break mid sentence and hear a man's voice finish what he was saying. Only we daren't laugh for he was not above clipping us about the ears if he felt like it.

"Who's for the flicks tomorrow then eh?" Tab said throwing himself down on the kerb.

"Gizza bit" Chas eyed the apple hungrily.

Tab took one last bite and threw his coggin in Chas' direction and both Chas and Jimmy dived for it. Jimmy won and crammed the remains in his mouth, chomping furiously lest anyone take it from him and swallowed it down, even to the pips.

"*We* can't go. Our mam's stopped our pocket money on account of 'er big gob."

Mickey had been playing with a stick, pulling and tugging at the filth round the edge of the street grate. He lifted the stick and pointed it at me and my face flamed anew. Tab asked what I had done and Mickey told him. He turned his head to one side to study Mickey's now fast and badly bruising legs and arms.

"Aw bleddy 'ell! All that for a bit o' cake? Don't sound much to be narked about does it? As she done that to you annall?" He looked at my arms and legs swelling up and colouring to match Mickey's. His face showed genuine concern.

"Bleddy 'ell," he said, "aw...bleddy 'ell. Your mam wants reportin'."

"Our mam never 'it's me, no matter what I done." Carol said. I knew that to be true, knew her to steal money regularly and she never got belted for it. Her mam didn't even shout at her. It was to be many, many years before Carol found out that her mam was in fact her grandma, her sister being her mam.

"What about you lot, you goin'?" Tab asked.

"I can't," said Winnie, "our dads proper poorly an' not bin to wok this week, so we ent got no money."

Dad had once said;

'Winnie's dad has indeed got a permanent bad back; the idle sod can't get it off the bed of a morning to go to work'.

"An' them", Mickey indicted the brothers and broke his stick in frustration. He stuffed the two bits of stick down the drain and went back to rubbing his legs.

"...they don't get any pocket money at all, not since 'itler killed their dad."

Mickey held Hitler personally responsible for their fatherless plight. I looked at the lad's faces, eyes downcast and for a split second I thought they were going to weep.

"Looks like it's just you and me then, eh Carol?"

"Oh yeah, I'll be goin' as usual."

I glared at her and felt anger rising in me. Some folks had it all.

It was an almost automatic move for me to look down the street to where the hill fell away out of sight only to rise again on the distant horizon in the green verdant fields of Mapperley. Dotted here and there were wide, lush green expanses dotted with cottages and tree's and smack in the middle of the view rose a large elegant pure white house which seemed always to be bathed in sunshine, even now on a fairly dull day it shone. I spent a lot of time looking at that house, wondering about the lucky people that owned it, lived in it... Even the bleddy sun wouldn't come and light our side of the street and the only verdant greenery we got was the odd blade of grass that pushed up between the dirt encrusted cracks in the kerbs and pavements or sometimes in the roof gutters far above our heads.

"Hey Tab" said Winnie, snapping me out of my daydream.

"Chas sez this is a mole, but its not is it, it's a beauty spot innit?"

He looked at it and replied tactfully;

"It's a special mole that's called a beauty spot."

Winnie and Chas raised their heads at each other, each claiming victory.

"Tell you what, "he said, "I know a way we can all get to the flicks AND..." he paused dramatically, "we'll even 'ave enough money left over to get some gobstoppers annall."

"How?" we said in unison.

"I'll show ya, you.." he prodded his finger in my chest, "...go inside and ask your mam if you can tek your Sandra for a walk, but in her pram mind."

I hung back, not liking the idea much. I was in mam's bad
books enough already, and whilst I didn't want to question
him, I was loath to do his bidding fearful of my reception.

"Winnie you go and bring your little 'un out in his pushchair
for a walk annall…."

Now if there was one thing our street wasn't short of in those
post war years it was babies. I stood up as he turned to Chas
and Jimmy.

"An' you Chas, go an' get your dad's axe, two if you've got
'em…

"What can I do?" asked Carol.

"Nothing, you'll spoil your posh new frock. You'd best go
home and we'll meet you for the flicks in the morning."

She happily skipped down the hill in those black patent shoes
with the crossed ankle straps, calling 'Tarrar…see ya..' over
her shoulder as she went. My eyes enviously followed her all
the way down the street. On the one hand I was glad she'd
gone, on the other mad that Tab didn't have anything thing
nice to say about my dress. I looked down it. It was not clean,
not nice and had two square patches of deeper colour where
mam had ripped off the pockets rather than sew them back

when the corners had come unstitched. There was not much chance of my ruining this 'Jackie Pownall's' special no matter what I did. And my shoes, oh yes, my shoes…

At the beginning of that summer, Carol got yet another new pair of sandals. The ones she had worn for a few weeks previously had been bought new for Easter and were now too small and scuffed, so she got new ones. I was asked to come home with her and see them that night but first I had an errand to run for mam and so made my way there an hour or so later. As I had walked into their yard, my heart had skipped a beat. Right on top of their overfull dustbin was her old cast off white sandals. White leather with daisies punched into the front apron and with peep toes and slim brass buckled ankle straps, they were simply enchanting. There they lay, settled on the newspaper wrapped kitchen scraps, empty food cans and coal ash, like the finest pearls in a trough of pig swill, I wanted to take them but was afraid they were watching me from the kitchen window.

I squinted into the kitchen, but all I could see was my own reflection. Reluctantly I walked down the yard and knocked on the door. There was no reply. I knocked again, still no reply. Turning to leave, I bravely put my face completely up to the window and peered right in. The house was empty. I turned and walked back to the gate, swiftly picking up the sandals and shoving them out of sight under my arm beneath my cardigan. Now I ran. By the time I got to the top of our hill, I was breathless, shaking like a leaf for the thief I was. I had stitch but ignoring the side pain, I stood in the jitty, eagerly tried the shoes on and found them to be a perfect fit. I had never owned anything like this in my entire life, they were simply gorgeous. Now I had to explain them to mam. I ran in and a much needed lie came easily to my lips as I told her that Carol's mam had given them to me. Mam said she hoped that I had thanked her for them and I said that oh yes I had. I looked down at my feet in rich girl's shoes a thousand times before I took them off at bedtime and even then I lay in such a way as to admire them over the edge of the mattress whilst the light lasted.

Such luxury would, I was sure, would fall into the 'Sunday only' category and would spend the rest of the week in mam's wardrobe alongside other, newer items. Wearing them for 'best' meant that Carol would never know I had them for I rarely saw her on Sundays, she being at the Sally Army most of the day and, as it was strictly upheld as a day of rest anyway, we were never permitted to play outside for fear of annoying our neighbours

The next morning I dressed and of course put on the shoes fully expecting mam to make me take them off. But she didn't. I was, I was told, to wear them all the time from now on...she had burnt my holed plimsolls. I swung my head towards the fire and saw the remains of a black gloopy mass bubbling in the depth of the coals. I nearly died of a heart attack. I had to go to school on Monday wearing the stolen sandals. Carol sat behind me in class and was sure to notice them. I had nicked her shoes from out of her dustbin and she would know, she was bound to know, bound to notice. Did I sleep that weekend? Did I thump. Monday I ran a fever, but mam was having none of it and sent me off with a stinging slap. Those light as a feather sandals weighed heavily on my feet as I dragged myself up the hill to school. I was so fearful, I dawdled and was late, and all the kids had already gone in when I got there. I now had to run the gauntlet of the class *all looking intently at me as I was apprehended at the door and admonished for my tardiness by my teacher. The short walk to my seat was several miles long and I was certain every eye was looking at my feet, seeing my sandals. All through the lesson my face flamed as I imagined Carol's eyes boring into my back. At lunch, we all piled out into the yard and Carol called to me.*

"Oi, Joy, come over 'ere and see my new shoes."

She pointed her foot out to me and turned this way and that, showing off the pretty summer sandals. Now she noticed my feet. She stared hard at them as my heart geared up for the inevitable full frontal attack I knew was coming.

"I used to have some like that," was all she said as she skipped away. Relief such as I had never known flooded through me. She never realised, never knew, until now....

I looked down at the shoes on my feet. Those once pretty sandals were now barely holding together. The toes were scratched and no longer white and the tiny pretty straps were blackened and ragged. Tab snapped me out of my reverie: "Oy, wake up yer dozy mare, Goo on then, what you waitin' for, bleddy Christmas? Goo indoors an' get your babby".

I snapped out of my reverie and in spite of my fear of mam, instantly obeyed and raced down the jitty. I jumped up the three steps in one leap and ran indoors. Mam glared at me. "Now what?" she barked. "Want some more cake yer greedy little bleeder you."

"No mam," I kept out of her clout reach, "….do you want me to take our Sandra for a walk in 'er pram fer a bit?"

She was crying lustily and mam was glad to be rid of her. Mam said she was badly, but I didn't think so, I thought her to be mardy. She was always cryin' day and night. With her mouth constantly open as she cried, saliva ran down her chin and onto her dress and snot joined in. Yeuk. Now mam wiped the snot from Sandra's face with a grimed teacloth as she struggled and burst out screaming afresh.

"Ohhh," said mam, "I shall gi' yo' summa ter cry *for* in a minute..."

She gave her a slap, put a cardigan on her and fastened her into the prams reins. I hurried back down the jitty pushing the pram and instantly Sandra shut up.

The enforced wait for her meant I was the last one back. They all stood waiting for me and Tab at once began to walk down the hill. Meekly we followed; a straggly group of kids pushing a motley wagon train of pram, pushchair and barrow. Unquestioningly we followed him with no idea as to where we were going or what we were going to do once we got there. It was Jimmy who finally mustered the courage to ask.

"Wher..wher..where we goin' then eh Tab?"

Jimmy stuttered and so didn't say much usually but his curiosity had got the better of him.

"Market."

"W..wh..wha..what we goin' the market for e…eh Tab?"

"We're going to get some wood."

Tab spoke as if he should have known what was on his mind. Jimmy persisted and asked the questions we couldn't or wouldn't dare.

"W..w…what we want w…w…wood for eh Tab?"

"To - chop – up - stupid." Tab sighed impatiently, then instantly ruffled Jimmy's hair by way of apology. The rest of us not wanting to show our ignorance kept shtum.

"W…w…w.."

"Oh shurrup, I'll tell you just now."

We followed like silent sheep.

Soon enough we reached the Sneinton wholesale market. It was a series of two storied store rooms built in square grid like alleyways and was predominantly a sprawling mass of fruit and vegetable sheds that were a noisy hive of activity from early morning till very late at night, with lorries coming and going, bringing and taking stuff away. Men carrying huge sacks of potatoes as if they weighed no more than a bag of sugar darted in and out of the doors, their thick heavy boots sparking on the cobble stones. Sometimes they loudly called out some rough banter to each other that caused raucous laughter as they loaded up the lorries standing patiently waiting. Boxes of neatly packed bluish black plums, giddy bright oranges and pale green pears, vied with the delicate shades of shiny red apples. The fruit attracted wasps which the men fearlessly batted away. The scent was divine. Just short of the market entrance, Tab stopped us dead and gathered us around.

"Right."

Sandra, lulled to sleep by the rocking motion of the pram, now woke and started screeching afresh again and rivers of snot coursed down her nose and into her mouth. I pushed her dummy in, rocked the pram violently and, struggling to hold on, she shut up.

"Here's what we do," the master spoke," each of you go to an alley and find the man in the shed and tell him your mam's doin' a moonlight flit, Gorrit? A MOONLIGHT FLIT, an' 'as 'e got a big wooden box to put yer mam's things in."

"Wha wh…what's a moonlight f…f…flit eh Tab?"

"Oh bloomin' 'eck, you'd better stay with me, the bleddy flicks'll be over before yo've got your words out."

Jimmy looked down at his scuffed charity boots and his face reddened. Tab did the hair ruffling thing again making him smile.

"Come on you lot, we aint got time to stand about gawpin' Get a move on and when you've gorra box, bring it back 'ere to me."

Everybody shot off down the alleyways that formed the market. I pushed the pram over the bumpy cobbles and stopped at the first stall. The owner was huge and I was afraid to even speak to him. He had on brown trousers tied at the ankles with string and held up by thick strappy braces, whilst a very wide leather belt cut across his middle and a dirty sackcloth apron tucked into it, covered an enormous stomach.

He finally caught sight of me and asked, not unkindly.

"Well, what d'ya want?"

"Please mester," I began in a very small voice, "erm..our mam's doin' a moonlight flit an' she needs a big wood box to purrus things in."

"You what?" he asked perplexed. "yo'll etta speak up."

I garbled the words out louder and quicker. He looked at me quizzically for what seemed like an age and then he threw back his head and roared with laughter, losing his hat in the process.

"Hey Geordy, ev yo ever 'eard owt like this? This kid's mam's doin' a moonlight flit an' she's sent her to ask for a box ter put all their things in. Aint that the bleddy cheek o' the devil eh?"

The other man joined in and the two of them laughed heartily. I looked on in astonishment and was just about to walk away, convinced I had failed, when he dumped a huge crate on the pram, stopping momentarily at least our Sandra in her screeching tracks.

"Eeyar…" he said, ruffling my hair and giving me two huge black juicy plums. "one each, mind she don't choke on the stone…" he warned me and still laughing, walked away.

I bit into the plum, removed the stone and put half the fruit in Sandra's hands. She pushed it into her mouth along with a string of snot, biting and sucking hard on the fruit.

She swapped screaming for loud lip smacking and I got a bit of peace! I managed to balance the box one handed and walk slow enough to eat the other half myself before breaking into a trot and heading for Tab. I had quite a job valiantly trying to steady the box on the pram and was the first back. He took the box from me, then to my surprise, jumped on it and he and Jimmy threw the flattened pieces into the barrow. I offered him the other plum.

"Well done, off you go and do the same again. Eat that, but save owt else they might gi' ya and we'll share em out later".

"Why 'ave you broke the box eh Tab?" I asked puzzled.

"We aint got time to talk, yo'll soon find out, now scoot."

I obeyed instantly and raced off.

I didn't know what I was saying but the result was always the same: a peal of laughter, a couple of pieces of fruit and a wooden crate. With the three of us working steadily, between us we amassed a huge pile of boxes and fruit. Tab decided we had enough and we set off for his back yard, hauling our bounty up the steep Bluebell Hill.

"Right, you two tek your babies home and ask your mam if my mam can borrow 'er bucket, you annall Chas. Mickey? You stop 'ere an' 'elp me an' Jimmy."

I shot off down the jitty, carefully lifted the pram up the three steps into the yard. I went indoors. Mam was asleep in the chair and Sandra was asleep in the pram, her face dress and cardigan heavily stained with the juice of the fruit I had been plying her with. I softly crept out. I knew about mam's 'let sleeping dogs lie' saying and parking Sandra under the window where mam would be sure to hear her if she woke. Pinching the bucket from under the scullery sink and praying I could return it before she missed it, I raced back to Tab's yard. Most of the boxes had already been chopped up by the time I got back and the yard was littered with hundreds of sticks and splinters. Mickey Jimmy and Tab were red faced and sweaty with the effort. Jimmy took my bucket and filled it to the very top with sticks. Tab, not stopping for an instant, gave me my orders.

"You...tek Turner Street, go to any house and ask them do they want to buy a bucket full of firewood for threppence."

As he revealed his plan he grinned from ear to ear! Now *that* was clever. A bundle of about 6 sticks from the Lizzies' shop was tuppence a bundle and folks had to buy them to light their morning fires, so a bucketful for three pence was an absolute bargain. I stood and looked at him with my mouth open. Tab the lad was an absolute genius.

"Don't just stand there gorpin' gormless, don't you want to go to the flicks? Gerra move on," he chided me, still smiling widely. I turned and ran out of Tab's yard at full speed, bumping into Chas on the way.

"Hey kid, it's dead easy…look…" he held out his hand to show me the pile of pennies he had, "…don't do Pym street, ah'm doing that," so saying, he shot into the yard to fill up his bucket again. At a fair old lick, I raced out and headed for Turner Street. Between us we had made quite a few bob and I could sill taste the bitter coating of the pennies on my hands as Mickey and I lay in our bed that night, the earlier argument now forgotten as we discussed the day's events and the coming cinema visit. One of the better days I concluded, with another one to come tomorrow was my last thought as I finally gave in to sleep.

The next morning we got our Saturday chores done in double quick time, and whilst mam and dad still slumbered, we went to the flicks. Mam had told us after the cake stealing episode, we would not be going to the cinema, so it was a defiant but indescribably brave couple of kids who tore down Pym Street that morning. Racing into the auditorium, Tab outed some kids who were sitting in our favourite places. We jostled for the right to sit next to some favourite someone as Tab divided the fruit up equally. We spat the stones and pips out at the heads of the kids in front and threw the near naked apple cores at bodies further afield, feigning innocence when they found their mark and the recipient angrily turned round. The noise was horrendous as the kids, let loose from their adult constrictions, charged round the cinema like maniacs, their feet thundering on the wooden floorboards, but as the lights dimmed, the kids settled and the silence was *instant*. Laurel and Hardy was the first film. We watched gleefully as the captors of our imprisoned pair ordered them to go into the kitchen and make something to eat. Stan looked round the room, nervously scratching his head as Ollie opened empty cupboard after empty cupboard in the hunt for food, until he spotted a box of soap powder in the last one.

"So-ap pow-der," he read slowly and out loud. His face lit up.
"So-ap that means its soup powder Stanley."
SOUP POWDER…, now – pass - me – that - pan."
The kids in the audience laughed uproariously as they realised
they could read and Laurel and Hardy couldn't.   A couple of
Mickey Mouse cartoons had us in stitches, followed by
another exciting episode of the 'Burn 'em up Barnes' serial
about a racing driver. A picture of our hero flashed onto the
screen and we deafeningly cheered him, immediately after,
came a close up of the evil anti-hero and we loudly hissed and
booed. Finally, the one we had been impatiently waiting for
since last week, 'The Perils of Pauline' starring Winnie's idol,
Betty Hutton, flickered onto the screen. The re-wound reel
took us back to the end of the previous week wherein she was
screaming in agony as the flames reached higher and higher
up those beautiful bare legs. Only now, her hero friend,
bravely rode his horse into the midst of the fire, cut her free
and threw her across his saddle as the Indians looked on
dumbfounded, much the same as we did. I didn't recall even
seeing him in the shot the previous week and now there he
was large as life, the deed done and she was free before the
Indians had time to blink. She had got away again.

Happily sucking and chewing, we watched the film and were left worrying how she was next to be saved from being pushed off the impossibly high cliff into the raging rapids below and this time, there was no-one in the entire scene there to see it, let alone rescue her. There then came the usual rush for the door as the national anthem began and we tumbled out, the bright daylight catching me by surprise at it always did. By the time the anthem had played out, the only things left standing was the spring loaded seats so recently and hurriedly vacated. I wasn't sure I would be going next week. My heart was thumping with tension from witnessing Pauline's latest predicament and it now lurched as realisation set in that I had yet to face mam's wrath after this morning's disobedience.

My mind tried to rationalise the situation. She hadn't actually said we couldn't go to the flicks, what she had said was we couldn't have our pocket money to go to the flicks. I tried to think of the exact phrase she had used. But all I could remember after the cake stealing incident was the severe beating she had ministered and which had now coloured my legs into bluish black, yellow and brown thick striped bruises. But even if I could justify the cinema trip, there was the question of my dumping Sandra on the doorstep and getting her clothes so filthy and she had also found out I took the bucket without permission yesterday, adding further to my troubles.

But 'home' was still a long unhurried stroll up 'effin 'ill' and for now I leisurely and easily climbed it, lost in the subtle delights of the ever changing colours of my last gobstopper.

CHAPTER 13

THE CHIMNEY SWEEP.

Our next door neighbours, to the left, just past the jitty going back down Moffatt Street, were first the Lee's and then the Boultby sisters who looked like identical twins. These adults kept themselves to themselves and as such were not really part of our social life and we were required to address them as Miss, Mrs or Mester. I was a fully and well paid up errand runner to both these households. The Lee's elder daughter Ethel was a pretty, smart looking, well groomed young woman who was the object of a lot of spiteful gossip from the street women. Many an errant husband got an elbow in his ribs and a mouthful in his ears for looking just a little too long at her trim ankles and long gravy browned legs as she tottered on her high wedged heels up and down the street. Each time she sashayed past the street aunts, with her film star looks and body, she ran the silent gauntlet of their envy for their own youthful figures now long gone.

"Jesus!" mam said as she passed, "did yo' see them bleddy

nails? They must be all of an inch long. And that colour? bright red? If ah wore owt like that on my nails, my Albert wouldn't eat owt I cooked that's fer sure." Mam had sniffed as she'd said it. I'd looked at mam's nails. They were no more than an eighth of an inch long and were bitten to the quick. She bit them so hard that most days they *were* bright red, caked with blood.

I will leave you to guess their reaction the time she emerged on a gloriously hot Sunday afternoon, her hair piled on top of her head, a la Patricia Roc and wearing *nothing* on her midriff. That time mam called her a stuck up, hoity toity, tart. That comment flummoxed me some. When I was in the company of and being spoken to by other adults, aunts, uncles, teachers etc, I knew exactly what they were saying, but mam spoke with a whole other comical and, at times, mystifying language she bought into play which I didn't understand at all. I knew what tart meant, I loved them and had home made ones quite often at the Boultby's house with either lemon curd or jam in them but what did 'hoity toity' mean and 'stuck up?' Did that mean Miss Ethel worked in a glue factory? Whether she was or not, did or didn't, she undoubtedly paid the best for running errands. Where others would pay me a penny for running a couple of miles, she would pay me sixpence for doing barely half that distance.

One of the most frequent errands I was required to do for her was to run through several streets to a lady up Carlton Hill who darned Lizzie's laddered silk and latterly nylon stockings. The woman had a houseful of screaming, crying, yelling kids. The crowded little back to back terraced home was a total tip but oblivious to the noise, disorder and general melee all around her, she would take the stocking from me, expertly pick up the thread with the finest of steel crochet hooks and with a jabbing motion, run it back up to the top as swift as the machine that had originally made them in the first place. Securing the stitch back in its rightful position with a carefully colour matched thread she'd break it off with her teeth and all this whilst a baby suckled at her breast! One stocking could and would be mended by her a dozen times or more times and all for the princely sum of one penny per stocking.

There were some people for whom I ran errands for nothing, albeit not willingly. These favours were not done from choice I might add, but we were not permitted to take money off the street aunts for example and I would always run for our gentle old next door neighbours though I had to keep it secret from mam. I usually got a home made cake, biscuit or handful of sweets from them as well as the customary penny. And there were some places I didn't like to go, the Home and Colonial stores for one. There was always a long queue and quite often, the adults would push in front of me as they were 'in a hurry'. But if I had been sent by mam, I was in a hurry too. Yet if I tried to stand my ground as mam said I should, I was accused of chelping and often clouted or pushed right to the very back.

Our nearest grocery shop was on Turner Street and fascinated me, smelling strongly and deliciously of freshly ground coffee, soap powder, disinfectant, biscuits and rich Gorgonzola cheese. The floor was covered in sawdust and there were a couple of bentwood chairs for old ladies to sit on whilst they waited for their order to be packed. I used to love to watch the grocer whilst he worked. Cutting off a lump of butter he'd weigh it, add a little or take a little off, pat it into the traditional shape, press it into a wooden block which left it with a rose or castle impression, before wrapping it in greaseproof paper and handing it to the customer. Weighing a half pound of sugar, he expertly poured it straight out of the scale's pan into the dark blue bag without so much as a lost grain. I'd shudder as he used the big powerful bacon slicing machine. At times the huge serrated toothed wheel looked a little too close to his hand and at any moment I half expected, half hoped, his thumb would be shorn off. Stuck in a never ending queue I would fantasise that if the heroine in The Perils of Pauline ever got tied to this machine, there was NO WAY she could get out of being sliced limb from limb. Dad once told me, that machine was painted red to hide all the blood as someone or other got their hands caught under those teeth every single week. After that I would wonder each time I saw one of the staff wearing a plaster.

This fiery red enamelled monster had a legendary thickness scale over the top and I thought, if ever he was to ask me what thickness of bacon I would like, number 28 looked just about the right size to me. But he never asked.

Don't you talk to me about a deprived childhood! The grocer himself was a kindly man and would sometimes give me a small bag of delicious broken and often stale biscuits or even the bits of cooked meat, bacon, raw sausage and cheese that fell off those evil teeth. Sometimes I was allowed to keep any errand money I earned, but mostly mam needed it for the gas, the electricity, bread or for fags and I willingly tipped it up to her on my return. *I can honestly say, hand on heart, I never begrudged her that bit of cash.*

The two Lee ladies and mam were stiffly polite to each other but Mr Lee however was a thorn in mam's side, having fallen out with him at the beginning of one cold winter. Every summer the sweep would come round the streets and set about cleaning all the chimneys, only not at our house. Since there was no need for a summer fire, there was neither sooty smell nor smoke filled kitchen to remind mam that this really did need to be done. Besides which, our summer dressed fire grate had its customary newspaper fan sat in a hearth clean enough to eat off and mam was not about to muck it up. Come the first winter chill however and the need became obvious. For a couple of weeks we all choked on the yellow foggy smoke that refused to be drawn up the chimney, even with the windows and doors wide open. The burning soot fell steadily onto the hearth and at times, onto the pegged rug. Mam and dad coughed and spat the blackened phlegm onto the fire. It slid slowly down the fire bars and crystallised into stalactites. Something had to be done.

One night she told dad not to bank the night fire as he came to bed, as was his winter wont, but to let it out as she would have to get the chimney swept. The sweep lived several streets away and early the following morning mam sent Mickey to fetch him. But he was unsuccessful having knocked on his door many times. He came reporting back to mam that there had been no reply. Mam scratched a hasty note on our 'stop press' stationary and sent him back with orders to try again and if there was still no reply, to shove this note through his letterbox. After waiting impatiently all morning, she came to the conclusion that now she desperately needed him; he could not, or more likely, would not come.

It was a particularly cold morning and the house was freezing. Mam decided there had to be an alternative. She went into the scullery and tipped all the dirty clothes out of the cane basket and kicked them out of sight under the sink. Now she bought it through into the kitchen and set it down on the table. Next she removed the clock and all the decorative items off the mantelpiece, took down the shelf runner, rolled up the hearth rug and now proceeded to stuff the whole washing basket up the chimney! As she did so, soot fell by the bucket load and quite a lot of it fell on my mother.

The basket went just so far and then would not budge further. Undaunted and covered in the resultant filth, she lay on the floor and shoved both her feet under the basket and bracing herself on the table legs with her soot blackened arms, pushed until it was right out of sight. Now she placed several twists of newspaper under the chimney hood and also in the grate and set it to fire. It lit and lazily emitted a smouldering, custard thick column of choking creamy yellow smoke, which slowly poured out of and undulated up the chimney breast and across the ceiling. She opened the doors and windows and we waited for what seemed to be some considerable time.

Nothing happened. Still it lazily crept and curled and folded in doldrums across the ceiling. It was not, it seemed, going to work. Spent black newspaper ash with creeping maggots of fire dropped here and there on the hearth and then WHOOSH! Such a bang. The still blanket of smoke on the ceiling now instantly reversed and was sucked back up and out of the chimney stack in a split second, as all hell broke loose. At the bang, folks ran outside thinking there to have been a resumption of war time hostilities and, on being faced with a soot storm, realised it was only that mad King woman and either stayed to watch or took themselves safely back indoors.

We kids ran outside after our soot covered mam, now looking remarkably like Al Jolson. We stared excitedly as animated stacks of smoke and fire puthered out of the chimney and raced into and polluted the sky. Burning soot fell like a black snow storm and coated everything it touched, roofs, window panes and sills, clothes lines, surrounding pavements, onlookers and unfortunate passers by. A deep, rolling, roaring, rumble shook the walls and vibrated the very ground on which we stood. Neighbours further up the street got wind of the drama and came hurrying out, gathering together, watched fearfully, excitedly even as the comedy unfolded.

Alerted by the noise and clamour, Mr Lees came to the window. He saw the crowd looking and pointing upwards and came out to see what the fuss was. He was horrified. There were only about 7 or 8 feet or so of jitty height that wasn't adjoined onto his property. He called mam all the silly sods he could muster and ran indoors to check on his house. He came back even more agitated than before yelling that his walls were now getting really hot! Mam laughed, treated him to a few choice words and he trailed back in and watched the proceedings with his face miserably and worriedly pressed into his window. Mam said for weeks after, he had lace curtain print on his forehead. The rumbling continued taking some considerable time to ease off before the last of the burning soot dropped into the hearth as dry grey ash.

The street aunts were not best pleased as this filth had permeated everything. The wash lines had to be thoroughly washed before use and there was hell to pay when a sheet blew onto a rather more than usual soot blackened wall. It took a good few downfalls of rain to finally wash away the soot. But mam had got her chimney cleaned and dad came home to a roaring bright fire. She did this one more time but this time, someone fetched the fire brigade and they pumped water into our kitchen to douse the fire. And boy, did they read her the riot act. Then she had the job of cleaning the ground floor of all that soot blackened water. After that, our chimney was swept along with the others in the summer and we joined the kids watching and waiting to cheer as the circular brush emerged from the chimney pot.

Right next door to the Lee's lived identical twins, Belle and Bunty the Boultby sisters. These ladies were *ladies*, full stop. Elderly they unquestionably were, spinsters they undoubtedly were but they came from a more genteel, graceful age and background and had maybe fallen on hard times. No one could really tell them apart for they were said to be identical twins and it was rumoured they had never even courted a member of the opposite sex let alone married one. Queen Victoria would have been proud of them. In retrospect, I could imagine them coming from the home of (say) a vicar or a mill owner, they had that sort of gentility, virtuousness and grandeur. Both wore their pure white hair scraped off their smooth plump faces, pinned back into a bun at the nape of the neck, which was in turn covered with a white hair net. 'Ponds' would have liked to think that their product had kept their English rose complexions shiny and wrinkle free, with apple shaped, pink coloured cheeks that owed nothing to rouge. They were stout, forever dressed in tiny print, all enveloping cotton overalls and wore – summer and winter alike – black velvet ankle strapped, button fastened, house shoes with lavatory pan styled heels and with thick, fawn coloured, lisle stockings covering their chunky legs. No way would their stockings ever need to have a penny ladder repair! I adored the Boultby's and happily ran my legs off for them and not just for the penny or so reward.

Their house amazed me and I loved to be invited in. It was a mirror image of ours but there the similarity ended. The second I walked into the scullery the differences were grossly apparent. For a start it smelled clean, visitors stepped onto thick, fawn coloured rush matting that was relatively soft underfoot and gave protection from the intense cold of the quarry tiled floor. Green and white gingham curtains hung at the windows and a matching curtain hung below and across the front of the sink hiding the spider hole beneath. The two shelves above the cooker had runners made out of the same cloth with points of decorative white lace running like a fence across the entire bottom edge. The shelves were weighed down with dated and colourful bottles of home made jam and preserved fruits covered with gingham tops and pretty bows. On the work surface at the side of the cooker was a polished wooden tea tray eternally set with an embroidered cream coloured cloth, two white china cups turned upside down into matching saucers and a highly polished silver teapot, matching milk jug and sugar bowl. The milk jug and sugar bowl had heavily beaded and crocheted, circular white cotton, anti fly covers. Their tiny scullery was as bright, cheerful, warm and beautifully neat and tidy as ours was dark, gloomy, cold and dreadfully untidy not to say dirty. I only ever went into the two downstairs rooms but young as I was I noticed the scullery smelled differently to the kitchen, one of disinfectant and the other of polish.

The ladies too smelled fragrantly of perfume and scented soap, not like mam who stank of cigarettes, baby sick and sweat. In the kitchen, the linoleum covered floor gleamed and laid on top of it was a large square of 'proper' carpet that reached right the way to the hearth and back almost to the wall.

As in our house, the oak table, gleaming in the sunlight, was dead centre toeing the line of the carpet perfectly. It was unfettered by any covering but in the middle, a round fat glass jug of fresh flowers sat on a doily, its image reflected in the polished surface. On the back wall an old fashioned dark oak, mirror backed sideboard stood, laden with sepia photos, vases and treasures; each one lovingly picked up and dusted daily. The windows shone and the net curtains, starched and pristinely set to the glass panes, were held in place with highly polished brass bands to weight them down. The hearth, identical to ours, always had a cheerful flame and never a bit of dust or slack was allowed to lay for more than a few seconds before being diligently swept up by one or the other of them. In the recesses either side of the fire, were two oval black pictures of beautiful tiny babies, one asleep and the other just waking.

On the mantelpiece a gold trimmed, purple satin cover ran along the shelf and dropped down either end to a gold tasselled point which swung gently in the heat of the fire. Sat in the middle of this was an elegant small brass clock with a white enamelled, flower decorated face and either side stood a pair of brass 'bell metal' candlesticks. Over the fireplace hung a large gold, fancy edged, mirror with attached candle sconces and either side of it a gaslight, mantled with what looked like dolls small white socks.

As they had a different landlord to us, their house hadn't as yet been wired for electricity and there were quite a few other houses, including aunty Bet's that still relied on gas and again, this was down to the landlord. The walls were unusually papered in a busy green holly leaf and red berry sort of pattern and either side of the fireplace sat two chairs with white lace antimacassars and matching arm covers. I was a just little girl and yet I never tired of going into their house. What could possibly keep me wanting to go back again and again? The home made cherry fruit cake I was often privilege to? No. The drink of creamy warm milk or sharp home made lemonade they sometimes gave me? No. Maybe the penny or so I got from a speedy errand run? No. Ok, so it had to be the extra handful of sweets I always got for an errand *especially* well run? It was all of these and something else that pulled me back again and again.

It was the exquisite, blue glass, bead curtain that hung twixt the kitchen and the front parlour. Strings of these beads some eight feet long hung from the ceiling and were gracefully draped back to the wall by a matching dark blue silk tasselled cord. I would edge over to it as soon as I got into the room. In time, I got to touch it, feel the silky smooth glass, and see how the room reflected back on the prisms of the different sized beads. I have bought some lovely diamonds these last few years. None of them come close to matching the beauty of those simple glass beads. The ladies knew my love of them and told me that when they died, I could have them. So they were mine. I was content that they continued to hang there, *but they were mine.*

They thought me very polite and well mannered and I loved the fact that I was able to call each of them Miss Boultby. Certainly I never knew which was which and addressing them both thus saved me from having to solve that problem. These sweet dear old ladies talked to me in an unfamiliarly pleasant way. If I asked them anything about themselves or their home, they readily answered, never telling me to mind my own business or chastise me for bothering them, or just telling me to shut up the way mam did. I once pointed to a photograph on the sideboard of a very pretty little girl with beribboned ringletted hair. She is limply holding a teddy bear by its arm and knowing they had never had any children, I asked who it was.

"That's my sister Bunty dear when she was just a little girl."

"Oh wasn't she pretty?" I had said.

"No prettier than you my dear," she'd replied.

"Ah'm not pretty." I said astonished, thinking of the image that looked back at me from our steam damaged mirror in the scullery.

"Mam says I've got a Roman nose an' sez it's so big it roams all over my face."

She cupped my face in her hands, looked deep into my eyes

and said;

"That's a very unkind thing for your mummy to say. You are beautiful and I wish I had a little girl as pretty as you," and she had kissed me.

(Whether meant or not, nobody before or since has ever said anything as sweet to me as that lady did that day. I found it hard to believe but I have never forgotten it.)

When they needed me, which was almost daily, one or the other of them would walk the few feet past the Lee's house to the end of the terrace, climb the three steps, cross the jitty with one tread and from the bottom of the next set of steps almost sweetly sing across to our back door.

"Hellooo, Mrs Kinggg…? Can Joy run an errand for us?"

Oh on winged feet ladies, on winged feet.

As I was privy to most of the houses in the street through playing with the kids or running errands, mam would sometimes ask me what they were like inside. I told her in detail about the splendour of the Boultby twin's home; described the scullery and kitchen carpet, the fancy antimacassars, the lace arm covers, the curtains at and under the sink and the shiny dust free hearth. I extolled the beauty of a home kept spotlessly clean and smelling of fresh flowers and perfume; of the wonderful treasures they had, of the blue glass bead curtain that one day would be mine…. I went on and on until eventually mam snapped and said:

"Yeah well, that's as mebbey. There's two on 'em an' they've got bogger all else to do wi' their time all soddin' day. It wunt be as bleddy clean and spotless as that if they 'ed yo' lot raund their feet every bleddy minute of the soddin' day an' night wantin' summat or other. They wunt ev the time to ponce abaht cleanin' like that then, ah can tell ya…an' don't yo' be thinking' of bringin' any bleddy rubbish back 'ere me lady, we gorr enough of us own junk….bleddy glass curtains indeed."

I had a sudden awful vision of what was to become of those glass beads if mam ever got her hands on them.

One day, mam had sent me on an errand to fetch some fresh bread which was still in short supply then, but the delivery had not yet arrived and I had begun to sing to entertain myself whilst we waited our turn in the long queue. I sang April Showers totally oblivious to the fact that everyone in the queue was listening. When I got to the end, the audience applauded and I blushed. The women around me began to ask what I wanted to be when I grew up. I answered as all little girls through the ages have always answered, that I wanted to go on the stage and become a film star.

I don't recall how, but the question of pretty dresses to sing and dance in came up. One lady told me if I went to her house I could have some dressing up clothes to wear. On the way home from school the next day I called and got a string tied parcel of what I had fancied to be film star glamorous clothes. My imagination had done its usual and I had visions of the wonderful outfits that Shirley Temple wore and I could not wait to get them home but when I did and eagerly cut open the bag, oh how our mam laughed. They were large ladies evening and bridesmaid dresses and as each one was pulled out, it looked even more ridiculous than the previous one. (Wish I had them now they would be worth a small fortune I'll be bound.) And mam was having a right old giggle. I noticed there was something dark in the bottom of the bag but before I could take it out and look at it, mam had snatched the other stuff up and still chuckling, took it off to show aunty Bet's. Sadly, I pulled out the black thing. It was a perfectly lovely circular skirted black cotton dress with several different coloured ribbons sewn around the hem. It had short sleeves and a small lace collar and it fit me like a glove. I whirled first this way and that, hugging it to me. I loved it. When mam got back in I proudly showed it to her. She sniffed and said I could keep it but not in the house. I took it out and hid it behind the big iron mangle in the backyard.

During school holidays, we often used to have a concert which I organised. Winnie's mam used to let us have her empty front room to stage our musical offerings. All the street kids were either participants or audience, although I did most of the entertaining! Now I had a new dress and for once, much to her chagrin, Carol found she was not going to be the centre of attention. It mattered not what she wore, mine, I forcibly informed her, was a proper stage dress. We began our plans for the show. Winnie had to be in it as it was her front room and I had to be in it for I could sing and I had the magic dress. We talked of having lemonade during the show and charging 2d a glass but where were we to get the money from to buy it? We decided to just go with a penny entrance fee.

Now, on the day, though they were meant to pay, most either pushed their way in and got in for free, or had relatives in the show, or had only a halfpenny anyway. Then those that did pay listened and learned that the other kids said they had got in for free and moaned so much we had to give them their money back. I don't recall us making a life changing profit but I do recall I practised long and hard inventing a dance that had me twisting and spinning every which way to show off the dress to its best advantage. In retrospect I would love to have seen me twirling away with those long elastic-less navy bloomers dangling round my knees! I suppose I wore that dress maybe twice and then I went for it one day and it had gone. From that episode, I knew those blue glass beads would face the same fate if mam got her hands on them and I found myself hoping I would be grown up before the old ladies died.

One Saturday morning I was sat on the back doorstep feeling really hard done by. Mickey and the other street kids had gone to the flicks but I had to stay home and get my head de-loused. Last night I had been given the dreaded letter by the school nit nurse informing my mam I had dicks! Most of the kids had come out of school waving their bits of paper making them look for the entire world like a cloud of yellow butterflies but I had sensed the shame of it and tried to hide mine up my coat sleeve. Last night, after she had read the note, mam had given my head a good rawking with the needle sharp nit comb, yanking clumps of my knotted hair out at the roots before covering it in a foul smelling lotion to kill off what she might have missed. She brushed so hard that the metal teeth scraped my scalp painfully and when I tried to pull away, she had whacked me hard across the face with the wire bristled hair brush. My face had burst into a hundred bloody holes and still she scoured my head. Then she poured a large amount of milky white Lysol lice killer on and rubbed it into my hair.

I had gone to bed with yet another reason not to sleep as the stuff seeped into the tiny holes in my face and stung horribly. The smell of that stuff was vile and I visualised whole families, armies even of insects running rampant through my hair and maybe going into my eyes or nose or worse, my mouth. Ugh! She had repeated the exercise again this morning and for once, I was looking forward to having my hair brutally washed by mam on washday and wished it could be right now. Having again been through the ordeal, the gruesome, icy cold lotion was uncomfortably dripping down the back of my neck. Indoors, Eileen was going through the same ordeal and was yelling. I heard mam give my young sister a resounding clout and yell;

"It's your own damn fault, ya shunt bring the bleddy things in then should you? For Christ's sake, will you owd bleddy still."

"The longer you wriggle, the longer it will take, just hold still for your mam, there's a good girl," dad said.

There was another resounding slap, immediately followed by another, louder yell. I wanted to go and play but mam said I had to wait as she wanted me to stay in and watch Eileen. Mam and dad were off to town to do some shopping. I had offered to go for her but she said it was something they had to do by themselves. I knew what that meant, I would be stuck with Eileen again all day and not be able to do what I wanted.

My head really hurt and I could feel fresh blood in some places where the lotion stung. Touching it gingerly with my fingers, I could SEE the blood, only now I had the awful lotion all over my fingers and when I nibbled my nails, as I always did, right down to the quick, I could taste the damned stuff. I tried to spit on my fingers and wipe it off on my dress to get rid of it but it didn't work. I stood up to go and wash my hands in the scullery sink and as I did so heard a singing voice call out;

"Hello sweetie". It was one of the Boultby ladies and I raised my hand in greeting and called 'Hello'.

She walked across the yard to the lavatory and closed the door shut behind her. I washed my hands and as I was trying to find a clean bit of the towel to dry them on, heard Miss Boultby's shrill cry;

"Joy, JOY, get my sister, oh do hurry…" this was followed by a crash and a thud. I cleared our yard in one step, the jitty in another and was knocking at the Boultby's door in just another.

"Miss Boultby…MISS BOULTBY," I called loudly, "come quick, your sister's shautin' ya."

She came running and began immediately to pound on the

341

lavatory door. Alarmed she called over and over,
'Belle'? 'Belle'? 'BELLE'? All the while pushing on the
door but something was wedged firmly behind it. Openly
panicking and sobbing, she frantically banged, pushed and
hammered on the door, rattling the latch, but all was
ominously silent.
"Fetch your mummy dear....quickly...QUICKLY."
Her face was white, her voice shaking.

Mam and dad came running and sent me to Lizzie's fruit
and veg shop on Bluebell Hill - the nearest person with a
phone in our area - and told me to ask her to ring for an
ambulance. I raced as fast as I could and was barely back
before I heard the ambulance bell ringing as I raced down the
jitty. In the couple of minutes it had taken me to go there and
back, a few of the neighbours had heard the commotion and
were standing watching as a couple of men tried to break
open the door. But it would not give. The men shouted and
called but there was no reply. The words began as a whisper
but soon gathered volume until all heard that it knew Miss
Boultby was dead. Somehow mam persuaded the other Miss
Boultby there was nothing she could do and took her

reluctantly back inside. A few of the other street women, not privileged to the insides of this fine house, followed to give ministrations to the devastated lady.

Dad said he was pretty sure an ambulance would not be of any use now and told me to go back to the shop and ask them to call the police. Again I made the journey as fast as I could and as I turned into the jitty the second time, I heard someone say something about
'Had she been when she went or did she go when she was going', and to my shock and surprise I heard loud raucous laughter. Half the street was now crowded round watching the useless attempt to open the door. I pushed my way through to the front and one of the men stood at the back said;
"I hear they are virgin spinsters… who said you can't take it with you when you go?"
"Judging by the size of them bleddy bloomers on the line, you'd ev a bleddy 'ard job findin' it."
"Ah, they don't call 'em 'and trappers' fer nowt yer know."
I was puzzled. I thought dying was supposed to be a sad thing. I didn't understand why they laughed and why this happened every time someone died. They always laughed. The

humorous remarks continued and so did the laughter but then it started to rain and a policeman came, cleared everyone away, and stood in the backyard with his arms folded, barring their path.

I ran indoors, raced upstairs and went into our back bedroom from where I had a clear view. I was quietly watching the proceedings but the policeman saw me and pegged something on the clothes line blocking the sight. It turned out, I later learned from the street aunt's gossip, that Belle had had a heart attack and died instantly. As she had gone down, she'd fallen wedging her legs and bottom into the base of the door and that was what the problem was. They had to break the door down to get to her and then break her legs to get her out. A day or so later, a new door was hung.

The funeral took place a few days later whilst I was at school and after that, all I ever saw of the other Miss Boultby, was a wraith like creature wreathed in black who seemed to drift across the window or up and down the yard to the toilet and back. Within a matter of weeks she was in hospital and never came out again. Each time I came up the hill en route home, I had to pass the Boultby's door which opened straight onto the pavement. The curtains remained closed, the house deserted and papers and letters hung out of the letterbox. It took on a dusty forlorn look with masses of spiders webs covering the windows and round the back, dust had blown up from the cliff below and gathered at the firmly closed backdoor, whilst the old toilet door was propped up on the iron fencing.

Then, one day, I was surprised to see the curtains gone and the room open to view. I peeped in and saw the parlour was totally empty save for a pile of papers on the floor, a two foot frieze of polished lino round the edges, and a pleated newspaper fan in the hearth. I ran as fast as I could, turned into the jitty and raced into our scullery.

"Mam, somebody's been in Miss Boultby's house and took all the furniture."

"Yeah, their relatives 'ave been in today an' cleared everythin' out. Folk's ave been tekkin stuff away as soon as they've put it out, an' I was at the bleddy doctors and missed it all. Them greedy sods must ave' ad a field day rummagin' about in the dustbins, trust me to miss out."

I dashed out and raced down into their yard. Standing on tiptoes on the very top of the three backdoor steps, I was just able to see that this room too had been cleared of everything; even the blue glass beaded curtain with the matching pure silk tasselled cord was gone. My heart sank. I know its silly but I still feel sad at the loss of those beads.

I missed the sisters enormously and not just for the pennies and little treats I earned from them. Within weeks the house was taken over by a Scottish couple who became notorious for their Saturday night boozy rows and the police became regular visitors to that once so elegant, peaceful house.

CHAPTER 14

BONFIRE NIGHT.

The next exciting social event of our year was bonfire night. To this end, Mickey and I set out to collect as much rubbish to build our annual bonfire with as we could. Mrs Quigley at the St Ann's Well Road 'beer off' had given us our best find so far, a double mattress. This treasure we knew would make a great blaze come the night a few days hence. With the two of us walking backwards, we struggled en route home with it and managed to haul it to the top of the steep hill of Livingstone street and round the corner into Moffatt street, where we let it lay awhile as we caught our breath. The side door of the cobblers shop across from us swung open and Mrs Abbott, popped her head round the door and called;

"Ay, yo' kids, are ya' collecting bonfire rubbish?"

"Yes missus," Mickey answered.

"Well ah got summat fo' ya'".

Mrs Abbott was both incredibly old and incredibly thin. Thinner even than aunty Bet's. She had snowy white sparse

347

hair covered by a net that struggled to keep the mess tidy. Her ears were enormous, and the earrings in her pierced lobes seemed determined to break free and by the looks of the tiny amount of flesh left at the very base, the heavy swinging gold adornments were just about to win. Dressed head to toe in black, her skirts sweeping the floor and with her shoulders covered by a vividly multi coloured crocheted shawl, she leaned heavily on a stick for support as she stood in the doorway and beckoned Mickey and me across the road. I nervously tried to hide my face as I had had a run in with her some months ago.

There were two cobblers occupying opposite ends of our street and though they both did the same trade, the shops and keepers were so different. The one closest to our house was run by a middle aged man with three kids all at school with me. He kept the shop smart, bright, organised and dust free. This one at the other end was actually closed. It had belonged to a stooped old man who was as deaf as a post. Mrs Abbott sat on a chair in the shop all day long, explaining to her hubby what it was folk wanted when they came in. Hanging outside above the porch door of this shop was a bundle of several pairs of boots and shoes all strung together. Some were ladies with sharp pointed toes and high heels, some were gents plain or patterned, one pair having black toes and heels on white patent leather, small children's shoes, impossibly heavy kids charity boots and a pair of brown leather clogs, all intertwined and swung gently and silently to and fro. But to a last one, they were all so very fuddy duddy and old fashioned.

"Dad" I had asked, as we walked past this shop one day.

"Why are them boots and shoes there?"

He'd looked up as though he had never seen them before.

"Ah don't know, ah suppose it's to show folk tharrit's a cobblers."

I trusted my dad completely and thought him to know everything but on this occasion, I was sure he was wrong, not that I dared tell him, having only just got over the wonderful black eye he had given me a couple of weeks previously.

(I had been out playing with my street friends and Mickey had come out with a huge crusty doorstep of bread. It was cut unusually thick and spread with a more than a generous amount of sparkling red strawberry jam, A veritable feast.

"Where'd ya get that from?" I had asked.

"Dad".

349

Ever hungry I had shot down the jitty in hot pursuit of the
same. Bursting into the scullery, I failed to see dad shaving at
the sink behind the back door and it slammed into him.
"Dad?"
I had called from the kitchen.
"...Dad?"
Louder this time.
"What?" he asked from the scullery behind me. I turned
towards him.
"Dad can I ev a slice o' bread and jam like you just gen our
Mickey."
"You'll ev ter wait a bit, ah'm shavin'."
"Aww, dad, goo on, yo' gen our Mickey some, it's not fair...."
I said those few words, in similar guise, several times over.
Finally, my beloved patient dad for once in his calm, serene
life, lost his cool and with faultless accuracy threw his
shaving brush through the doorway some 10' and it hit me
sock in the eye! He was mortified. Make no mistake, he was
horrified. I was kept off school for a few days and when I
went back had to tell all who asked after the fast fading bruise
that I had fallen downstairs and I was happy to do so.)

But his explanation of the hanging shoes was undoubtedly wrong. It was *obvious* that this was a cobblers shop, the windows were covered in huge adverts for Cherry Blossom Boot Polish and Phillips Steel Segs. The window display was an untidy arrangement of stick on soles, shoe laces, tins of polish and shoe cleaning brushes. What else could it have been *other* than a cobblers? His reply had created more questions than it had answered. I tried another tack.

"Well where thi' got them boots an' shoes from then eh dad?"

"They are what folk tek in to get repaired an' then never fetch back."

I was dumbfounded. Folk who lived round here had more than one pair of shoes and could afford to leave them in the shop? It was unbelievable.

"But why wunt they fetch 'em back eh dad?"

He sighed.

"Ah don't know, p'raps thi' just forgot, or maybe thi' couldn't afford to fetch 'em out, or p'raps somebody died an' nobody in the family knows thi' were there."

"But.."

"P'raps they'd bought some new ones an' didn't want them any more."

"But...."

"But nowt. **Ow the 'ell should ah know?** Fer Christ's sake shurrup bleddy natterin'. Oh you're enough to mek a parson swear yo' are."

So each time I had reason to walk past this shop, the swinging line of boots and shoes continued to intrigue me.

Then, one day a year or so earlier, I had been sent by Miss Lee to take some shoes in for repair and she had stipulated it had to be this shop for this particular job and not the one just a hundred yards down from our house. I stood outside momentarily looking up at the shoe display. One side of them had been sun bleached but the other side still maintained much of their original colour and now I noticed there was a pair of ladies dark red, velvet shoes with a dusty gold buckle on their front hidden in there too. As I pushed the door open and went in, a brass bell tinkled above my head and the horrid fishy smell of glue hit me. There were piles of shoes stacked up on the floor, the counter, everywhere, some in pairs and some odd ones. Behind him rows of shelves were packed tightly with boots and shoes of every colour, size and genre. The floor was awash with tiny tacks, bits of cut off leather, broken shoe buttons and street dirt that had blown in on this windy corner.

Mrs Abbott sat on her usual chair, the crochet hook in her hands darting in and out of the shawl she was working on. As I came in she let them fall onto her lap. Alongside her, busy tapping away at a boot, a tall stooped old man stood behind a dusty, tool littered counter. I gave him Miss Lee's shoes and told him what she wanted doing. He examined them through little glasses lodged on the end of his nose. His wife shouted loudly to him what was required.
"Thi'll be ready Friday." He boomed at me.
"Mester.." I began, determined to ask about the shoes, but the old lady shooed me away as the shop bell tinkled and she looked up and greeted the next customer, effectively dismissing me.

Come Friday I had to go again and fetch back Miss Lee's shoes. As I had pushed the door open, the overhead brass bell had given a muffled response and I looked up and saw it was puzzlingly bound by a piece of sack cloth. To my surprise the shop front was full of neighbours all commiserating with the old lady who was sitting quietly on the same spindly old chair and looked as if she had not moved since I'd left. Just listening in was enough for me to learn that the old man had died the previous night and the old lady was in floods of tears. I instantly recalled my previous visit just a few days ago and such a sadness hit one of the nerves mam said I didn't have and I wept. Full of all the sorrow in the world, I said passionately;

"Eh, Mrs Abbott, he worr such a nice man, ah wish it ad been me instead o' 'im."

And for that wonderful, selfless moment, I really meant it; the whole shop could see I was genuinely sad for her and her intense grief. One of the ladies squeezed my shoulder in something resembling praise. Mrs Abbott looked at me and sobbed afresh, burying her face in her hands. Then she rose unsteadily, scrabbled about in the cash drawer and handed me a whole shiny sixpence.

"Here," she sniffed, "go an' get yourself some sweeties you lovely little girl."

I bought a big bag of Cherry Lips!

A few days later, I passed the shop again and the memory of those delicious fruity sweets made me think it might be worth another try. I popped my head round the door, put on a not so quite sincere face and said again 'I wished it had been me', then ran for my life as it very nearly was. On my scrawny little legs, I easily outran her, but lived in terror for the next few days waiting for the knock on the door that was sure to follow and wouldn't be long in the coming. After all, I was easily identified; small, scruffy and stinking of pee. But, after a few days, when the knock hadn't come, I gratefully realised she didn't know where I lived and eventually forgot about it.

Now here she was seemingly looking straight at me. My heart sank. But if she recognised me she didn't seem to show it. Even so, I was still a bit wary as I crossed the street with Mickey to her door and eyed her stick much as I eyed the punishment cane in our hearth.

"Come in 'ere yo' kid's an' get this."

We followed her as she limped into the darkened passageway, took us into the brighter back room and indicated a desk on the opposite wall.

"Tek that.." she lifted her stick and pointed at it, "then ya' can come back fer them."

She tapped the top of one of two brown leather suitcases on the table. The desk, an elegant, highly polished piece with thin spindly legs was surprisingly heavy. But Mickey removed all the drawers, turned it on its side and somehow the two of us managed to get it out into the passageway. We half pulled and half tugged it to the all the way to the door to the accompaniment of Mrs Abbott beseeching us to watch her 'paintwok'. There we stopped. There was no way those legs were going through that front door.

"Can we chop the legs off eh Mrs Abbott?" Mickey asked.

"Ah gen it yer ta burn, ah don't care what ya do wi' it. Ah just want it out of my way."

"Eya gorran axe then?"

"No I ent. But 'urry up, its cowd wi that door open."

Not to be outfoxed, Mickey climbed up on top of the sideways on desk, braced himself by stretching both hands out on either side of the corridor wall and jumped down hard on one leg. The leg splintered and fell and he moved over and did the same on the other leg. Now he turned the table upside down, repeated his actions and it was a piece of cake to pull out what was now effectively just a flat table.

Dragging it across the road he laid it flat on the mattress. We turned to go back and found the two suitcases and four table legs thrown out on the pavement and the door firmly closed. Together we hauled the legs onto the mattress, then Mickey took the large case and I took the other. The bigger one was unlocked and Mickey opened it. It was full of what looked to be the deceased Mr Abbot's clothes and they were not much more than rags. There was a couple of combinations (an 'all in one' cream cotton or wool, neck to ankle suit with a fly front and in this case, a less than salubrious square flap at the back for toilet access), a couple of old jackets, a pair of striped pyjamas, a pair of men's black shoes with holed soles and some dark blue greasy overalls. The clothes smelled 'dead'. The small case was firmly locked and though we tried, there was no way we could open it. Mickey bid me sit on the desk top and he would pull the mattress up the gently sloping hill by its handle and give me a ride. It was wonderful! As we reached the brow of the hill I saw mam in the distance talking to aunty Bet's...*and she saw us*!

Guiltily I jumped off the mattress and stood, unsure what to do next. I knew we were in trouble and I mentally went through all the chores I should do each day and ticked them off one by one as having been done. So the only thing I could be in trouble for was handling this by now filthy mattress, although it was no dirtier than the one we slept on but then the 'our muck is different' rule came into play and that meant trouble. We had no choice but to continue up the street and meet our fate. As we neared, we got her full attention.

"Wot the bleddy 'ell ave yo' got there nah?" she called.

"Its bonfire rubbish mam," Mickey called back.

The two women watched as we edged nearer. It was hard to read mam's face but she didn't look too angry as we drew to a stop just out of clout reach.

"What's tharr on top?" she asked.

"Two suitcases mam off Mrs Abbot at the cobblers."

"What's in 'em?"

"Owd clothes in that one but that little 'un is locked."

"Lets evva look then".

She opened the big case up and began to rifle though the contents. If there was anything of value, mam would find it. Pursing her lips in distaste, she looked at the pyjamas, pulled the cord out of the waistband and stuffed it into her pinny pocket.

"Want some jackets for your lad to go to work in?" mam asked.

"Gi' over Feera, my lad wouldn't be seen dead in them."

"Well, ah'll ev the buttons off 'em then."

Mam twisted them expertly till the thread snapped and she put them one by one into her pocket.

"Mam, can we ev these owd clothes to mek our Guy." Mickey pleaded.

"Ay, don't bring 'em into the house though, leave 'em outside in the case."

Now she turned her attention to the smaller of the cases.

"Mmmm, it is locked. Come on indoors an' ah'll gerrit oppen."

We all trooped down the jitty and I began to realise that, at least for now, we were off the hook – had we ever really been on it? It was hard to tell. Once indoors mam lost no time in springing the lock and opening the case. It was full of letters tied with a thin blue ribbon, some with funny stamps. Mam took the earliest one and began to read, her eyes widening as she did so.

"JESUS Bet's just listen ter this…" seemingly unaware of us kids wigging, she began to read out loud, her voice getting more excited by the second:

"My Darling Doll, How are you? I miss you so much my sweet. I think about you every minute of every doggone day and kiss your dear sweet face on your photograph. The other guys think I am crazy and I guess I am, crazy in love with you. I just exist until I see you this weekend. Honey I got you some silk stockings, bags I get to put them on you, you Jezebel you. "

All the letters were pretty much the same. Mam raised her eyebrows in astonishment and finally said;.

"Doll? Honey? Jezebel? Who the bleddy hell is he an' who is he writin' to?"

"Beats me," said Bet's, "burr ah've bin called woss things in my life."

"What's the address Bet's?"

Bet's studied the envelope.

"Livingston Street."

"Ohhh bleddy hell," mam's voice was in awe as she finally realised to whom the letters had been written.

"Ah know who it is, its that Dot Abbott as was! What's 'er

married name?"

"Oh you mean young Dot at the cobblers? Marshall, Dorothy Marshall." Bet's replied.

"Ahh, that's it, Marshall. She married that George Marshall off Turner Street din't she? What bleddy date was this then?" She snatched the envelope up and squinted at the faded date. "June 12th 1942? She was married an' evvin' it off wi' a yank! Miss Prim and bleddy proper was playin' away from 'ome, while 'e was fightin' fer King an' country! Well bogger me!"

There was not a chance of anything getting done whilst just one of those dozens of letters went unread. By now, both women were reading a letter each and both had some salacious detail to report to the other. As we kids alternatively watched with widened eyes and wigged with expert hearing, we kept the ladies lubricated with copious cups of tea. Depending on your point of view, a love story or a sordid affair was revealed in our kitchen that day. As the letters were opened one by one, they were perused by the two women and cast aside as the whole sorry story tumbled out. But as the two women continued to read, we realised we were really off the hook. Now we turned our attention to important matters, like the coming celebration and set to in the backyard preparing and making the Guy who was to be the chief guest and centre of attention at our coming bonfire night fire.

It must have been some considerable time later when mam called us in to help her get tea ready for dad's imminent arrival from work. We had to help by peeling the spuds and cutting them into tiny cubes for quick cooking, as mam hurriedly sliced up a large cabbage and fried sausages and onions together. As I have already told you, our scullery was miniscule and with three of us in there together, we had virtually hip to hip contact and should mam lash out at any time, there would be no ducking or flinching and we would cop it. But her mind was busy elsewhere that night and in no time, the house smelled as though cooking had been going on for hours and dad walked in to a busy warm house and an excited mam. Even before he had both feet through the backdoor, she said;

"Boy ave ah got summat to tell yo. Yo' just wait…"

"Well let me get in and tek me coat of fust an' ah'm that starved ter death, ah could eat a scabby dog." Dad said.

Over dinner mam related the tale.

"She's got such a 'holier than thou' attitude, struttin' about as though she owns the bleddy place."

Dad waited until he had emptied his mouth before asking;

"Who? Who's this Doll? Do ah know 'er?"

"Dorothy Abbott as was, Abbott at the bottom o' the street, the cobblers."

He still looked perplexed.

"Ah'm boggered if ah know who yer on about."

He cut into his sausage and chomped on it.

"Ohh, you're bleddy useless you are. Long dark hair, always curled, Married George Marshall off Turner Street."

The penny finally dropped

"Oh I know who ya' mean. That young gel wi' long dark hair!"

"That's 'er. Yo've gorrit."

"Ah know now. Pretty gel, ad twins din't she?"

Mam sniffed.

"Pretty is as pretty does is what I allus says, 'an what she's done in't so pretty. Mek's me wonder just who them bleddy kids belong to."

"Yo' be careful what ya say." Dad all but snapped at her,

"Yo' know nowt an' yo' could do a lorra damage if yo' aint careful."

"Ah do know summat. Ah know 'ow as at one point she is prayin' for yo' know what to happen…"

"What 'yo' know what'?"

"Ohh, fer gods sake gi' me strength, yo' drive me potty yo' do. Do I 'ave to spell it out? Think on a bit will ya, little pigs have got big ears."

She glared at me.

Here she goes again with those meaningless sayings. I searched the room for something connected with little pigs but came up blank and not for the first time. Grrr!

"Ah drive yo' potty? That's rich coming from the likes of yo'… Everybody meks mistakes Vera, everybody. Yo' ev, I ev! Them were funny days an' folk din't know if they would be alive or dead bi the mornin'. Let well alone will ya? Just leave 'em be. Ow would you like it, if folk round 'ere discovered stuff about us? What would they say if they knew about Sandra an' that one eh?"

He cast he his eyes down at mam's huge belly.

"No, ya wunt like it would ya."

"Shush," she snapped, "…remember the kids."

"Ahh, burrits more than these kids we gorra think about innit? Yo' think about the kids lady, yo' think."

Mam jumped up, her eyes blazing. She grabbed her fags and matches and made for the door.

"Ah'm gooin' to Bet's. Sod ya."

And with that, she exited and slammed first the kitchen and then the scullery doors making the very house shake.

Over the next few days, there was a queue of people wanting to read those letters and much sport was made of them. As each aunt had read the contents, they had been returned to mam and there had been ceaseless gossip over endless cups of tea and boundless fags. Then the next neighbour got to read them. Each time they were returned, they were a bit more dilapidated and tattered, especially the ones that seemed to have hidden meanings. Mam took charge of them and hid them under the sink in the clothes basket. Gradually, by putting the little bits of information we heard together, we kids were able to glean, if not actually understand, that there had been some sort of affair which had ended when George Marshall had come triumphantly home from the war to find he was the father of twins.

November the 5th seemed to take forever to arrive and when it did, the dark could not come soon enough for us. There was always much competition between rival streets as to who had the biggest bonfire. Every house had something or other to get rid of and this was an ideal way to dispose of it. It is a measure of poverty that anything given for the fire was rarely if ever worth salvaging. Ours looked as though it was going to be a whopper this year and most of the rubbish collection had been scavenged by me and Mickey. The adults packed the bonfire as high and as tight as possible smack in the middle of the road opposite our front window. With the old clothes in the case, we had set out to make our guy and he'd turned out to be the best ever. For the main body, we had stuffed one jacket with another, used the trousers from the pyjamas as legs and made a good papier mache head. Dad sat him in an old baby's high chair right on the very top of the fire.

Each of the aunts added something to the festivities; Mam made trays of toffee apples and then added cream of tarter from her store cupboard to the remaining toffee and allowed it to bubble away to the bitter rich dark cinder toffee peculiar to bonfire night. Aunty Bet's had made a huge batch of ginger beer, there were plenty of mushy peas bubbling away on the neighbours fire trivets, whilst dozens of large potatoes were set aside ready to be heeled into the glowing embers. It was going to be a night to remember. As soon as dads' bike squeaked its way down the jitty we were off and running, begging him to light the fire. Even at this not quite dark early stage, the occasional rocket streaked overhead and wrote across the twilight sky. Mam took her fireside chair out and sat it squarely under the front window, being joined by the other street aunts with their chosen seats placed close by her, a comfortable distance from the fire. For once the front door was not only unlocked but left wide open and we had free access in and out of our front room. Dad lit the fire......

One by one, people began to gather in small groups and there was a lot of laughter and bon homie. We King kids had sparklers and all the fun of bangers and rockets bought by other, richer households like Carols. The warmth of the fire permeated the fronts of our November cold bodies whilst our backs froze. After about an hour or so, a couple strolled up the street and stopped awhile leaning against the lamp-post, their faces lit by the gas light. She had her back to and was leaning on him and he linked his arms around her waist. It was George and Doll Abbott. The women folk gathered around mam, stretching their necks to see them and began not so quietly cracking raucous jokes amongst themselves. Someone in mam's group evidently did not know what was going on and was quickly bought up to date.

Now many curious eyes were on the couple as their faces danced in the firelight. Dad looked at mam and almost imperceptibly shook his head. She lifted her head defiantly, called Mickey over to her and sent him into the house. Dad followed him. A second or two later dad came out hugging the small brown suitcase to his chest. He stopped a couple of yards away from mam and just looked at her. Then he turned on his heel and threw the case into the very middle of the fire. Mam half jumped out of her chair as if she was going to try to fetch it out and then slumped back defeated. It flared for a few minutes and died. Mam looked across at George and Doll but they had gone.

The fire burned for several hours, refreshed from time to time with newly donated rubbish and eventually, when the last rocket had streaked across the black sky and died, when all the food had been eaten and the toffee apples just a tooth destroying memory, mam sent us to a very late bed. We lay in the attic, the room and us stinking of cordite and smoke and we talked about the night and the burning of the letters. As tiredness finally overcame Mickey and he dropped into a peaceful sleep, I drowsily listened as the folks below our window chatted. I clearly heard mam's voice say:

"Eee, it'll soon be bleddy Christmas again! Ah don't know where the years gone ah'm sure. Christ on'y know's where I'm goin' to get the money from this year. I ent done payin' fer the last bogger yet! Ay, it's just round the corner an' then we be in the thick o' winter, ah c'n smell snow on the way already…"

A few seconds later I went to sleep, pondering how on earth mam could possibly *smell* snow.

The next day mam stirred the fire up once more and sank potatoes for our dinner into the glowing embers so by the time we got home from school they were ready. We sat around chomping into the hot goodies as our neighbours piled yet more stuff on the fire to give us a second bonfire night of community pleasure. At the appointed time, dad came up the hill wearily pushing his bike before him. As the glow of the fire came into view, he stopped and drew his breath. Mam turned to face him, arms crossed over her ample bosom. Every other face also turned round to see his reaction, for sat on the very top of the blazing fire, was his armchair.

CHAPTER 15

ANOTHER MOUTH TO FEED.

Somehow, I had reached the age of ten and survived all my many worries, the war and post war years, the poor diet, the beatings and thrashings, the illnesses and at times, the bitter, bitter cold. But in the middle of that year, our morning rituals changed. Mam was now up before us. With a fag in one hand and a cup of tea on the table by her side, she was throwing up time and time again into the coal bucket. And oh boy, God help us if we did anything to upset her. For now, her temper was so short she would throw whatever was close to hand without a second thought. At this point in time, things that the aunts had said within our hearing were just so much gobbledygook!

Things like;

"Ah c'n tell ya know, I can see shitty nappies in yer face."

(WHAT?)

"Yo carryin' different this time Vera. Ah betcho it's a lad."

To which mam replied;

"It'd better not be else ah'll shove the bogger back. Lads is trouble."

And, the other legendary foolproof way of finding out the sex, holding a sewing needle over her growing mound of a stomach and watching which way it swung! Bet's said;

"Look at the way this needle is turning, that's a gel. That's definitely a gel! Yo' mark my words."

"Bet's ah don't really care too much worr it is. Ah'm just frightened its goin' ter go the same way as the last 'un."

But it wasn't all sad, sometimes mam's sense of humour came to the surface and I remember her once having the aunts in stitches as she told them that having a baby meant extra milk, butter and meat on her rations and a bit more on the cock rent book.

It was during an icy cold early December, that our next baby was to make an entry. When we got home from school one night, mam was in a fouler than usual mood. We dashed around trying to do as much as we could whilst she held her side and moaned as if in agony, terrifying us. Dad came home and immediately fed us a bowl of tea pobs and put us to an

early bed. We were both reluctant and ready to go. I slipped
into an uneasy sleep and woke sometime later to hear mam
loudly groaning. A strange woman's voice, the midwife, was
talking to her. The baby began to make an entrance. Dad was
sent to fetch aunty Bet's. There was much hustle, bustle, toing
and froing. Curious, I got out of bed and silently made my
way down the attic stairs, stopping just short of the bend in
the staircase so I was hidden from view. Once again, being a
light sleeper was a good thing as it meant I was in the thick of
it, albeit tucked out of sight.

I got to see and hear an awful lot over the next hour or so.
This was far better than sleep. There was no light on the attic
stairs and the lower stair light was off too, but mam's door
wasn't quite shut and although I could see them quite well,
passing to and fro on the landing, they were far too engrossed
in what they were doing to notice me. Aunty Bet's was
helping by running up and down the stairs carrying cups of
tea and other essentials, stopping now and then to give mam a
bit of encouragement.
"Come on Pal," she said, "… what's tekkin' ya so long? I
should 'ave thought it were like shellin' peas to yo' be now."

"Thanks a lot mate, you wait till it gets to your turn again....OWWWGGGNN."

"You gotta 'ave that that makes 'em to get in that state and them days are over for me."

"They are for me annall after this...Ohhnngggg"

Nurse Gilding the midwife began bustling around mam and before long she and dad were either side of her urging her to push. Hearing her moaning and groaning so, my stomach churned into a knot and I bit into my knuckles, sharing her pain, hoping they weren't hurting her. This went on for a short space of time and then I heard another different sound, a slap. If I hadn't known better I would have said someone was hitting someone. Then a different sort of cry, a thin wavering sound like a kitten's mew and dad's voice saying;

"...we've gorra little lad Vera..."

Aunty Bet's voice pleaded.

"Shift over an' gizza look Al....oh 'e's a a proper little blondy."

"Well, yo' got what yo' wanted din't yer dad? Think ah'da sooner ave had another gel. You can dress em so much nicer."

"Aw don't say that Feera, don't ever say that. All babies are welcome. Lad's are lovely, ever so lovin'.'"

Bet's voice sounded odd, tearful.

"I worr only joking Bet's, only joking, It's just that ah got all Sandra's baby close an' wunt ev ter buy owt new. Giz 'im 'ere nurse…has he got all his fingers, toes, tackle? Oh he's well enough, 'e'll do ah suppose." mam's voice too sounded odd, sort of strained, as if she had a bad cold.

"Oh yes, they're all there, I counted them myself and so's 'is tackle. Is 'e a chip off the old block then eh Al?"

Dad chuckled.

"You can have a little gel next time," said the midwife.

"Yo' can piss off annall, I'm not goin' through that again. 'im and 'is tackle aint comin' near me no bleddy more."

I was somewhat relieved to know that mam was back to her usual cussing self.

"Ohh… if only I had one penny for every time I have heard that…."

(She was yet to hear it from mam again! THRICE!)

Nurse chuckled, her words hanging in the air.

"That's you sorted mam, lad just wants a bit of cleaning up now and we have done, then we can all get some sleep, won't we my little precious."

"Giz a fag Bet's…" mam said and I heard the match flare and then the all too familiar scent of tobacco drifted out.

"'ow many's that yo've delivered then eh nurse?" asked Bet's

"More than the fags you've offered around!"

"Oh I am so sorry, I didn't realise you smoked, Eeyar nurse, evva a fag."

Bet's proffered the packet.

"In a minute, just let me finish."

"Pass 'im over Feera whilst you finish your fag. …oh int he gorgeous…look at 'is white 'air…"

Mam mumbled something. Aunty Bet's voice sounded weird, tearful even,

"Our Patty's hair was this colour when she were born…what yer callin' 'im Feera?"

"David."

"Awww, that's nice…."

"Tell you what Bet's, he'll be needing a Godmother, would you like to do it."

I heard such a howl of anguish coming from aunty Bet's that I dropped down the last few stairs and peered though the crack in the door. She was sobbing fit to burst, her whole body

376

shook as she held onto the new baby. Dad went to her side, put both his arms around her and held her tight, shushing her the while. Nobody spoke and I learned that day there are times when there really are no words. Gradually her sobs abated and became mere sniffles.

"Well, what do you say then? Are you alright being Godmother?" now mam's voice cracked.

"Eee, I am that. Thanks," the words came out strangled.

"I think we all need that cuppa now Al," nurse said, "…and take this downstairs and burn it, heel it well into the fire mind."

Dad made for the door and I shot back out of sight round the bend in the stairs. I peeped at him as he went down. He was carrying a large brown paper parcel.

By the sound of it, the women seemed to be taking it in turns to hold the new baby and it was too much, being so close yet unable to see my new brother. I again crept down the remaining few stairs and peeked through the gap in the door. Aunt Bet's was still cradling the baby but had her back to me so I could not see. Then dad began to come back upstairs with the tea tray, I didn't move fast enough and was caught.

"What are you doin' outta bed at this hour?"

Dad's tread on the stairs was slow and measured and he sounded dog tired but not at all angry.

"I can't sleep, cos I 'eard our mam cryin'."

"She's been avin' the baby, well go in then and take a look at ya new brother."

I pushed open the door, fearful of mam's anger but she bid me come sit on the bed and see the new baby. Aunty Bet's laid him carefully in my arms and with her support I held him. He was amazing. I can still see and smell him even now. I marvelled at his tiny shell like finger nails and impossibly tiny feet. His doll sized squashed face seemed red and angry but he lay peacefully enough in my arms, looking up at me, his mouth a perfect little o.

"Come on you, let's get you back to bed now."

"Aw, just another minute dad….eh dad?"

"Go on then, one more minute an' then its bed."

"It's been a tough time for the baby as well as you, you know Mrs King, I have a feeling he'll be hungry." Nurse said, sipping her tea.

Mam nipped the end off her ciggie and popped it behind her

ear. Dad gently took the baby from me, handed him to mam and headed me towards the door. I never took my eyes off my new brother. Mam thrust a huge bosom into his mouth and he sucked contentedly. Even as I reached the door, I was still watching him. Then he smiled.

"He smiled mam," I said in astonishment, running back to the bed,

"...I saw him and he smiled!"

"No you didn't you silly sod, it was wind, he can't see, he's blind...."

A river of shock ran through me as dad scooped me up in his arms and carried me off to bed. I cried myself to sleep for the poor blind baby. Eee, if it isn't one damn thing, it's a – bleddy –nother.....

David proved to be a good baby and thrived. We all loved him and took it in turns to walk him in his nice shiny, albeit second hand, pram. The pram was difficult to fit into the back room and it had to go up the three steps into the front room. Gradually the china cabinet got scratched as we struggled to manoeuvre it. Mam started moaning that the house was far too small since his arrival......dad started to look worried.

CHAPTER 16

CHRISTMAS

Me and our Mickey were not happy. It was Sunday and mam had said it was now far too cold for us to go to the Sally Army. When she went into the scullery to peel the potatoes for lunch, Mickey took me to one side and said he thought it was because Christmas was coming, she had no money and would not be able to give us the bus fare or a penny for the collection box. Perhaps if we offered to walk there and back and maybe just put a halfpenny each in the box, she might relent. It seemed like a good idea and I went to the scullery door and suggested what Mick had said.

"Oh go on, wear your shoes out some more why don't you. Don't yo' think your dad's got more to do wi' 'is bleddy time than keep mendin' your bleddy shoes every soddin' week?"

It was far too important an issue to both of us to let it be and I further persisted with my hastily thought up compromise.

"What if we wear us plimsolls instead eh? Can we go then mam?"

"'What if pigs 'ad wings then eh mam'?" she parodied me.

"It's the bleddy winter you dozy idiot, it's far…too…bleddy … cowd… for…plimsolls."

She strung out her words, this usually was a sign that she was getting really angry. Still I pleaded our case.

"Well, if we bussed it just one way and…?"

I got no further, she had the steel colander in her hand full of Brussel sprouts and I didn't see it coming. I took the full brunt as she whacked me on top of the head with it. Blood began to trickle down my face and neck. I ran upstairs lest she came at me again and staunched the blood on my frock. I was gutted. Oh we had no more love for the place now than before, but in less than three weeks it was the Christmas party and today was the signing in day. If we weren't there today, we would not be included in the list. It was so unfair. The other kids had stopped going a couple of weeks after we started and Mickey and me had been going religiously for several months now and with less than three more weeks to go to the famous party, we, the only kids who had really earned the right to go, would not be going. My throat ached with unshed tears.

Once bonfire night was over, the Christmas festivities began in earnest. At school we practised for our carol service and the baby classes rehearsed their nativity play. I had played Mary one year and disgraced myself by dropping the pot doll baby Jesus and smashing its head, and in the fuss that followed, I wet my knickers on stage! Now I was older and quite content to simply sing 'Away in A Manger' solo out front of the school choir. Preparations for the party had started some weeks previously and we had made crackers out of pages of the Mirror by rolling and gluing the painted newspaper onto a tube. In the morning class, we had hand written some silly jokes on slips of paper which we now slipped inside. Once they had dried, we pulled the tube back out and decorated the 'cracker', by painting and sticking on stuff meant to look like holly leaves or bells. I put a lot of artistic effort into mine and looked forward to receiving it on the day. We also made a paper hat and once again the Daily Mirror came into its own. Painted and glued, they were quite passable and again, I made sure the one I made was the best I could do. Then Miss collected them all up in a huge box ready for the feast.

On the day of the party, we had to take a cup, spoon, dish and plate all duly labelled and we left the house with dire warnings to return all the items in good order and not to lose anything or there would be no Christmas at our house. When we got to school, the hall had been prettily decorated with ancient baubles and tinsel and there was one huge table down the centre which had plates of curled at the edge potted meat sandwiches, fairy cakes, jelly and custard, all of which was served by the dinner ladies. When we got to sit down, we found we had got a squashed hat and cracker that someone else had made. They weren't a huge success as the hats didn't fit, the glue didn't glue and the crackers didn't 'crack'. We had a sing song and then Santa, looking suspiciously like Mr Martin the head master, made his entrance and began to give out parcels to every child. Once I got a small flat package wrapped in green painted newspaper and I could not wait to open it. Inside was a cellophane packet and within this, a white satin hair bow. It was sealed and remained so as I treasured it and kept it safe for many years.

At home also, Christmas preparations were in full swing. Mam followed the traditions, passed on faithfully by previous generations, to the letter. Boxes of dates and figs appeared either side of a huge bowl of nuts on the sideboard. The dried fruits were in no danger whatsoever of being eaten since nobody liked them and when dad questioned why she had bought them, mam replied it was traditional to have them and Christmas would not be Christmas without them. Slowly in the heat of the kitchen the fruits dried out totally over the next few months and sometime in the following spring, mam would cut them up, soak them in cold tea and add them to a bread and butter pudding. The nuts were definitely not to be touched until 'Christmas', though the quantity did seem to lessen as the days went on.

We kids turned our attention to the festive garland that would hang from the ceiling. Mam bought us a few packs of coloured strips of paper that had glue on one end. These had to be made into interlocking circles. Oh how eagerly and quietly we concentrated on getting the colours right for the ceiling swag. "One red, one blue, one green and one yellow." mam patiently explained showing us how lick and stick the strips of coloured paper together to make it.
"Red, blue, green, yellow, blue...BLUE? Somebody's put the

wrong colour in mam."

Mr Nobody, who seemed to permanently live at our house, had been busy again and nobody would admit to the error and, as it turned out, it wasn't the only mistake, though they could only be seen once they were drawing pinned in situ along with a giant faded gold tinsel bell, above the table!

It has to be said and with much more than a little gratitude, mam always gave us a magic Christmas. Come the eve, she would be in unusually high spirits and would spend the day laughing joking and singing with and to us. We sat round the table and wrote our traditional notes to Santa and watched with open mouths as she pushed them up the chimney for him to collect, though we worried how he would cope with the roaring coals below. With the radio in the background playing festive carols and songs, mam sang along as she made a start on the 100 or so mince pies that were a must for the coming day.

Before long, the scent of mam's delicious goodies permeated the whole house and she began to turn them out onto cooling trays ready to be put away for the coming days.

Now she turned her attention to the coming repast. She peeled and cut dozens of potatoes, parsnips, carrots and Brussel sprouts, took out the plum pudding she had made and which had been maturing on the top shelf for several months and carefully pushed inside it several silver threepenny pieces and sixpenny bits. There was such intense happiness and joy in that house at that time. Mam would tease us, telling us what Santa might bring. Finally when as much as possible had been done, mam sat down and told us stories of her childhood Christmasses many years ago. We sat companionably round the fire waiting for dad to come home, the sense of excitement wrapping us up a cocoon of expectancy. Only when, earlier than usual, the squeak of his bike heralded dad's return did a feeling of completeness descend. *I can feel that utter one day of the year contentment even now.*

Down the jitty he wheeled his bike bearing a small but real fir tree dangling on one handle bar and a chicken on the other. Somehow he always managed to appropriate a tree for us every year and we happily set to and decorated it with the old faithful baubles that emerged from dusty boxes like long lost friends. Oh how we squealed with delight as these beautifully coloured fragile decorations once more took their rightful place on the tree. Now we knew it to be Christmas proper. Meanwhile, Mam attended to the chicken. Removing the last of its tiny feathers with the chewed remains of her finger nails, she cut off its feet and pulling on the guiders, made them move and chased us round the kitchen with them as dad laughed out loud.

Christmas Eve always began the same way. The walls began to sing. Sent to bed earlier than usual, we had lain awake for hours and listened to the carols being sung in the pub further up the street, the coats and bedcovers pulled up to our noses against the intense bone searing cold. We huddled together and lay chatting about the coming morning. After a couple of hours, the street noises began anew as the pub began to call time and the inhabitants unsteadily made for home.

"Merry Christmas and a happy new year Ted" a man's voice slurred, "…tarrar midduck. 'ope Santa brings ya what ya want."

"Ahhh, an' the same ter yo' anall".

"G'night Evelyn, nannight and don't let the beg bugs bite."

"Ah won't ev time ter get ter bed ternight, I gotta stuff that

chicken an' gerrit ready fo' the mornin' an' ave gorra do all
them stockin's annall yet…eh, its all go innit?"

"'Appen yo'll still be up when Santa comes an' yo' might
gerran extra present eh?"

Laughter filled the still night air. Gradually it tailed off and a
few moments later began again as the last stragglers climbed
the hill and headed for home from the city centre.

I shot out of bed and crossed the floor to look out of the
window. Dressed only in a vest, the cold went to my very
core and made me shiver unpleasantly. Frost had already
begun to etch its exquisitely intricate lace pattern on the
window panes and I knew they would be completely covered
with a solid sheet of ice by the morning. This was the one and
only night of the whole year when the attic ghosts and
gremlins that blighted my life would not be walking. I stood
at the window bathed in the friendly moonlight and watched
as the last person left the pub and the lights were turned off.
Now just the moon and the lamp below lit the night and the
silence was total. I watched as a lone cat, its tail erect, walked
slowly and stealthily up Upper Beacon Street and disappeared
into a jitty. Above, the moon rode high and bright in a star

studded sky. There was nothing more to see and I clambered into the warmth of sleeping Mickey's back. Almost immediately I heard;

"Oh come all ye faithful, joyful and triumphant…"

It was close. Not from the street, it was much closer.

"Mickey, MICKEY" I gave him a hard nudge.

"Them walls is singing, just like they did last year."

"No they're not, its old man Lee next door. He's pissed again. Yo' just listen a bit an' she'll start shahtin' at 'im."

Sure enough, a few minutes later, Mrs Lee began to call loudly to him from upstairs.

"Fred…FRED, come on up to bed an' stop mekkin' a row, yo'll ev them kids awake next door."

"Ohh, come lerrus adore 'im, oh come lerrus adore 'im, oh come lerrus adoooooorrrrr 'iii - iim…Chri..i..ist the loooord…."

A few seconds later, we heard a shuffle as Mrs Lee went downstairs and then some bumping as she struggled to get him upstairs and into bed. After a further minute or two of mumbling, a blessed silence finally descended. I knew I would never sleep this night…. From my hard as nails lumpy pillow, I watched the moon. At some time in the middle of the night, there came faint rustling noises, but I just rolled over....

I had woken and yet hadn't, some little time ago. My mind had not quite grasped that it was morning and not just any old morning, but THE morning of all mornings. Still I lingered in the warm fug of the bed, reluctant to bring my head out of the acrid smelling, urine scented steam. Mickey still snored gently beside me. Then it hit me with a bang. IT WAS CHRISTMAS DAY!

I woke Mickey by jumping on him and we both stumbled, he still half asleep, to the bottom of the bed whereupon two stockings hung. I eagerly snatched mine up, sat on the bottom of the bed and began to explore its seemingly never ending treasures; a book, paint set, sewing set, crayons, Ludo, snakes and ladders, an orange, apple, huge bar of chocolate, three bags of sweets, a card with a pretty silver cross necklace on it, some nuts and right at the very bottom in the toe, three bright as new, shiny pennies. Wow. I glanced across at Mickeys pile. He had an airplane which he had to glue together, a set of soldiers in a box, a book, paints, crayons and the same sweet goodies I had. Choosing a small packet of the sweets, I began to tuck greedily into it. My teeth were chattering, as I got off the bed and began to get dressed. Only now did I notice there were also two boxes at the foot of the bed, a small one my side and a larger one his. I yelled.

"There's another box Mickey…look, 'ere..one fo' you and one fo' me. "

I picked mine up and opened it and felt my blood drain into my feet. It was a small china headed doll with brown sleeping eyes and lipstick red smiling mouth complete with tiny white teeth. It was dressed in a white and green printed frock and over it was a green felt coat fastened with the tiniest buttons I had ever see in my life. Its head had painted on brown hair and was encased in a matching green bonnet with two tiny feathers at the side. Oh Lord, Santa had really heard my prayer this year for I recognised the doll as the one that had been in Slater's shop window on the corner of Turner Street for weeks. Oh how I had hankered after it, looking at and admiring it every chance I had got until one day saw that it had gone and it broke my heart. Carol had said that she was going to get it for Christmas and I hadn't argued, knowing it would be so. But no, here she was, in my hands. So engrossed was I in my new friend, I didn't even look at the huge new soldiers fort our Mickey had got. She was mine and even before I went downstairs I had fallen in love with her and called her Patty.

Mam and dad were already up by the time we came downstairs. The radio was belting out a Christmas edition of the Armed Forces Radio show, baby David was asleep in his pram in the front room, Sandra and Eileen were sat on the hearth rug playing with the rag dolls Santa had bought them, mam was in the scullery putting the plum pudding on to simmer for the required several hours - on her feet the new pink furry slippers dad had bought her - whilst dad was tamping down the roaring coal fire and banking it with enough slack to make it last the whole day.

Already the scent of the coming feast filled the air and made us realise just how hungry we were. She asked us to show her the gifts Santa had bought us and did we like them? She told us that the sweeties and chocolate were strictly for after dinner and I was somewhat relieved mam didn't cotton on to the fact that one of my sweetie packs was already missing. We tore outside to join our friends and excitedly exchanged 'I got' stories and, clutching Patty safely to my chest, I headed downhill to a certain Carols house.

I ran round the back to their door and pounded on it. Someone let me in and in a glow of excitement I showed Carol my doll, not any old doll, but THE most coveted of dolls. She barely looked at it and lifted up the doll Santa had bought her. It was huge, could walk when you held its hand, said Mamma when you tipped it up and was double jointed. I would like to say I didn't care and I didn't.

I loved my doll and played with her endlessly until I came home one day a few weeks later and found it with a hole smashed in its head where Sandra has managed to pull it off the chair. Mam stuffed the hole with newspaper and made it a bonnet to hide the damage but I was always aware of it. Some many months later, the doll was taken to the dolls hospital and a new head put on it and I had it for years.

Eventually, after hours of stomach grumbling impatience, we sat down at last to dinner. Oh such bliss. Mam said she found it hard to imagine that some folks ate like this every single day of their lives and dad said that nobody ate any better than this on Christmas day. Oh that delicious once a year chicken, that crunchy home made sage and onion stuffing, those wonderful brown crispy baked potatoes, Brussels and mashed potatoes, carrots and rich thick meaty gravy. And oh how quickly the food was downed and the plates were cleared. Mam said it had taken her months to save the money, weeks to prepare, hours to cook and we had devoured the lot in minutes. She got up and scraped every little bit of bone – chewed or not - gristle and skin off the plates straight into the stew pot already bubbling on the fire trivet as the start of tomorrow's dinner.

She took away the empty plates and dumped them into the scullery sink for later, much later consideration, and with all eyes on her, she proudly came back triumphantly holding aloft the steaming Christmas pudding. Placing it centre stage on the table, she turned it upside down onto a plate. The aroma tickled our noses and whetted our appetites afresh. Digging into the glutinous sticky mound, she gave us each a huge heaped spoonful of this tar black, ear tickling pudding and poured a copious blanket of hot, saccharin sweet, Monk and Glass custard all over it. She reminded us to make a wish and to watch out for the silver coins and not swallow them. Now she waited with outstretched palm as one by one, they were excitedly discovered and somewhat reluctantly returned to her. The luck was in the finding of them, not in the keeping of them, mam said!

Do you suppose that maybe, just *maybe*, on this one occasion of the year I *did* leave my mothers table unable to eat one more morsel? Oh no, I still had room to start on the sweets and chocolates of my stocking. And there was still tea to come. At this second repast, the chicken carcass was bought to the table, along with jars of varying sharp pickles. Mam and dad picked it clean and the remains of that too was put into the now nicely stewing pot on the hob. On the table a huge fresh cream sherry trifle decorated with glace cherries and crunchy hundreds and thousands sat centre stage, along with a home made iced Christmas cake, ham and tongue sandwiches and we could finish this wonderful repast with one mince pie. Melt in the mouth delicious, rich, golden brown, sugar drenched, crumbly flaky pastry, filled with a

black fruity mixture so powerful as to hurt my ears and make
my eyes water. Ohhhh! We could have eaten a dozen, but no,
we had to be content with just the one. The day had been so
wonderful, so bountiful, it seemed to me to be as good a day
as any to take my life in my hands, do an Oliver Twist and
politely ask; 'please mam, may I have another one?', but mam
snapped,

"You greedy little cah yo' fer yer nowt else. After all yo've
just ate? There's another bleddy day to come termorrer ya
know!"

Then the next day being Boxing Day, we were allowed
another mince pie, and yet again the 'there's another day' rule
came into play, not that I dared play Oliver for a second time.
But eventually, as Christmas slipped effortlessly into
memory, folks finally stopped mechanically wishing each
other a 'Happy New Year' and started to think about hot cross
buns for Easter, it was about now, mam turned her attention to
the mince pies still mouldering and patiently waiting for
'another day'. Peering into the tin, she pursed her lips and
said;

"It were a waste o' me bleddy time, effort and moneh to make
all these soddin' mince pies an' thi've still not been eaten. Ah

won't be botherin' again next year, yo can count on it.'   So saying, she chucked the tin on the table, where it landed with a loud clatter sending up a white talcum like cloud of stale icing sugar, she said they had better be eaten and eaten quick! Then we could have a dozen all at once if we wanted and *oh I wanted. . .*

THE END?

PS....it was around about that time mam suddenly and inexplicably became a model tenant and started paying her rent religiously. In order to do that, we were told to tell the ever growing army of door knockers 'shintin!' even more often than usual and she started avidly studying the 'House Exchange' column in the Nottingham Evening Post and News. Dad continued to pour cold water on her many queries as to this street or that area, until....

"Where's Broxtowe Al?"

Dad opened his mouth to speak and then snapped it shut as he realised to his horror, *he didn't know.*

He looked worried and he had good reason to.

THE BEGINNING......?